KT-144-716

gardeners' question time
techniques & tips

C333893211

gardeners' question time
techniques & tips

Matthew Biggs, John Cushnie,
Bob Flowerdew & Anne Swithinbank
with a foreword by Roy Lancaster

Kyle Books

special photography by Mark Winwood

other photography by Jonathan Buckley

This edition published in 2015 by Kyle Books,
an imprint of Kyle Cathie Ltd
192-198 Vauxhall Bridge Road
London SW1V 1DX
general.enquiries@kylebooks.com
www.kylebooks.co.uk

First published in Great Britain in 2005 by Kyle Cathie Limited

by arrangement with the BBC
BBC logo © BBC 1996
The BBC logo is a registered trademark of the British Broadcasting Corporation
and is used under licence

ISBN 978 0 85783 365 5

© 2005 by Matthew Biggs, John Cushnie, Bob Flowerdew & Anne Swithinbank
Photography © 2005 by Mark Winwood & Jonathan Buckley
(see also other copyright acknowledgements on page 319)

All rights reserved. No reproduction, copy or transmission of this publication
may be made without written permission. No paragraph of this publication may
be reproduced, copied or transmitted save with written permission or in
accordance with the provisions of the Copyright Act 1956 (as amended). Any
person who does any unauthorised act in relation to this publication may be
liable to criminal prosecution and civil claims for damages.

Project editor Caroline Taggart
Design Geoff Hayes
Copy editor Catherine Ward
Picture research & editorial assistance Vicki Murrell
Index Sarah Ereira
Production Sha Huxtable & Alice Holloway

Matthew Biggs, John Cushnie, Bob Flowerdew & Anne Swithinbank are
hereby identified as the authors of this work in accordance with Section 77
of the Copyright, Designs and Patents Act 1988.

A Cataloguing in Publication record for this title is available from the
British Library.

Printed in China by C&C Offset Printing Co., Ltd.

contents

dedication

This book is dedicated to all our listeners, without whom there would be no *Gardeners' Question Time*.

acknowledgements

Thanks to Caroline Taggart, who is so patient and a pleasure to work with; Geoff Hayes for the splendid design; and Vicki Murrell for imaginative picture research.

Thanks also to Mark Winwood for all his work on the step-by-step photography and Jonathan Buckley for supplying most of the other photographs. And to the staff and students of Sparsholt College Hampshire, particularly Ray Broughton and Mark Ekin; Rachel Foster of Exbury Gardens; Steve Bradley; and Roy Prior of the British Clematis Society, all of whom provided expertise, enthusiasm, plants and materials for the step-by-step photography.

Matthew Biggs would also like to give many thanks to the following for their help: Johnny Mobasher and Michael Thornley at Hartley Botanic Glasshouses; Joel Mellor, for helping to construct the glasshouse; Ted Holmes at Butterfields Building Supplies Limited, Luton; StoneFlair Limited, Newark (Decorative Landscape Products); Robert Field of Robert Field Landscapes.

foreword

by Roy Lancaster

One of the advantages of being a lifelong and successful gardener, professional or amateur, is the sure knowledge that beginner gardeners are liable, if not likely, to make the same mistakes as you did when you were in their shoes. An experienced gardener is therefore in an excellent position to provide the kind of advice needed to deter, if not prevent, newcomers from wasting time, energy and most of all money on doing the wrong things or making the wrong decisions.

Gardening today has never been more exciting or challenging, nor more fashionable. Add to this the fact that there are now more people interested in gardens and gardening and far more garden plants to choose from than ever before. What better time to publish this book? Its authors are regular panellists on Radio 4's long-running and popular *Gardeners' Question Time*, a show enjoyed and respected for its mixture of hands-on practical advice, bang-up-to-date information on gardening matters and sense of humour.

For several years I had the privilege and pleasure of working with the *GQT* team travelling throughout Britain, visiting garden clubs and societies, and I can vouch for the quality of the advice given and for the authors' enjoyment and sense of fun in sharing their experiences with their audience. A shared experience is the perfect start to solving and correcting problems and avoiding them in the future. That is why the authors, all long-time professionals respected by their peers, deserve our attention as they discuss each subject, assess our needs and dreams and advise us accordingly.

This book is not nor was it planned to be a guide for experts, though even they may find in these pages reminders of basic facts long since forgotten. It is, rather, a thoroughly practical, easy-to-follow guide on how to take the heat and the anxiety out of gardening by adopting the right approach at the right time. Readers will not have to travel far into its pages before realising that its advice is based on good old-fashioned common sense, an awareness of new trends and ideas and the experience that accrues from years of experimenting on your own patch. It is an enthusiastic, reliable and confident combination that can only bring success.

Above: An imaginative container for a herb garden – an old wine box planted with chervil.
Opposite: All gardeners love the feel of rich soil and well-rotted compost.

introduction

Let me take you behind the scenes of a *Gardeners' Question Time* recording. If you could hear the banter and chatter that goes on in the 'green room' before the team file on stage for an evening recording you would be amazed. Eavesdrop on their conversation after a show as we tuck into an Indian meal, usually the only restaurants open after ten at night, and again you'd be stunned.

So what dominates the conversation of these gardening icons? It's gossip, that's what dominates. But it's not the usual 'who's doing what with whom' that keeps the average office and workplace buzzing, oh no. The gossip which gets these tongues wagging is all about their favourite topic, gardening. A tip for this, a technique for that; they can't wait to share their latest discovery or recommend something they've been doing for years. They all have hot pieces of 'gossip' that need to be spread, and what more fertile ground than fellow panel members?

Most of our recordings follow a similar pattern. The outside broadcast engineers, Gabby Tewson and Ted Teasdale, arrive first and start to rig the venue with all the technical paraphernalia needed for today's high-tech digital radio recording. Bob Flowerdew, usually the first team member to appear (he hates being late and always allows plenty of time), will turn up clutching a long-since out-of-print gardening tome. While he waits for the others he'll consume several chapters. John Cushnie, fresh off the Belfast flight, arrives next with a joke and a hug for Jo King, the programme's assistant producer. Regular listeners will not need reminding that Bob's passion is growing organic fruit

and vegetables, while John can't abide vegetables in any form. It's not long before the two of them are giving each other the benefit of their opposing gardening wisdom and Jo ducks for cover.

Anne Swithinbank, battling with a less than reliable car, turns up third and flings herself into the throng. Her beaming smile starts to bring calm. Matthew Biggs, who times his arrival with minutes to spare, erupts into the room clutching goodies for us all… cuttings of plants he's grown and is keen to share.

This gossipy group is now at critical mass and woe betide anyone who tries to stem the flow at this stage. The momentum is so great that nothing will stop it – so no point trying. To an observer it's priceless. If only I could record it. The times I have wished I had a microphone handy to capture this torrent of tips, techniques and teasing – it would make a great programme. It's a heady mix; a fertile blend of great first-hand knowledge culled over many years, enriched with the sort of banter and joking that can't be scripted but just tumbles out when people are on the same wavelength, are passionate about their subject and genuinely thrive on each other's company.

All this happens while, in the background, with no fuss, Gabby and Ted complete the technical rig. They need to 'balance' the voices and we have long since learnt that trying to get the team on stage for the technical rehearsal while they are in full flight is a lost cause. Best to let this initial flood ebb away before we attempt to do the sound check.

At last the team take their places. The chairman this week is Eric Robson, who puts on his most schoolmasterly voice and attempts to get quiet. The class are not listening – there's still too much talking going on. Bob and John are never going to agree on organic growing nor vegetables, but neither will they give up trying to convince each other. Matt and Anne are getting worked up about the merits, or otherwise, of hormone rooting compound.

Eventually calm descends, the technical tests are complete, Gabby and Ted are happy with the balance and we can return to the green room as the questions start to arrive. The team don't see the questions and while the chairman and I sort through what's been submitted they're off again. More chatter at the back of the class.

Half an hour later, clutching the questions chosen for the recording, we step on stage and now, instead of an audience of half a dozen, there are around one and a half million keen gardeners with whom the team can share their tips and techniques.

What more could an evangelical gardener want? Well, there is just one thing and that is a book which records and captures all those moments backstage, and onstage, and compiles them into one comprehensive, easy-to-read title.

This is that book – we hope you enjoy it as much as we love making Britain's favourite gardening programme.

Trevor Taylor
Producer
BBC Radio 4 *Gardeners' Question Time*

Gardeners' Question Time can be heard
at 2 p.m. on Sundays and 3 p.m. on Wednesdays
BBC Radio 4 (92-95 FM, LW and Digital)

A colourful woodland planting of snowdrops, cyclamen and hellebores.

a note from the authors

For more than a decade I've been on the *Gardeners' Question Time* panel and I've been rewarded time and time again by the curiosity and enthusiasm of our querists. Gardeners most sincerely wish to do a proper job, to tend their plots and plants better, to be 'good' gardeners. We on the panel try to help, to guide and explain the intricacies of horticulture not only to the querist, but also to the millions of gardeners, and non-gardeners, listening to us on the radio. But simply because it is a radio programme, we cannot indulge ourselves, or a tiny fraction of the audience, by dealing with many gardening subjects in anything like the depth that can be offered in a book. Hence *GQT Techniques & Tips for Gardeners*, in which four of us from the panel have written chapter and verse depending on our specialities – and have not been limited by three minutes of airtime. We have written it to be accessible, so although it does not pretend to be a comprehensive technical manual for the professional, we hope it is a complete guide for the keen amateur. This book explains the practical ways we have found to manage the various tasks involved in making and tending our own gardens competently – with the aim of making it easier for you to do the same.

Since Adam and Eve began to dig and delve, gardeners over the millennia have been perfecting their techniques, aiming to increase their success rate and ease their load. The knowledge gained through experience has been handed down through the generations to become the vast volume of accepted gardening principles found in most books today. However, such is the scale of the subject and the inherent ingenuity of gardeners that everyone has their own 'tricks of the trade' gained from practical experience or prompted by a desire to experiment.

These nuggets rarely find their way into practical books – except this one!

Gardeners never stop learning; Thomas Jefferson, the third President of the United States of America and a keen fruit and vegetable grower, observed, 'But though an old man I am but a young gardener.' The experience of a lifetime barely rakes the surface of this vast, enthralling subject. I've been gardening for over 25 years and although I'm not an old man yet, this book has been a great opportunity to share some of my practical understanding in the hope that it will increase your sheer delight in the art of gardening – the greatest pastime in the world!

Matthew

Techniques and tips are the backbone of *Gardeners' Question Time* and we are good at it. We have had lots of practice. Our secret is that we are gardeners. The panel members have been there, done it and got the blisters and the sore back to prove it.

It's not that each of us knows all the answers, but collectively we can offer a solution to most problems. Any three panellists have a combined minimum of sixty years of gardening experience and I can think of one combination where there is a hundred years of know-how to be drawn on.

All the advice and instruction offered in this book will work for you. It has been written in a no-nonsense manner without any fancy frills. Gardening terminology has been kept to a minimum and where technical terms have been used they have been explained in layman's language.

It's said that knowledge freely given is never wasted and that is what I believe. I have tried to cover all the tricks of the trade and offer tips and techniques accumulated from a lifetime of gardening experiences.

In turn, I have learnt a lot from the ideas and methods of Anne, Bob and Matt. If you get as much good gardening advice out of this book as I have then the two of us will be very happy. Good gardening,

John

I love to hear my fellow panel members answering questions on *Gardeners' Question Time*, because we all have varying ideas of what our gardens should be like and how we ought to behave in them. In horticulture, there are two kinds of wisdom – the received and the acquired. Most of us start with the former, from books, courses or a formal training. Then, when hours spent working in the garden turn into years, we learn to apply that stored information and mould it to suit our personalities and plots. I often think that gardeners are bombarded with technical information, leaving them scared to touch a plant for fear of 'getting it wrong'. Hopefully, in this practical book, the four of us are giving the reader not just the accepted version of how to think through a problem or tackle a certain job, but our own personal views on how that version should be applied.

In a way, this is what listeners can hear when they tune in to *Gardeners' Question Time*. You might be surprised at how much we sometimes disagree with each other. After all, surely there's a right way to do everything? Well, yes and no. The more I garden, the happier I feel about the relaxed style I've developed over the years, and that's what's important. You need to feel comfortable, confident and open-minded for your talents to blossom. Use textbook information as a springboard, but have the courage to trust your instincts and try out new ideas. If they work, they're right.

Anne

Chapter 1

planning your garden

Anne: A new garden brings with it so much potential. There, out of every window, at dawn and dusk, is the raw material just waiting for you to breathe life into it. Planning a garden from scratch can also be quite daunting, because even in a small plot, there are thousand of permutations to try and thousands more plants to consider for starring roles and supporting cast. Should you have a lawn or not? Be formal or informal? What planting style will you choose and what are the limitations set by aspect, soil and climate?

planning on paper

Some of us are good at designing on paper and others have difficulty transferring what they see on a flat plan to a three-dimensional plot. If you have a small garden, especially on level ground and visible from the house, you can probably plan quite adequately without drawing anything. Your garden is small enough to peg out lawns and borders and put canes in to indicate trees. You can fiddle about to your heart's content until it all seems right.

When it comes to larger sites, especially those that disappear downhill and out of sight like mine, planning on paper is definitely a good idea. The first job is to survey the site and plot the boundaries on a large sheet of graph paper, to scale. This is not necessarily as straightforward as it sounds and involves a lot of patient measuring using a long tape. Plot on the trees, borders and other features you plan to keep or adapt. Sometimes it's necessary to divide a huge plot into several sections. Delve into your house records to see if there

is a plan of the house and garden in your deeds. Consider employing a surveyor, who will make quick work of the job by using sophisticated equipment and a computer.

The benefits of a plan include being able to sketch out what you want and make the whole plot flow together. Use it as interior designers would a mood board by noting down all kinds of peculiarities special to the plot and attaching ideas for colours, seasons and favourite plants. When you see an idea you like in a newspaper or magazine article, cut it out straight away and keep it in a garden folder before you forget. Ideas can be as simple as innovative kinds of mulch, such as sea shells or slate. Using colours like steely blue and silver to cool down hot areas is effective. Or perhaps using a multi-stemmed tree instead of one grown as a standard.

When you have settled on a basic design, decide how you are going to carry it out, perhaps dividing the scheme into different phases. This is particularly relevant to larger gardens where you may not be able to find the time and money to develop the whole lot at once. Our last garden covered roughly one third of an acre and we divided it into four sections. There were three in the back garden, each revolving around a section of lawn as you progressed to the bottom and the front garden made up the last section.

Terracing is one way of coping with an uneven site. This luscious mixed planting includes osteospermum, artemisia, perovskia, achillea and cardoons.

A well-maintained path through the middle of the garden enables you to create two very different 'garden rooms' on either side.

analysing your plot

Before getting too carried away by the aesthetics of your design, note down particulars of what your garden can offer. By analysing aspect, exposure, the lie of the land and soil type, it is surprising how many microclimates you can find, even in a small garden. Identifying and understanding these not only helps when it comes to choosing plants, but is significant when siting garden features like patios, shady nooks, ponds and sunny, Mediterranean-style borders. I like my borders to have strong identities and to help with this, I give them descriptive names. This is how we come to have a spring border, a late border, woodland garden, winter garden, sea garden, tropical border and so forth. They sound rather grand, but are just small areas of the garden where I've chosen a certain type or style of plant to suit what's on offer. These names help

concentrate the mind when choosing plants or finding homes for those you've bought on impulse or been given.

Where the sun shines

The aspect of your garden affects how much light it receives in different parts and at different times of the day, so the first step is to note down the points of the compass. In the northern hemisphere, a south-facing garden catches the most sun, especially during winter when the sun travels lower in the sky. Gardens facing north are often well lit, but parts lying in the shade of buildings and trees can be dark and cold, especially during winter. A west-facing garden catches evening sun, an important requirement for patios designed for use at the end of a hard day's work. An east-facing garden should be flooded by morning light, but loses its sun by late afternoon.

In towns and cities, the shade cast by neighbouring buildings is significant and needs careful observation. In the country, trees and hedges cast shade and rolling countryside throws up some interesting variables. Where river valleys are running mainly north to south, down to the sea, they often create hills and valleys. There's no use buying a garden on the east-facing side of the hill if you want good evening light. Similarly, if you are an early bird, you won't be enjoying much morning sunshine if your garden faces west.

Baking hot sun and light soil

These two make a surprisingly good combination, because you can grow the full range of Mediterranean-type plants which thrive on sun, well-drained soils and low fertility. The trouble with heavier, more nutritious soils is that the plants make too much sappy growth and are then vulnerable to winter cold and wet. Should you want to conserve moisture in summer, the best mulch to use for these plants is shingle, stone chippings or slate. John suggests some good plants to try in the section on page 45.

Hot sun and clay soil

This is a much more difficult combination, because sun bakes clay soil into a solid lump, with cracks forming during droughts. Heavy winter rains can cause waterlogging, ruling out a lot of Mediterranean-style plants. The best mulch here would be a thick layer of well-rotted organic matter to feed the soil and trickle down into gaps.

Light and dappled shade

Light shade is often found in north-facing positions, where there is little direct sunlight, but not too much dense shade

cast by buildings either. Good light often shines in from the sides during morning or evening. Similar, diffuse but not dense shade can be found under trees with light canopies. The effect here is of the type of light found at a woodland edge, or where trees have been thinned. This quality of light provides an ideal home for a wide range of woodland plants. These like a good, but well-drained soil, so add plenty of well-rotted organic matter or leaf mould. In small gardens, raised beds against north-facing walls make superb woodland-style areas. Here, roots will stay cool in the heat of summer and wide, flat leaves remain unblemished by the scorching effects of sun.

drought-tolerant plants for clay

Campanula takesimana
Mexican orange (*Choisya ternata*)
Hawthorns (*Crataegus*)
Angel's fishing rod
  (*Dierama pulcherrima*)
Euphorbia characias subsp. *wulfenii*
Geranium 'Ann Folkard'
Golden hop (*Humulus lupulus*
  'Aureus')
Himalayan honeysuckle (*Leycesteria
  formosa*)
Liatris
Malus 'Golden Hornet'
Mock orange (*Philadelphus*)
Silver pear (*Pyrus salicifolius*)
Roses
Stachys macrantha

Leycesteria formosa

plants for dappled shade

Wood anemone (*Anemone nemorosa*)
Camellias (on acid soil, but not facing
  morning sun)
Dog's tooth violets (*Erythronium
  dens-canis*)
Fothergilla major (on acid soil)
Blue Himalayan poppy (*Meconopsis
  betonicifolia*)
Rhododendrons (only where the soil
  is acid)
Bloodroot (*Sanguinaria canadensis*
  'Plena')
Wake robin (*Trillium cuneatum*)
Merry bells (*Uvularia grandiflora*)

Meconopsis betonicifolia

hints for clay

● Add lots of organic matter.

● Cultivate wide patches for planting and don't dig small planting holes in the clay.

● Avoid walking on the soil.

making shade

● Create shady areas for underplanting by pruning off the lower stems of shrubs to create a trunk or trunks with a head of growth on the top.

plants for dry shade

Alchemilla mollis
Mrs Robb's bonnet (*Euphorbia amygdaloides* var. *robbiae*)
Geranium x cantabrigiense 'Biokovo'
Geranium nodosum
Mourning widow (*Geranium phaeum*)
Helleborus argutifolius
Honesty (*Lunaria annua*)
Mahonias
Foam flower (*Tiarella cordifolia*)

Lunaria annua planted among peonies

Dry shade

Impoverished soil sucked dry of water and nutrients by tree roots and shaded by a dense canopy of leaves must be one of the most difficult planting situations. Well-drained, dry banks are similarly challenging. Even the tough plants listed below will only ever look poor and stunted unless constantly watered and mulched.

Under trees

Ivy grows even in the densest shade, so take a cue from nature and plant a few roots around the outer rim of shade cast by the tree. Then train the shoots inwards to cover the soil. The Chinese creeping bramble *Rubus tricolor* will perform a similar role if you want something a little more sophisticated. Periwinkles (*Vinca minor* and *V. major*) would add their starry blooms.

Stand a container or group of containers under the tree. Filled with good compost, that just leaves the problem of shade. For summer colour, busy lizzies (*Impatiens*) would be a good choice or, more appropriately, a hardy fern like the soft shield fern (*Polystichum setiferum*) or many-eyelashed fern (*P. polyblepharum*). These are nearly evergreen, though they look a little shabby in winter. For winter interest, a brightly coloured evergreen such as *Euonymus* 'Emerald Gaiety' or *Aucuba japonica* 'Crotonifolia' would fit the bill.

Plants for walls

Nowhere is the effect of aspect more marked than against a wall. Plants for walls divide into true climbers and shrubs whose preferences and shape make them ideal for growing against a wall.

Support

Relatively few climbers successfully support themselves by clinging onto walls and fences. Virginia creeper (*Parthenocissus quinquefolia*) clings by means of disc-like suckers on the tips of its tendrils. Ivies and climbing hydrangeas (*Hydrangea. petiolaris* and its close relatives *Schizophragma hyrangeoides* and the evergreen *Pileostegia viburnoides*) grip by sending roots from their stems into their support. Most other climbers, including twining and scandent, draping types as well as wall shrubs, should be tied in to a support system (see pages 222–26) at least until they get going.

planting climbers

It is tempting to plant climbers flat up against the wall or fence, but this more often sets them into poor, rubbly soil and in the rain shadow created by the wall. Although when a plant is small it looks a bit daft, do plant it a good 30cm (12in) away from the base of the wall and make sure it is watered when the soil is dry, until established.

Some climbers (notably ivies and climbing hydrangeas) are slow to take off, so don't lose heart if they appear to flounder at the base of the wall for a year or two before they really get going.

Hot, sunny walls

Walls and fences facing south (in the northern hemisphere; north in the southern) will receive good light all day and catch winter sun too. Choose your plants carefully, not only to maximise the benefits of light, but to avoid those that don't appreciate a sizzling hot aspect. West-facing aspects are well-favoured too and receive good light through the second half of the day.

plants for hot, sunny walls

True climbers
Kiwi fruit (*Actinidia deliciosa*)
Actinidia kolomikta
Chocolate vine (*Akebia quinata*)
Trumpet vine (*Campsis radicans*)
Evergreen clematis (*Clematis armandii*)
Clematis (west-facing positions ideal)
Summer jasmine (*Jasminum officinale*)
Honeysuckles (*Lonicera*)
Passion flower (*Passiflora caerulea*)
Chilean potato vine (*Solanum crispum* 'Glasnevin' and *S. jasminioides* 'Album')
Star jasmine (*Trachelospermum jasminioides*)
Grapevines (*Vinis vinifera* cvs)
Wisteria sinensis

Passiflora caerulea

Wall shrubs
White forsythia (*Abeliophyllum distichum*)
Californian lilac (*Ceanothus* spp. and cvs)
Pineapple broom (*Cytisus battandierei*)
Fig (*Ficus carica* 'Brown Turkey')
Fremontodendron californicum
Itea ilicifolia
Evergreen laburnum (*Piptanthus nepalensis*)
Rhamnus alaternus 'Argenteovariegata'

plants for shadier walls

True climbers
Clematis (those with pale, interesting colours won't fade in the shade)
Ivies (*Hedera helix* cvs and *H. colchica* cvs)
Climbing hydrangea (*Hydrangea petiolaris*)
Honeysuckle (*Lonicera periclymenum* cvs)
Boston ivy (*Parthenocissus tricuspidata*)
Virginia creeper (*Parthenocissus quinquefolia*)

Wall shrubs
Camellia
Japanese quince (*Chaenomeles*)
Herringbone plant (*Cotoneaster horizontalis*)
Euonymus fortunei 'Silver Queen'
Silk tassel bush (*Garrya elliptica*)
Winter jasmine (*Jasminum nudiflorum*)
Firethorn (*Pyracantha*)
Sophora 'Sun King'

Camellia japonica 'Mercury'

sheltered or exposed

Look around in rural neighbourhoods and you'll notice that on the whole, older properties are tucked away in sheltered valleys away from cold winter winds. When they were built, there was no double glazing or central heating, so farmhouses and cottages had thick walls and small windows to reduce heat loss. These days, houses are often built in higher places to take advantage of far-reaching views. The trouble starts when their owners want to make a lovely garden and find themselves both fighting the wind and in a dilemma. Planting windbreaks shields gardens, but at the same time reduces views.

City gardens are no less prone to exposure, as they will grow and spread regardless of topography. The hard surfaces of a city tend to absorb and retain heat, so that on the whole, they are warmer than the surrounding countryside. Yet solid buildings create wind tunnels and plants growing on balconies and roof gardens have to put up with extremes of heat, wind and light.

When frost is forecast, some gardeners have more reason to quake than others. Gardens by the sea will rarely suffer frost, whereas further inland and in higher places, frost is often severe, penetrating and longer-lasting. Then there is the strange, often unpredictable phenomenon of frost pockets.

While planning and designing your garden, look out for every nuance of climate and note it down. Not only will this help when it comes to choosing plants and the most sheltered areas for seating, but it might suggest what look parts of the garden might have. If what you have resembles an open prairie, a Mediterranean hillside, a boggy ditch, a woodland or an enclosed area ideal for scented plants, go with the flow and capitalise on your conditions rather than fighting them.

Cold gardens

Frost pockets are caused by cold, frosty air rolling downhill and sinking into hollows, or stopping in front of a solid barrier such as a hedge, wall or fence. The cold air hangs and damages plants uphill of the barrier. Frost takes a variety of

tip

● Leave the old, dead stems on your perennials instead of tidying them up at the end of the growing season. They protect the crown of the plant and act as a home for overwintering insects which, in turn, provide a food source for birds (as do seeds). Best of all they look fantastic in a hoar frost.

forms and is prettiest when the air is humid and crystals of ice form from condensed water. This is known as a hoar frost.

Less visible, black frosts happen when the air is dry and ground frosts penetrate the soil. After a prolonged ground frost, evergreens look dreadful because they cannot take up water and their leaves hang as if experiencing a drought. They usually return to normal after a thaw unless their roots are particularly shallow and vulnerable.

Frost damage

Plants vary in their ability to withstand frost and if you push the limits by growing too many tender types outdoors in your garden, you run the risk of suffering losses after a particularly hard winter. Some plants are killed by cold air collecting just above soil level, others by ground frosts. Sometimes the effect of a frost is made worse when soil is waterlogged at the same time. Tender plants almost always survive winter better when planted into well-drained soil.

Spring frosts are particularly damaging, especially in a maritime climate where warm weather starts early in the year, bringing new growth on, only to be clobbered by one or more sudden, sharp late frosts. This variability can be a shock to plants whose wild ancestors come from areas where more defined seasons are normal. Some, like Japanese maples and many magnolias, would enjoy sheltered woodlands protected by a canopy of taller trees. Take plants like these and make them the specimen tree of a rather bare front garden and this puts their fresh new leaves or flowers at risk. Failure to fruit in early-blossoming peaches, pears and plums can often be blamed on a late frost destroying their flowers.

Protecting tree ferns from frost in winter using hessian wrap.

tips for preventing frost damage

Damage from late frosts often occurs when thawing takes place rapidly with sun shining on the leaves or buds. If you wake one morning to find vulnerable shoots and buds frozen, try watering them gently, using a rose (sprinkler) on the end of a can and cover with sheets of newspaper to shade them from the sun. This will slow the thawing process and your precious plants might emerge unscathed.

Tender plants can survive winter frosts when they are carefully wrapped to protect their vulnerable crowns and roots. Many gardeners find they can successfully overwinter bananas, tree ferns and palms by tying the leaves and branches together, packing straw, bracken or horticultural fleece around the plants and then wrapping with hessian. Done neatly, these wrapped plants can enhance a winter garden, but tatty wrapping looks awful and is likely to come adrift in high winds. Tender plants in pots have vulnerable roots as well as tops, so the pot will need wrapping too.

Should a tender shrub be cut down by severe cold during winter, don't give up on it until summer. Sometimes plants like bottlebrush (*Callistemon*) and *Pittosporum* grow back from the base or almost from below ground surprisingly late. Once new growth appears, cut all the dead stems away.

Timing is all when it comes to judging the weather. Tender plants won't tolerate frost and there is no point trying to push things by planting them too early. Annuals and tender perennials used as summer bedding plants and tender crops like runner beans, courgettes and pumpkins should only be planted outdoors when there is no more danger of frost, usually in late spring or early summer.

Wind

Strong winds have a damaging effect on plants, breaking their branches, pushing them over, loosening their roots and drying out their foliage. Plants constantly lose moisture through their leaves and under normal growing conditions, this is replaced by an even uptake from the roots. But wind causes an increase in evaporation, whipping moisture away faster than the roots can cope with. Certain plants have evolved physical characteristics to help them deal with this, including shiny, leathery surfaces or protective hairs to cut down on evaporation. Succulent foliage able to store moisture and tiny leaves putting up little resistance to the wind can withstand both wind and drought better than large, thin leaves.

Strong winds can affect insect pollination and where fruit trees like pear, apple and plum are grown in exposed positions, there can be a bad set of fruit if winds were high at blossom time, as insects would not readily take to the wing.

Hazel hurdles make an attractive, natural-looking screen in a windy garden.

Sheltering a windy garden

The virtues of hedges as wind screens are explained on page 164. Hedges are effective because wind is filtered, rather than deflected by a solid screen only to bounce back down into the garden further on. Woven fencing works well too, for the same reason. Woven willow hurdles are particularly useful in windy gardens if they are maintained as mobile sections. This way, they can be put up where needed to shelter new plantings while their roots establish. Our garden, perched on the ridge of a hill only 2km (1 mile) from the sea, has a dreadful wind tunnel. Carefully chosen plants will withstand the wind in this vulnerable part of the garden, but they need help in order to anchor themselves into the ground with new roots. We planted three New Zealand flax (*Phormium* 'Alison Blackman') and had to laugh when they were literally blown out of the soil. Short screens pushed into the ground on the windward side solved the problem. Alternatively, a less aesthetically pleasing solution is to fix netting or special windbreak membrane between supports to act as a screen. Windbreak screens should consist of roughly 60 per cent solid material to 40 per cent tiny gaps and holes. A screen reaching

1.2m (4ft) will provide shelter for some distance (about 20 times its height), after which the wind picks up speed again. To succeed in slowing really high winds, a series of windbreaks may be necessary.

High rise

A number of high-rise dwellers create fabulous small gardens on their balconies. Being able to look out onto greenery from a 20th-floor flat must be a real bonus when you are so far from the ground. Exposure to both sun and wind are extreme at these heights and high-rise gardeners have to employ all the tactics used by owners of larger plots at ground level, but concertina'd into a narrow space. They have to anchor everything securely against the wind, for the safety of people below as well as their own plants. The weight-bearing capacity of the balcony is also extremely important.

Most start by creating a windbreak for their smaller plants by erecting a trellis along part of the balcony (not all, or the views will be obscured). Growing in pots and secured to the trellis are a line of wind-resistant trees and shrubs such as rowan (*Sorbus aucuparia*), honey locust (*Gleditsia triacanthos*), birches, cotoneaster and evergreen *Elaeagnus* x *ebbingei*. With pruning and root restriction, they will not reach their usual heights and spreads. Within this windbreak, all kinds of smaller plants will grow, with places for shade-lovers and sun-

There's no reason why you can't have a satisfying garden in the heart of a city.

lovers, including pelargoniums and even tomato plants. I have even seen lawn grasses grown in seed trays clipped with scissors and miniature ponds created in waterproof pots and containers. Small trees, shrubs and herbaceous perennials can stay in the same, lightweight pot for many years as long as they are watered regularly and fed adequately. I'd opt for a slow-release fertiliser added to the top of the pot every spring. Top dress with fresh compost when space in the top of the pot allows.

some wind-tolerant plants

Field maple (*Acer campestre*)
Erman's birch (*Betula ermanii*)
Nootka cypress (*Chamaecyparis nootkatensis*)
Thorn (*Crataegus* x *lavallei* or *C.monogyna* 'Stricta')
Euonymus japonicus
Holly (*Ilex* x *altaclarensis* and *I. aquifolium* cvs)
Laburnum watereri 'Vossii'
Larch (*Larix decidua*)
Magnolia x *loebneri* cvs
Mountain pine (*Pinus mugo*)
Mock orange (*Philadelphus* 'Beauclerk')
Coyote willow (*Salix exigua*)
Whitebeam (*Sorbus aria* 'Lutescens')
White-berried rowan (*Sorbus cashmiriana*)
Western red cedar (*Thuja plicata*)
Lime (*Tilia cordata*)
Guelder rose (*Viburnum opulus* 'Xanthocarpum')
Laurustinus (*Viburnum tinus* 'Gwenllian')

Coastal gardening

Seaside gardening is a mixture of extremes and deliberations. On one hand, there is the joy of being able to grow tender plants on milder coasts where proximity to the sea means there are rarely frosts. On the other, gardeners have to deal not only with harsh winds, but those laden with salt, sand or both. So to persuade a wide range of plants to grow, windbreaks are needed for shelter, but not at the expense of sea views. On a large scale there are plenty of stalwart windbreak trees such as ash, sycamore, hawthorn, oak, evergreen oak (*Quercus ilex*) and Monterey pine (*Pinus radiata*), but those with modest gardens will have to make do with a tough hedge and perhaps a few shrubs to filter salt-laden wind. While these are establishing, protect them with woven fencing or screens as described for windy gardens. Young specimens adapt better than older, larger ones.

Salvage style in the garden: a weathered breakwater provides protection for santolina and valerian.

Inside the shelter, a wide range of smaller plants will live happily and tolerate a lesser degree of wind and salt spray. Conjure up pictures of seaside holidays in your mind and you'll quickly remember hardy fuchsias, hydrangeas, the rounded heads of blue and white-flowered African lilies (*Agapanthus*), pink belladonna lilies (*Amaryllis belladonna*), red hot pokers, Cape fuchsia (*Phygelius capensis*) and Californian fuchsia (*Zauschneria californica*). Separate banks of colour are made with silvery foliage plants like *Artemisia ludoviciana* and *A.* 'Powis Castle', cotton lavender (*Santolina chamaecyparissus*) and pungent curry plant (*H. italicum* subsp. *serotinum*).

tips for coastal gardens

● Don't be upset if your windbreak plants take a hammering during wild, wet winters. They will often look ragged on the windward side by spring, but usually make better growth during spring and summer. They are there primarily to do a job and if they look good in the process, that's a bonus.

● Shingle and seashell mulches look particularly appropriate near the sea, or can mimic a seaside garden inland. They are also particularly good at conserving moisture, suppressing weeds and acting as an attractive background for low-growing coastal plants.

● Many plants from New Zealand have proved themselves tough and resilient in the face of salty winds. They are not usually able to tolerate severe cold, but make fantastic choices for milder coastlines where temperatures are unlikely to reach much below –5°C (23°F). Try daisy bushes, including silvery-leaved *Olearia traversii*, *Pittosporum tenuifolium* cultivars., barbed wire bushes (*Corokia cotoneaster* and *C.virgata*), *Elaeagnus*, *Griselinia littoralis*, the evergreen climber *Muehlenbackia complexa*, hebes and New Zealand flax (*Phormium*).

other tough shrubs & hedging plants for coastal areas

Escallonia rubra 'Crimson Spire'
Sea buckthorn (*Hippophae rhamnoides*)
Hedgehog rose (*Rosa rugosa*)
Elder (*Sambucus nigra*)
Spanish broom (*Spartium junceum*)
Tamarisk (*Tamarix ramosissima*)

Plants with the sea in their names!
Sea thrift (*Armeria juniperifolia maritima*)
Sea cabbage (*Crambe maritima*)
Sea holly (*Eryngium planum, E.alpinum*)
Sea lavender (*Limonium latifolium*)
Beach aster (*Erigeron glaucus* 'Elstead Pink')

Slopes

Gentle undulations make for an interesting garden, but steep slopes can be the stuff of nightmares. Do you cut a zig-zag path down through and spend your entire gardening life balanced on one leg? Or is it better to terrace? Terracing is going to be time consuming and expensive, with plenty of attention needed to drainage at the base of the beds and firm walls to support the soil. But once you have them, steps can lead onto the flat surfaces and each will be backed by a retaining wall, offering wonderful planting opportunities. Hopefully, by doing this, terracing manages the worst of the slope, leaving only a few banks to plant.

planting on banks

The success of banks largely depends on their aspect and whether they happen to be viewed mainly from the top or from the bottom. Your best angle is a south-facing slope viewed from below, all the better to admire the shimmering, rainbow colours of sun-loving plants laid out in front of you. From above, you tend to look into the backs of the plants. Shady slopes are by no means a disaster, especially where trees cast light shade, creating perfect woodland conditions for hardy ferns and woodland plants with lush foliage and dainty flowers.

● The soil on banks is easily eroded, so covering the ground with plants is a good way of stabilising the soil by knitting it together with roots.

● Banks are inherently dry, so consider installing an irrigation system (a seep hose would be ideal) to make life easier for you and your plants.

● Condition soil thoroughly before planting and create a level planting pocket with a rim to hold water.

● To direct water straight to the roots, bury a short piece of drainpipe or even a flowerpot beside the plant, leaving the top poking out. Water can be applied through this so it doesn't run away down the slope.

Plants for sunny banks
Abelia x *grandiflora* 'Francis Mason'
Californian lilac (*Ceanothus thyrsiflorus* var. *repens*)
Rock rose (*Cistus* x *purpureus*)
Convolvulus cneorum
Foxgloves (*Digitalis purpurea*)
Genista lydia
Sun rose (*Helianthemum* 'Wisley Primrose') and others
Beauty bush (*Kolkwitzia amabilis* 'Pink Cloud')
Lavenders of all kinds
Toadflax (*Linaria purpurea*)
Mock orange (*Philadelphus* 'Manteau d'Hermine')
Jerusalem sage (*Phlomis fruticosus*)
Phlomis russelianus
Rosemary of all kinds
Verbena bonariensis

Plants for shady banks
Bear's breeches (*Acanthus mollis*)
Japanese maple (*Acer palmatum* 'Dissectum')
Elephant's ears (*Bergenia* 'Sunningdale')
Anchusa (*Brunnera macrophylla*)
Centuaria montana
Clematis x *jouiniana* 'Praecox'
Cotoneaster horizontalis
Bishop's mitre (*Epimedium* of all kinds)
Euonymus japonicus 'Emerald 'n' Gold'
Geranium nodosum
Snowy woodrush (*Luzula nivea*)
Lungwort (*Pulmonaria saccharata*)
Foam flower (*Tiarella cordifolia*)

Genista lydia

personal priorities

Anne: Part of the planning stages of a garden must include an analysis of your own personal needs. These will change as a family grows up and gardens usually mature and change along with their owners.

Time constraints

Gardening should be a pleasure, so the gardener must have enough time to look after what is there. If you can't win and are always chasing your tail, gardening becomes a chore, which is a shame, as it should be rewarding and fulfilling. When planning a new garden from scratch, think hard about how you will maintain what you intend to create.

Low-maintenance tricks

Bare soil is the bane of the busy gardener. Leave it unfilled and weeds grow. Bare soil also needs a lot of tickling over (usually with a border fork) to keep it looking really good. The answer is to cover as much of it as possible, in the early stages by mulching (see pages 114–16), and later by allowing ground cover plants to knit together both above and below ground (see pages 114–15). If you like to see gaps between your plants, use permanent mulches to protect the soil surface. Choose either well-rotted organic matter to resemble soil, shingle (large grade is less messy than small), stone chippings, seashells or other hard materials.

If you've inherited a garden that might have been someone's hobby, but you don't want to make it yours, plan some changes to make life easier.

● If there are too many borders, grass them over. Mowing is easier than maintaining borders and can be delegated to non-gardening family members or a contractor.

● If you've a very large garden, yet don't want to move, have the top part near the house fenced, hedged or walled off in some way. Keep this tidy and turn the rest into a paddock. Plant a few good trees, surround with stock-proof fencing and allow local horse or sheep owners to graze their animals there.

● In tiny gardens, a paved area with no lawn and plants in raised beds and containers will make life easier.

● Instead of apologising for an untidy garden, create organised chaos, introduce log piles and more plants to attract bees, butterflies and birds. Call it a wildlife friendly garden and everyone will be impressed (see pages 31–33).

children in the garden

There is no reason why gardening cannot continue around your children and their enjoyment of a plot. I admit this is easier for me because I now have a large garden of about 0.6 hectare (1.6 acres). This allows for a productive kitchen garden (fenced), borders around the house, a rabbit run, a wide flat lawned area for trampoline, badminton, football and so forth. There is still space for an orchard and wild area. We used to enjoy a meadow, but this has now been turned into a paddock for a Shetland pony.

When we had a smaller garden, I banned football and took children to the local park instead.

Many children love to be given a bed or border of their own; this must have good soil and enjoy an open position or they will be put off for life. As a rule children prefer to grow large, fun and edible plants.

plants for children to grow

Pumpkins
Sweetcorn
Herbs
Sunflowers
Dahlias
Ladybird poppies (*Papaver commutatum* 'Lady Bird')
Squirting cucumbers (*Ecballium hirsutum*)

An unusual red variety of sunflower, *Helianthus annuus* 'Velvet Queen'

In my experience, children tire quickly of houses built for them in the garden, but love the creativity of making their own dens. Leave a wild area for them to roam about in (the bottom corner of a small garden will do). Provide a variety of twiggy sticks, planks and assorted wood and they'll do the rest themselves. Lawns are great for children, as they're the basis of many games and entertainments. Again, they'll make their own camp cities out of folding chairs, old curtains, blankets and pegs. Keep the main activities in view of the house so you can keep an eye on your offspring.

Safety for children

Ponds are a danger area for small children, who can drown in as little as a few centimetres of water. As such, they are best avoided. Fortunately you can install water features that don't involve a depth of standing water. But for older children, ponds are a great source of fascination.

Many garden plants are poisonous and if we eradicated them all from our plots we'd be digging up rhododendrons, box, daffodils and lupins as well as more well-known suspects like laburnum and yew. When my children were little, I made sure tempting poisonous berries were removed from the likes of marble-leaved *Arum italicum* subsp *italicum* 'Marmoratum'. Spurges (euphorbias), whose sap can be irritating to sensitive skin, were moved to the back of borders. Plants of extreme toxicity such as monkshood (*Aconitum*) were banned altogether. At the same time, the children were taught not to experiment with plants and to ask before they ate. But everyone must find their own solution to this problem. Should you suspect your child has eaten a poisonous plant, remove any remains from their mouths and take a sample when seeking help.

Gardens can be dangerous places, so always keep chemicals under lock and key, and make sure that children are not wandering about while mowing is taking place, sharp tools are not left lying around and the tops of canes are softened by plastic guards to protect eyes.

Children can learn to love gardening at an early age if you give them jobs of their own and make it seem like fun.

elderly or disabled gardeners

Raised beds are the answer for gardeners who find bending difficult, or are restricted to wheelchairs. Built of brick, or attractive stone, they raise both the plants and the soil to a height where they are easily appreciated and worked on. (See pages 68–72 for Matt's tips on making raised beds.)

For elderly gardeners, installing ramps instead of steps, or shallow steps with rails will help considerably in preventing an accident.

Garden users with impaired sight need plenty of sensory stimulation for the nose, ears and fingers. Rails to guide them round the garden should bring them into contact with scented flowers, aromatic leaves, soft, furry foliage, smooth bark and the rustling of bamboo or rattling of seed pods.

Anne's suggested plants for the visually impaired

Scented plants
Lawson's cypress (*Chamaecyparis lawsoniana* cvs)
Moroccan broom (*Cytisus battandieri*)
Pink (*Dianthus* 'Mrs.Sinkins')
Gum (*Eucalyptus dalrympleana*)
Magnolia grandiflora
Narcissus 'Quail'
Climbing rose (*Rosa* 'Etoile d'Holland')
Lilac (*Syringa vulgaris* cvs)
Viburnum x bodantense 'Dawn'

Prunus serrula

Tactile plants
Pelargonium tomentosum
   (soft leaves, peppermint scent)
Bhutan pine (*Pinus wallichiana*)
   (smooth bark)
Tibetan cherry (*Prunus serrula*)
   (smooth and peeling bark)
Lambs lugs (*Stachys byzantina*)
   (furry leaves)

entertaining

Not all garden owners are passionate about plants, but most do want their plot to look good and to function as an extra room, especially for entertaining. A patio or deck is likely to be the focus of a garden, hopefully encircled by plants to give privacy. Site patios carefully to make the most of sun and shelter, but think about the need for summer shade as well. The main patio should be large enough for cooking, table and chairs, but, if space permits, plan in a couple of smaller seating places for winter sun or morning sun (see also John's thoughts on garden rooms on pages 45–49).

Above: An ideal evening oasis: a patio next to the pond, where you can enjoy the sight and sound of water, and the warmth of the last rays of sun.

evening oasis

Those who return late in the evening to enjoy their gardens should bear that in mind at the planning stages. Design a secluded seating area near the house, with perhaps a small water feature to add sound and when choosing plants, opt for scents and pale flowers to shine at dusk. Many lilies are scented and their perfume intensifies as light falls. Stagger bulb plantings during late winter and spring, to provide a succession of lilies in pots, including my favourites *Lilum longiflorum*, *L.* 'Casa Blanca', *L.* 'Marco Polo' and *L.* 'African Queen'. True evening-scented tobacco plants (*Nicotiana alata*) don't open their white flowers fully by day, but come evening, they pump up and open fully, belting out a sweet fragrance. Most honeysuckles are at their most powerful in the evening and I can recommend *Lonicera* x *americana*, *L. periclymenum* 'Belgica' (the early Dutch) and *L. p.* 'Serotina' (late Dutch) and the semi-evergreen Japanese honeysuckles *L. japonica* 'Halliana' and *L. japonica* var. *repens*.

self-sufficiency

If you only have a small or modest plot and want to grow a wide range of crops in an attractive, kitchen garden style, then I suggest you make your whole garden into a potager. This is where vegetables, fruit, herbs and flowers are grown together in beautiful and harmonious ways. We have fenced an area of our garden off as a kitchen garden and I often think how well it stands on its own. It contains an attractive wooden greenhouse with a patio by the side of it. The plot is irregular in shape, but divided roughly into four to make crop rotation easier (see pages 134–35 for more about crop rotation). Paths give access and there is a more or less central water feature.

As well as growing vegetables, we have soft fruit and apple trees trained as upright cordons. These are great if you want to fit lots of fruit varieties into a small space. Each tree is secured to a stake and fruit grows on short spurs growing from the single main trunk, all controlled by summer pruning. The trees are spaced about 1.8m (6ft) apart and make good vertical accents. Rows of flowers such as antirrhinums, gladioli and zinnias are grown for cutting and sunflowers are planted wherever they will fit in. The paths are lined with thyme, sage, lavender, golden feverfew and other herbs, many raised cheaply from seed.

Winter interest in a kitchen garden needs some work, but if you are clever with your path edgings and use evergreen herbs, there will always be some structure. A surprising number of crops stand during winter, including the winter brassicas (Brussels sprouts, Savoy cabbage, kale, sprouting broccoli) and leeks. Don't be scared to use props to full advantage, but make them appropriate, such as terracotta rhubarb and seakale forcers or lantern cloches.

For more on the practical aspects of planning a kitchen garden, see pages 46–47.

gardening for cut flowers

Any garden can yield a surprising quantity of material for flower arrangers with regular jobs decorating churches, or supplying material for flower clubs. I am not a skilled flower arranger, but I do make up little posies of what's in bloom for a small vase on my desk, so that I can enjoy the essence of my garden while I am working. Grander arrangements seem to require a framework of shrubby material, fleshed out with fillers of foliage and small flowers, with larger, more sumptuous blooms carefully placed to provide the main impact. The latter can be bought or grown, but gardens come into their own as providers of foliage and fillers. Skeins of ivy, fern fronds, hosta leaves, the long sword-like foliage of New Zealand flax (*Phormium*) and stems from shrubs such as *Elaeagnus* and *Pittosporum* are all useful. For pretty posies and tight, domed tussie mussies, *Brachyglottis greyi*, bay, hyssop, rosemary and lavender are ideal.

For flowering filler material, members of the cow parsley or carrot family come in useful. Try growing bishop's flower (*Ammi majus*) or dill (*Anethum graveolens*) as annuals. Spurges, too, are useful, such as caper spurge (*Euphorbia lathyris*), sun spurge (*E. cyparissias*) and *E. oblongata*. Colourful fillers might include biennial sweet rocket (*Hesperis matronalis*) and tobacco plants (*Nicotiana*) grown as annuals from spring-sown seed. Don't be afraid to use the kitchen garden to raise plants specifically for cutting. Try Iceland poppies (*Papaver nudicale*), dahlias and rudbeckias.

Papaver nudicale (Iceland or Arctic poppy) in the cutting garden.

tip

● I like to lift tulips that have flowered once in my borders and remove them from the equation before they can spoil next season's colour combinations. Give them a good six weeks in leaf before lifting and drying the bulbs off. Replant in late autumn, about 13cm (5in) apart into rows in rich soil. They will then yield excellent cut flowers the following spring.

what kind of gardener are you?

Anne: Having taken into account the practical implications of your plot and what you need from it, now think about what approach you will apply to your newly renovated garden. There are all kinds of gardeners in the world, going about their hobby in vastly different ways and all enjoying it immensely. I can recall a retired miner who liked his bedding plants. In a tiny garden, he created dazzling displays of begonias backed by fuchsias and set off by a narrow river of fine lawn cut closely twice a week. Dead flowers and leaves were assiduously removed, any insect that moved was sprayed, as was any disease that dared blight his plants. In the autumn, plants were cleared and the ground rested, with nothing in it. In early spring, seeds were germinated under glass, plants pruned and started into growth and the cycle repeated itself. Not my style, but you could not help but admire what he did so well. And he loved it.

At the other end of the scale, you have gardeners whose plots are a cultivated wilderness. No garden chemicals are used, native plants are carefully introduced according to the habitats available and wildlife of all kinds cherished.

Many gardeners tread a middle ground, intervening with a few garden chemicals, but only as a last resort and having thought through all the implications they may have on garden life. As far as my own garden is concerned, we want to grow exotic plants, but try to match them with prevailing conditions so we can garden as naturally as possible without altering our soil type or using undue quantities of water. Rather than lining plants up in rows, we experiment by trying the naturalistic approach. You can observe and copy plant associations found in nature, creating woodland glades or prairie-style plantings of perennials and grasses in loose drifts.

Organic gardening

The decision to garden organically means recognising and respecting the small environment over which you have control. In a way, you are making a decision to stop dominating your plot, and instead casting yourself in the role of caretaker. You may own the land, but it is already the home of countless other living creatures.

The organic movement started in agriculture back in the 1940s, as a backlash against the increasing use of chemical fertilisers. The basic premise is that you feed the soil not the plant, by adding organic matter in the form of compost, manure and other materials. This increases the numbers of soil micro-organisms and they in turn break down the organic material, releasing nutrients for plant growth.

You garden thoughtfully, without polluting your environment and as a result, it will be teeming with life. Most of this will be beneficial, and a surprising number of problems vanish because there are natural predators in place to keep control over pest populations. Healthy plants, not overfed with artificial fertilisers, tend not to suffer from diseases. When there are problems, these can generally be solved by lateral thinking rather than reaching for a chemical solution.

Most organic gardeners extend their philosophy by trying to lead sustainable lives, use renewable resources, reduce waste and recycle.

To become an organic gardener

● Stop using chemical fertilisers and pesticides, because they will jeopardise your efforts to grow organically. Your local authority will advise you as to how unwanted products can be disposed of.

● Feed the soil with organic matter.

● Encourage all the wildlife in your garden to flourish.

Encouraging wildlife to the garden

Making sure your garden is visited by as much wildlife as possible will make it healthier as well as more interesting. Some of it – the slugs, snails, greenfly and blackfly for

Ponds for wildlife should have sloping sides or marginals in raised containers around the edge to help all sorts of creatures to reach the water safely. Long-stalked plants such as water iris enable dragonfly larvae to climb out of the water before shedding their skins and flying away as adults. Quality planting around the pond not only looks great, but provides shelter for amphibians.

but these can be dealt with by applying a biological control harmless to the environment but devastating to slugs. Millions of slug-killing nematodes are watered into the soil, severely reducing their population.

You can have a tidy garden and still attract wildlife, but generally you will create more habitats by being relaxed enough to allow for areas of long grass, planned areas of wildflowers (weeds if you like) and log piles of rotting wood to encourage insects. Thicket-like hedges provide roosting and nesting sites for birds. I even turn my back on what I've been taught are 'good' horticultural practices. A little dead wood on my trees gives the woodpeckers and other birds who inspect bark for bugs (usually beetle larvae) something to go at. Windfall fruit left lying on the ground provides late food for butterflies, blackbirds, fieldfares and pheasants. Leaving old stems on herbaceous perennials over winter has become widely accepted.

Ponds are vital in providing a permanent source of water for a variety of creatures. Make sure the sides slope, or are decorated by pots of marginals so that animals can access the water without drowning.

instance – are certainly infuriating. But they are all food for other animals whose presence makes sure pests rarely reach plague proportions. Eradicate the pest completely and you are taking away food from the predators, who will then go elsewhere. Worse, by killing pests with chemical sprays, you are potentially killing natural predators in the process.

In my garden, aphids on fruit trees and honeysuckles are usually removed promptly by the large bird population and the myriad beneficial insects for whom aphids are also food. We suffer from relatively few slugs and snails, probably because there are so many birds and toads in the garden. We have a problem with underground slugs infesting potatoes,

Mammals

Some gardeners are infuriated by the rabbits, moles and squirrels who visit their gardens. True, they do nibble your plants, make hills in your lawn and dig up your bulbs (often while planting acorns at the same time, ensuring an interesting oak plantation the following year). You won't get rid of them by getting angry, but a change of attitude will make you feel better. I have rabbit-fenced my kitchen garden; if I had moles, I'd collect up their molehill earth to use as potting compost or lawn top dressing and I laugh at the antics of squirrels, even when they steal food put out for the birds. Voles can be a nuisance, but their populations seem to sort themselves out. If mice infest my sheds and greenhouse, I use mouse traps rather than poison and I long one day to find some hazelnuts with tell-tale holes in them, suggesting that there are dormice in the garden. Hedgehogs do no harm at all, but eat lots of slugs.

Attract blue tits by putting out fat balls or nuts and they will also pick your plants over for aphids and other bugs.

Birds

Birds bring a garden to life with their song and flight, and the insect- and mollusc-eaters among them are great for keeping plants clean of pests. Many birds prefer to fly short distances from tree to tree, so bring them right into your garden by planting a bird corridor of trees and shrubs across open spaces. If your garden lacks good nesting sites, put up a variety of nesting boxes to encourage birds to stay. Dense hedges are valued as roosting sites. There are many seed- and fruit-bearing plants birds find attractive. They'll probably find your blackcurrant bushes attractive too, but in our garden we never want to eat all the fruit and neither do the birds, so we share.

Anne's recommended 'bird plants'

For fruit
Virginia creeper (*Ampelopsis quinquefolia*)
Spindle (*Euonymus europaeus*)
Wild strawberries (*Fragaria vesca*)
Ivy (*Hedera helix*)
Holly (*Ilex aquifolium* cvs)
Crab apple (*Malus* 'Golden Hornet')
Elder (*Sambucus nigra*)
Rowan (*Sorbus aucuparia*)
Guelder rose (*Viburnum opulus*)

For seeds
Ornamental onions (*Allium* spp.)
Michaelmas daisy (*Aster novi-belgii*)
Birch (*Betula pendula*)
Teasel (*Dipsacus fullonum*)
Sunflowers (*Helianthus* spp.)

Sorbus aucuparia

Reptiles and amphibians

Finding these fascinating animals in the garden is always a thrill. Here, we have lots of newts and toads and the occasional slow worm. Frogs are common and some gardens are lucky enough to be visited by lizards and grass snakes. Between them, these creatures eat a lot of slug and insects. Undisturbed places like log piles and compost heaps are favourite.

Beneficial creepy-crawlies

To attract hoverflies, just grow a wide range of flowers. Hoverfly larvae are strange little articles, like almost translucent greenish-brown maggots. They may not be pretty, but they eat huge numbers of aphids, as do the adults and larvae of lacewings and ladybirds. Adults of both these insects hibernate during winter, searching out dense, dry material in which to rest.

Beetles are handy pollinators and some eat slugs. Wasps are surprisingly good for the garden during spring and the first half of summer, when their diet is high in protein and they eat lots of pests. Unfortunately, come late summer and autumn, their preference changes to sugary foods and they are out in force eating jam sandwiches and fruit. Bees perform a starring role in pollination and without them we would have a much poorer set of crops like runner beans and on our fruit trees. There are many different kinds, easy to attract by growing a variety of nectar-rich plants throughout the year. Bring these flowers right into the kitchen garden and orchard so the bees are drawn to the flowers most in need of pollination. Aubrieta, *Alyssum saxatile*, pulmonarias, wallflowers, clover in lawns, buddleja, most herbs including lavender, thyme and marjoram, sedums and fuchsias are just a few of the many flowers bees love.

Butterflies and moths, like birds, bring a garden to life, though the larvae or caterpillars of some can be pests. The worst are undoubtedly those that feed on cabbage, and the only real answer is to cover your plants in tents of mesh to prevent the butterflies from laying their eggs. Some moth larvae attack fruit trees by eating their leaves or, worse, their fruit. But on the whole we love to see these insects on the wing. A wide range of plants, including areas of grasses and wild flowers, should ensure plenty of food plants for the larvae.

Spiders do a tremendous job in the garden by catching many flies, including aphids. The orb webs of some are beautiful when strung with dew in the autumn. In their turn spiders provide food for many birds.

Wildflowers

Patches of wildflowers suit some areas of the garden and if you have a wild area under trees, or a meadow of long grass, you might decide to restrict yourself to native plants in these areas, so that it seems as if your garden contains a small piece of countryside. There are plenty to choose from and they will thrive as long as you introduce them into the appropriate habitat. Wildflower gardens are not self-maintaining, though. In the wild, you can see how other, thuggish natives push out the prettier wildflowers. You will still need to weed out brambles, nettles, ivy, thistles and docks to enjoy your 'improved' wild-flower area.

John will have more to say about planning a wild-flower garden on page 46.

Top: Bumble bees emerge earlier in the season than honey bees, so are important for the pollination of early-flowering plants.
Right: Don't clear the thistles away from a wild patch in the garden – butterflies like this brimstone love to feed on them.

the inherited garden

Anne: On moving into a property, few of us will be faced with either a blank canvas or the garden of our dreams. Usually, we inherit the efforts of previous occupants, ranging from meticulously kept beds and borders to a completely overgrown jungle of rough grass and old shrubs. Sadly, even the loveliest of gardens is unlikely to meet the exact needs of a new family moving in. Everybody has different tastes, requirements and time available for maintenance. The time-stricken would struggle to look after high-input, cottage-style gardens or large potagers of vegetables and fruit. Feeling that you will never win in your garden is a miserable state and new owners should assess what they have inherited and adapt the garden to suit their own lifestyle.

Unless you want to be radical, the accepted wisdom is to leave the garden for a year and learn about its little foibles before launching in with new designs. Although a clean start might be compelling, there's a lot to be said for maturity.

Charging in to rip out established trees and shrubs will affect shelter from wind, shady refuge from sun and how birds use the garden. For assessment purposes, a complete year is needed to discover whether you love or loathe the rose flowers, whether the apples are cookers or eaters and what flowers materialise on herbaceous perennials and spring bulbs.

By the time a year is up, new owners will also have worked out how they use their garden space and can apply this to drive new designs or alterations. Wild areas with trees might become the children's private forest and a more natural playground than anything planned by an adult. A fragrant old climbing rose, having stood the test of time, may well be the best, most disease-resistant type for the garden. Use it as the inspiration for an arch, pergola or arbour. Maybe the smart front door is never used and the path from car to back door is all-important. Well-used paths need to be of generous width and well-planted with year-round appeal. Particularly sunny, secluded parts of the garden may not, at first, be obvious. When they are, then they become sites for patios or seating areas.

Jobs for the first few months

A year's grace from radical alterations is no excuse for laziness, however, as there are always plenty of jobs to get on with.

Lawns

Most gardens have a lawn and even the roughest can be easily improved. If the grass is 8–10cm (3–4in) high on moving in, new owners must react quickly, before it grows beyond the capabilities of an ordinary domestic lawnmower. Longer, rougher grassy areas can be tackled by hiring a special type of mower suitable for the job. Long grass looks terrible when it has just been cut, as all the green part is removed, leaving coarse, yellowish stalks behind, but it will soon recover if you mow again, this time with an ordinary mower, and apply a lawn weed and feed during spring and early summer. One application followed by regular mowing should restore even the ghastliest lawn to a usable sward. If the lawn still has a definite edge to it, continue to trim the edge and push the soil back away from it as described on page 157.

Trees and shrubs

Identifying trees and shrubs can be difficult, even with the help of books with pictures. As they come into leaf and flower, take photographs of their distinguishing features and note the date. By taking the photographs to garden centres or nurseries with advisory desks, or with the help of a garden club or society, it should be possible to determine what they are.

Examine trees to make sure they are safe, with no rotten trunks or branches liable to fall. Where too many trees have been planted, some might have to be removed to benefit the rest. If in doubt, engage the services of a qualified tree surgeon. Check tree ties on young trees to make sure they are not constricting the stems as they grow. Pull out weeds growing around their bases of trees and spread a mulch over their roots, though not piled up around the trunk.

Keeping a cottage garden beautiful might be too much work for some busy families. But wait a year while enjoying the roses, dusty miller (*Lychnis coronarius*, the deep pink flowers to the left of the sundial) and sea hollies (*Eryngium maritimum*, the spiky white ones to the right) before making drastic alterations.

Overgrown shrubs sometimes block paths or cover windows and will need pruning back in the short term. Rather than reduce them to stumps, or prune them like topiary, I would thin them out by removing one third of the oldest and wildest stems. Trace these back either to the base or to a healthy side shoot and cut them out, starting with those most in the way. Stand back and check the shape of the shrub now and again, trying to keep it as natural as possible. This method may not be textbook perfect, but can safely be carried out at any time of the year and on any shrub, regardless of its identity.

Weeds

Leave them too long and they will multiply and cause havoc, so I'm afraid the year's grace does not include exemption from weeding. Preventing annual weeds from seeding, and digging out the larger perennial types such as thistles, nettles, docks and creeping buttercup, is good damage limitation. Borders infested with pernicious weeds such as ground elder and bindweed need more thought. Do your best to prevent the spread of these weeds to other areas, and read pages 109–11 to plan an eradication strategy.

Hedges

Well-kept hedges make fabulous boundaries to your garden and backdrops for your plants. Those with lovely shapes and tight growth will have been clipped regularly and at the right time, and this regular upkeep must be maintained to keep them in good condition (see pages 170–73). Renovating neglected hedges is a job worth tackling before the year's rest is up. Should untended beech, hornbeam or yew hedges have grown halfway across the garden, they can be pruned back hard during the winter months. Should you own both sides of the hedge, prune one side and then wait a couple of years before tackling the other. By doing this, you will gain valuable time, as neglected hedges can take three years to regain their former beauty. Cypress hedges cannot be cut back into old wood and should only be renovated by trimming into green shoots.

defining your terms

Bob: Gardeners use a lot of more or less technical terms to describe plants and how they grow, so if you are new to gardening it makes sense to learn and understand some of the vocabulary.

Annuals are short-lived plants that germinate from seed. They grow, flower, set seed and die all within a year or thereabouts. Although some may have a life cycle of only a few months, and others may germinate one year and flower the next, all die afterwards. Annuals may reach 60cm (24in) or so in height (or bigger if they are sunflowers), but generally less. Their brief growth means they are often used to fill gaps in beds – Virginian stocks and pot marigolds, for example. Some longer-lived plants may be treated as annuals, especially summer bedding plants such as pelargoniums and busy lizzies (*Impatiens*).

Biennials are plants that take more than one growing season to complete their cycle – for example, they may be grown in the first summer or autumn to flower the following year and then be thrown away. Many biennials form spires of flowers and are useful for adding height to beds – foxgloves and Canterbury bells are typical examples in the flower garden. Some short-lived perennials such as hollyhocks and wallflowers are treated as biennials, because they quickly become leggy or ugly and flower less well after the first couple of years.

In the vegetable garden, many crops such as onions and carrots are biennials, although after making their big stores full of reserves in the first year they don't usually get to flower and seed in the second year as we have eaten them before then.

Perennials are plants that ought to live longer than a year or two. Some are naturally very long-lived, but most have a much shorter useful gardening life. Many plants that would be perennial in another country are treated as annuals in the UK: zonal pelargoniums, for example, dislike the merest suggestion

Nepeta (the purple flowers) is a perennial that will look good for a number of years, but foxgloves (*Digitalis*, the tall pink spikes) are biennials and will need to be replaced after the second year. Fortunately, they tend to self-seed, so may replenish themselves with no intervention from you.

of frost, so are best restricted to summer displays, whereas in warmer climates they would survive several years out of doors. Most perennials take a while to reach flowering size – two to five years for the smaller and more herbaceous plants; anything from three to 30 for trees and shrubs, with the bigger examples generally taking longer – so trees take longer than shrubs, and fruit trees grown from pips take longest of all. Most perennials benefit from having their dead flower heads removed to save them wasting resources on seed production.

Herbaceous plants, whether annual, biennial or perennial, have soft stems – unlike trees and shrubs, they do not form hard, woody parts that endure for more than a year. The perennial ones mostly die down in winter (though there are exceptions, such as hellebores) and are often grouped together in beds with other herbaceous plants, including bulbs. Clumps of herbaceous plants tend to grow wider but rarely taller year by year, making them more convenient than shrubs and trees.

Deciduous plants are those – mainly trees and shrubs – that lose their leaves in the winter, often having provided us with a brilliant display of autumn colour before they do so.

Evergreens are perennials that do not lose their leaves in winter as deciduous plants do, nor die down like herbaceous ones. They are of most value during winter, providing shelter, colour and often flowers and scent, too. Many are coniferous (pine-like) or have hard waxy leaves, such as laurel. Most dislike harsh winds, especially if on frozen soil. Evergreys are the sub-group of silver- and grey-foliaged (or nearly so) plants. Many of these are Mediterranean in origin and some – including lavender, sage, santolina and thyme – are among our best herbs. These all need sunny sites and well-drained soils.

Top: Holly (this is the horned variety, *Ilex cornuta* 'Red Robe') is an evergreen shrub but may lose its leaves temporarily if distressed.
Right: Although normally classed as a shrub, *Yucca gloriosa* is one of those plants that blurs the edges of the definition and can look very elegant in a herbaceous border. It is normally grown for its sword-like foliage, with the bonus of long-lasting spikes of white flowers any time from mid-summer to late autumn.

Shrubs, bushes and trees

Perennials with enduring woody parts are classed as shrubs or bushes – unless they use other plants or structures for support, in which case they are climbers, or are grown on a single stem or trunk, in which case they are trees. A shrub is usually classed as an ornamental, but a bush may also bear fruit.

Shrubs are often grouped together in their own border to prevent them choking out everything but climbers. They usually need pruning to keep them under control and can rarely be left to grow into their natural forms – which is by far the most beautiful way to have them. Pruning is best done well or not at all (see pages 208–12). Most deciduous subjects are best pruned in winter, except for the stone fruits and most evergreens, which are done in spring or summer. Sensible gardeners choose their shrubs as the dwarf forms to save on growth and pruning requirements. Most shrubs and trees can be trained into more ornamental forms, such as espaliers or cordons, for extra effect or for bigger flowers or fruits (see pages 200–02). Some climbers such as kiwi and wisteria can also be trained to espalier or even tree forms and many others will form bushes if cut back continuously.

Bulbs, corms, rhizomes and tubers

Many biennials or perennials store their reserves as bulbs, corms or rhizomes so they can go dormant and re-grow the next year. Botanically they are very different, though to most of us they are almost interchangeable terms. Technically, a bulb is a swollen, leaf-based storage organ you find with tulips and onions, for example; a corm is the swollen base of the stem of plants such as crocus and gladioli; and a stem tuber is something in between the two, such as a potato. A rhizome is a swelling that connects roots and leaves and that extends horizontally in plants such as flag iris, lily-of-the-valley and Solomon's seal. Short, erect rhizomes can be used as rootstock for plants such as primroses (but the rootstock for a tree, shrub or any grafted plant is a special set of roots grown to affect the qualities of the top or 'scion' grafted onto it.) Great care needs to be taken over the handling and storage of bulbs, corms, rhizomes and stem tubers, and with planting depths; read the paperwork for each new one you come across.

Hardy, half-hardy and tender

Hardy plants are ones that can typically stand the commonest miserable winter weather and spring frosts and survive without extra protection. The extent of this group is uncertain, since really hard winters kill many plants normally thought to be hardy. As a general rule, most hardy shrubs survive most years and most hardy annuals can be sown in autumn to give earlier flowers than spring-sown batches. Hardy does not mean vigorous or immune to wind sear!

To be more precise, in the UK we consider plants to be hardy if they will endure the light frosts and freezing temperatures that are experienced in our maritime climate most winters. However, every so often a harder winter comes and many so-called hardy plants are lost – oaks have been known to burst their trunks! In North America, where greater extremes of temperature are common, the Department of Agriculture (USDA) publishes a map that divides the continent into zones defined by maximum and minimum temperatures, and plants are sold as 'hardy to zone 3' or 'suitable for zones 4–9', etc. Even plants considered hardy in the UK are best confined to the maritime regions in the northern zones of North America, as the central continental winters have far lower temperatures than anything we normally have to contend with.

Half-hardy plants are not tough enough to endure any real frost or winter weather. Some, such as lobelias and salvias, are usually started under cover, often with extra warmth, then hardened off before being planted out for the summer and dying in autumn.

Tender plants are just that – they cannot endure any cold. Even so, many can be hardened off and brought outdoors in the middle of summer. Others may be grown under cover for more of the year and all year round with heat.

Alpines, aquatics and marginals

Alpines mostly grow wild in mountains. The ones we buy for our gardens are predominantly natural species, rather than

Iris pseudacorus 'Variegata'. Irises are herbaceous perennials that grow from bulbs or rhizomes, spread freely and soon form attractive clumps.

Nymphaea 'Rose Arey'. The waterlily is one of the most familiar – and spectacular – aquatic plants.

man-made selections. Alpines are often small specimens with charming flowers but are usually scentless. They do not mind cold or wind, but hate damp – most need superb drainage and a cool root run. Alpines are best grown on screes (flat piles of small stones), in pots or in raised ornamental beds.

Aquatics are plants adapted to life in water. Pay careful attention to planting instructions, particularly water depths (see pages 80–81).

Marginals stand by water and like to have their feet wet – most resent drying out. Bulrushes are native to Britain, and are a good choice because they attract wildlife. The vaccinium fruit bushes such as cranberry and blueberry make productive marginals.

Different roles for different plants

An ornamental is a plant grown for its aesthetic appeal. In other words, we get no actual use from it. The opposites are esculents (edibles) or utilitarian fruit and vegetables. Skeleton plants are ones that form the structure of the garden, especially in winter. They will mostly be deciduous or evergreen trees and shrubs, and are often planted as the

backdrop or backbone to beds and borders as their bulk and outline remain fairly constant for other plants to show up against.

The pretty alpine plant *Polygala calcarea* 'Lillet' growing through rocks – a reproduction of its natural environment.

Fillers form the larger part of most planting schemes, with groups of plants in threes, fives and sevens, fleshing out the beds and borders. This may sound odd, but planting odd numbers produces a more pleasing effect than even numbers. Believe me – try it with anything. Fillers are more often composed of herbaceous plants and smaller shrubs.

Bedding plants are temporary fillers of beds and borders, enabling more use to be got from the same area by changing the constituents wholesale. Usually this is just for summer display, but it is possible to make three or more separate and different 'shows' on the same ground in the course of a year. 'Carpet bedding' is the term used for a colourful, relatively low and flat display such as that required for filling flowerbeds on roundabouts and other municipal sites.

Spot and dot plants are ones with visual impact. They are used singly and are usually of contrasting colour, height and form. Used sparingly, they are effective; done badly, they are revolting.

Specimen plants are usually single, finely grown examples of a particular plant. A good way to set them off is to place them in a lawn or against a uniform hedge.

Cosmos bipinnatus – a useful summer 'filler' or bedding plant.

types of garden

John: So you have inherited the space and you want to garden. What type of garden do you want? There are many styles to choose from, and the good news is that you are not restricted to one type. Armed with all the information that Anne has given and your scale drawing you may be able to fit a series of mini-gardens or garden rooms into an average-sized plot. They need not be large. A secret garden, for that quiet cup of coffee or snooze where you won't be disturbed, need be no more than 3m (10ft) square – sufficient for a table, a couple of chairs and a screen of plants scrambling over timber trellis walls. The various compartments can be linked by steps or paths, an arch, pergola or a central lawn.

You may well have a favourite part of the garden, but as the seasons change your preference may move to another compartment. The patio complete with fragrant summer-flowering shrubs may give way in autumn to a seat under a single rowan tree clothed in fiery red, orange and yellow foliage. A small woodland area may be your pride and joy in late winter and early spring, carpeted with winter aconites, wood anemone, hardy cyclamen and snowdrops.

Some mini-gardens naturally complement each other. A pergola or timber arbour in the secret garden enables you to relax under a canopy of colourful, sweetly scented climbers and provides an air of romance. Positioning an aromatic garden close to the patio or other area for relaxation allows the fragrances to be appreciated fully. Bear in mind that while summer is usually considered to be the season for scent, with heady aromas from favourites such as roses, mock orange and lavenders, other seasons contribute with their own fragrant specialities. In winter, the Christmas box (*Sarcococca confusa*) is indispensable. It produces, in the middle of the season, tiny white flowers with an incredible fragrance that will be noticeable at a distance downwind of up to 6m (20ft). Planted under a low opening window, a single plant will be sufficient to fill the room with fragrance. Other shrubs such as mahonia, wintersweet (*Chimonanthus* spp.) and witchhazel (*Hamamelis* spp.) all brighten up dull winter days and are

worthy of the highest accolade simply for the fragrance of their flowers.

Vertical surfaces, such as fences and walls, have an important role to play in the garden. Walls of outbuildings and garages are excellent for training wall plants and climbers such as roses. Plants that twine or cling will soon hide an unsightly surface, but bear in mind that many favourites such as wisteria, Virginia creeper, montana clematis and 'Kiftsgate' rose are vigorous growers and require a lot of wall space.

House walls with opening windows can play host to fragrant shrubs. The perfume of pineapple broom (*Cytisus battandieri*) or lemon verbena (*Aloysia triphylla*) wafting through an open window is what gardening is all about.

Maintenance

When planning which 'rooms' to incorporate into your garden, think about how much maintenance they will need and when the busiest periods are likely to be. Many of the projects will require regular or even constant weeding for the first season. Note the priority times and, where possible, try to set aside time for the pruning of shrubs and climbers without it clashing with other urgent jobs such as lawn care.

Quite often the type of garden, rather than its size, determines the amount of regular labour required. For example, a modest-sized lawn may demand your every waking hour, while a carefully planned and well-planted border surfaced with landscape fabric and a deep mulch of bark will look after itself for months on end.

Most established gardens can be summed up as a blend of several different types of garden. Many of them have sort of happened over the years, through a series of planned and unplanned changes, both improvements and mistakes. There may well have been the best of intentions at the beginning, but over the years compromises have been made depending on how much time is available to manage the garden. As

Buddleja 'Dartmoor' drapes itself over the roof and wafts its scent through the window, while *Hydrangea* 'Ayesha' flourishes below.

family circumstances change, so does the garden – this might mean amending the original beds and planting schemes one year to cater for a children's play area and altering them again a couple of decades later as the need diminishes, only for them to reappear again as a priority if grandchildren descend.

Fruit and vegetable-growing areas tend to expand and contract as the family grows and shrinks. If such areas are underused they may eventually revert to lawn or some other type of garden more suited to current needs.

Beds that were originally designed solely for shrubs or perennials may become mixed. Impulse purchasing of plants in flower means that any available space is often planted with species not originally intended for that particular bed.

Usually the result is pleasant and in no way detracts from the overall picture, but if mistakes are made they should be rectified. A bad design is one where the planting has been carved in stone. Shrubs that become too large for the allocated space and perennials that spread like weeds may have to be removed, but that allows something different to be put in its place. The result is an ever-changing garden scene, which adds interest to a satisfying hobby.

The problem for some people with gardens is that the amount of uninteresting, tedious work they create is too much. They become disheartened and never become gardeners. Let's make sure that doesn't happen. Design the garden for your enjoyment, not as a means of keeping fit!

Large gardens

Large and very large gardens need to be planned carefully since everything is on a much grander scale. Buying plants singly won't make an impression. Even if you bring them in by the wheelbarrow load, the scene won't change much. Over the years, lorry loads will be needed. Thinking big allows you to introduce trees which, when mature, will change the landscape. Beech, oak, lime and chestnut may be added to the shopping list, where in a smaller garden any one of them would be ridiculous.

Lawn becomes parkland and for pond read lake. Paths may be designed sufficiently wide to permit two or three people to walk together rather than in single file.

With labour costs high, the large garden should be designed with low maintenance as a priority. A small area close to the house may be developed as a formal garden with shrubs, perennials, bedding, hedges, patio and water features included. Beyond that, and separated by a hedge or wall, drifts of woodland and banks of bold shrubs such as rhododendrons may be used to direct the eye to the distant landscape.

Small gardens

At the other end of the scale, town houses are often restricted to small front and rear plots. While there isn't the same scope for a range of features, thoughtful design will allow you to develop an individual and enjoyable garden. Place interesting plants at the furthest point from the house, front and rear, to make the areas appear larger. Resist purchasing trees and shrubs that will, eventually, become too large for the plot. Aggressive carpeting perennials such as dead-nettle (*Lamium* spp.) that tend to smother other well-behaved plants nearby should be removed from your shopping list or, if the mistake has already been made, eliminated from the garden.

Balconies and roof gardens

Balcony gardens have always been popular, but as property developers in inner-city areas are forced to build up instead of out, these small, hard-surfaced areas are becoming more and more commonplace. The secret of success is to grow plants that are happy to remain in a pot. Choose as large a container as possible, after checking that the balcony can support the weight. Where the balcony is in a windy, cold situation, you will have to rule out permanent plantings of tender climbers and shrubs. If possible, connect an irrigation system to the mains water to save carting water through the rooms. Soil-free composts are lighter than soil-based ones, but when used in containers are prone to dry out more quickly.

Rooftop gardening can be a real challenge and is not for the faint-hearted gardener (if there is such a person). A priority is to check that the roof has been designed and built to carry weight. Then all the materials – compost, plants and containers – have to be carried to the roof. Elements including wind, cold blasts, sun, shade and drought will be taking it in turn to attack your plants and some will succeed in killing the most tender. Those plants that manage to grow and thrive, however, will make the whole operation seem worthwhile.

In a small urban space like a paved garden or this rooftop, planting in pots may be your only option. But it has the advantage that plants can be moved around to protect them from too much sun or wind.

garden rooms

John: Some of the styles of garden you might like to choose from are:

Mediterranean-style gardens

For most of us, a Mediterranean-style garden will need to be constructed. What you will finish up with is a free-draining, open-textured soil with lots of added grit and gravel. The soil need not be rich in nutrients. A position in full sun with shelter from cold winds will keep the plants happy and help ensure their survival through an average winter. Think of herbs with aromatic foliage such as sage, lavender and thyme. Include silver-leafed plants that tolerate strong sunlight: cotton lavender (*Santolina chamaecyparissus*), the New Zealand daisy (*Celmisia semicordata*), lambs' lugs (*Stachys byzantina*) and *Convolvulus cneorum*. The African lily (*Agapanthus campanulatus*) will love the hot dry conditions. To add structure and architectural shape, plant a *Yucca gloriosa*. From the centre of its rosette of long, broad, sword-like leaves rises a 2m (6½ft) high spike of creamy-white, bell-shaped flowers.

Rock roses (*Helianthemum* spp.) and sun roses (*Cistus* spp.) will maximise your summer colour. Formality may be introduced with a trained and shaped bay tree. It will become a favourite spot for relaxing, so leave room for a garden seat.

Planning a Mediterranean-style garden
Plants that are at home in a Mediterranean-style garden require:

● a sunny site.
● shelter from cold winds and late spring frosts.
● light, free-draining soil that warms up quickly.

Key tasks Late autumn: applying straw mulch over crowns for winter protection. Late spring: pruning.

Woodland gardens

A woodland garden needn't be on a grand scale. It may be no more than an extension to a perimeter planting of quick-growing trees and shrubs designed to screen the garden and offer protection from strong, cold blasts. Add to your tree-planting list a selection of interesting deciduous and evergreen species with coloured bark (birch), shaped foliage (maple), flowers (hawthorn) or fruit (crab apple). Under the tree canopy, it will be possible to grow shade-loving plants such as camellias and azaleas. The rampant, climbing, highly fragrant wild woodbine, otherwise known as honeysuckle, is another woodlander.

Low-growing plants for the woodland floor include a range of early spring bulbs. There are English bluebells, wood anemones and winter aconites, all of which love a shaded, weed-free floor littered with a mulch of leaf mould. A small area of woodland can be made to seem larger by meandering the path through the planting and doubling back to give the impression of a walk through a larger area. In the early years, it will be necessary to deal with weeds by mulching, chemicals or hand weeding. Eventually, as the canopy of leaves shuts out light, the ground will become weed free. Laying a deep mulch of bark or wood chippings will help beat the weeds and provide a forest-like feel. Small trees will become established and grow more quickly than expensive, large trees. As the trees grow, trim off the lower branches for better access.

Magnolia stellata is often grown as a specimen shrub, but has happily adapted to this woodland setting.

Planning a woodland garden

● Plant climbers to scramble through the canopy. Honeysuckle, climbing roses and clematis should all succeed in these conditions.

● Plant spring bulbs that will die down before the soil becomes dry in summer.

● Avoid fast-growing conifers such as the Leyland cypress.

● Use vermin guards for a few years to stop local small mammals eating your young trees.

Key tasks Spring: tidying up, pruning, freshening paths. Autumn: pruning.

Wildflower gardens

If you have room for an unmown area at the bottom of the garden, a well-established wildflower meadow is a thing of rare beauty. From spring until autumn it is a palette of ever-changing flower colour. And it doesn't have to be an entire field – almost any small patch that you mow only once or twice a year can produce good-quality, well-behaved wildflowers such as cornflowers, native daffodils, cowslips and ox-eye daisies. An impoverished soil with no added fertiliser will result in a wide range of wildflowers becoming naturalised.

Having said that, a wildflower garden does need considerable attention unless you are going to allow it to become really wild, if you see what I mean! Refrain from cutting the herbage until the flowers have set seed. Then leave the hay for a few days and, if the weather is dry, toss it on site to make sure the seed is dispersed before adding it in thin layers to the compost heap. Many of the annual flowers that set seed will germinate the following spring and continue the cycle.

Key tasks Late spring: planting. Late summer: hay-cutting.

Cottage gardens

A cottage garden is a labour of love. Any extra work spent looking after lots of different plants is more than compensated for when the garden is in flower. There are no set rules; however, by tradition many of the plants will be herbaceous

perennials, biennials and annuals. Roses, vegetables, fruit bushes and herbs are allowed to mix and it is no shame to have plants such as lady's mantle (*Alchemilla mollis*) tumbling over the path.

Planning a cottage garden

● Start with ground free of perennial weeds.

● Allow space between perennials to reduce the need for annual thinning.

● Remove dead flowers before they seed.

● Seedling plants may become as troublesome as weeds – keep an eye on them and remove as necessary.

● Include plants with fragrant flowers and aromatic foliage.

Key tasks Spring, summer and autumn: weeding and staking. Spring: dividing plants. Summer: removing dead flowers. Cottage gardens need fairly constant maintenance and perhaps are not for those with little spare time.

Kitchen gardens

For me a kitchen garden is an intimate area where the best of food is grown. It is not to be confused with a vegetable plot that takes up a large part of the garden with endless rows of all sorts of cheap and mundane vegetables.

Planning a kitchen garden

● The site should be in full sun. A free-draining loam soil is easy to cultivate in spring, allowing early sowings to be made. Choose a site that is free of perennial weeds, or clear it carefully (see pages 109–11).

● Raised beds are useful where the soil is heavy, wet or a sticky clay that dries hard in summer. Avoid stony ground for root crops such as carrots and parsnips. The stones result in forked and misshapen roots.

● A small patch is easier to keep tidy. Select the choicest of vegetables, growing sufficient for your needs without a surplus to feed the neighbours. Salad ingredients such as lettuce and spring onions are always in demand. Sow small amounts every fortnight for a continuous supply.

Kitchen gardens traditionally mix vegetables and flowers, like these cabbages and marigolds.

● Longer-term vegetables such as asparagus and globe artichoke will benefit from a deep, light soil. Onions grown from sets, garlic, parsley, early peas and a row of beans will use up most of the space.

Key tasks Early to mid-spring: the busy period, with soil to cultivate and sowings to be made. Late autumn: the last of the harvest.

Fritillaria meleagris, the snake's head fritillary, makes an interesting short-term early-spring display in a container, and you can move it out of sight once the flowers fade.

Container gardens

Container gardening allows you to grow a wide range of plants in a small garden, or one that is covered in paving or concrete. Tender shrubs can be moved to a more sheltered position or indoors during the winter. Salad crops, herbs and strawberries will thrive in pots. All but the most rampant ornamental shrubs, climbers and trees will succeed, provided they are fed regularly.

One good piece of advice is to buy the best containers. Many plastic pots are plain ugly and some of the cheap earthenware ones will crack during the first frost.

Key tasks Spring: re-potting. Summer: watering, watering and more watering. Container gardens are not for those who summer abroad.

Knot gardens

Knot gardens are fun and need not be large, but can be time-consuming during the growing season. A low-growing, formally maintained hedge is first drawn to scale on paper and then planted to an intricate design. The pattern forms a series of 'knots' and the spaces enclosed by the hedge are planted with colourful ground-cover shrubs, perennials, annuals or herbs. The finished area will still be as pretty as a picture if, instead of plants, the spaces are surfaced with various coloured gravels. Box is the usual choice for a knot hedge and needs to be clipped at least twice during the summer. A word of caution, though – snails love to hide in a box hedge. It acts like a five-star snail hotel.

Planning a knot garden

Dig out a continuous trench for your box plants, rather than individual planting holes. A layer of well-rotted farmyard manure or compost in the base will get the plants off to a good start.

● Space your plants at intervals of 20–25cm (8–10in).
● Beware of snails. They do no harm to the hedge itself, but maraud every night munching their way through most other plants in the garden.

Key tasks Late spring: re-planting annuals. Summer: clipping.

Rockeries

A rockery is exactly that – an area of rocks built to resemble a small-scale mountain. Rock plants or alpines are planted in pockets of soil and between cracks. The rockery doesn't have to be high, although height allows you to use larger rocks. Use soil that is free of perennial weeds to make the mound, since once weed roots become established under large rocks they are difficult to eradicate.

Planning a rockery

● Restrict the planting areas to pockets of weed-free soil among the rocks.

● Soil should be free draining.

● Mulch the soil surface with a 5cm (2in) layer of clean, coarse grit for drainage and as a weed control. This will also help keep the collars of the alpine plants dry and prevent rotting.

● Choose plants that are not aggressive or prone to smothering neighbouring alpines.

● Stick to one type of rock, making sure that the strata (lines) of sandstone or similar lie in the same direction.

● Lay each piece of rock on a firm base to prevent movement. For more information on building a rock garden, see pages 73–77.

Key tasks Spring: tidying up and applying grit. Autumn: cutting back and protecting tender plants.

This low-level rockery adds height and interest to the garden. Having the rock edge flush with the lawn facilitates mowing.

Chapter 2

construction & hard landscaping

site clearance

Matt: Sites fall into two basic categories: clear sites, like those on new housing estates with weeds and debris; and established gardens that need modifying or clearing to make way for a new design.

Buried material can be found in any garden, so knowing the history of an established plot is useful. The decision to work with, without or around immovable objects lurking below ground level influences cost and design – buried air-raid shelters might be unsuitable locations for flower borders, but they are fine beneath patios and paths. Whether to leave or remove rubble depends on the time, effort and expenditure, and the impact it has on the garden. You must decide if it's worth it – removing debris in large volumes leaves you with a space to fill and your next dilemma will be whether to replace it with soil (the most obvious solution) or to create a new feature, such as a pond or a change of level.

The best time to clear a site is in spring, early summer or autumn, or when the soil, especially heavy clay, is most workable. Avoid wet weather because walking or driving over wet soil will damage its structure and make work difficult and dirty. Before starting, decide which plants and features are to remain and do not remove anything worth incorporating into your new design, particularly if it makes the garden look established. Check if trees have preservation orders before removing them. Unwanted ponds can be filled with rubble and topped with a decent depth of soil, depending on the type of plants you choose to grow.

Most garden debris can be removed using hand tools. Before starting, make sure you have a tetanus jab, and wear overalls or old clothes, heavy-duty gloves and clothing, particularly footwear. Build up your fitness slowly, don't overdo it and aim to create a 'rhythm' when working. If you can persuade someone to help, two people do three times the work (or talking!), make it more enjoyable and are invaluable for brainstorming sessions.

Mark out the areas where plants will grow, where you will put grass, borders or trees and concentrate on these first. There's no need to dig where paths and other hard-landscaping features are planned, so mark them out beforehand. Systematically dig over areas where plants will grow as deeply as possible (see page 142), removing stones and debris as you dig. Take out any old roots or stumps to avoid problems with honey fungus in the future (see page 273), as well as the roots of perennial weeds. A fork is often better than a spade and a mattock is invaluable. If there is sharp debris, use a wheelbarrow with solid, rather than pneumatic, tyres to avoid endless punctures.

Hiring machinery
An appealing alternative to digging by hand, particularly on larger sites, is to hire machinery. Although it will increase costs, it will speed up site clearance, save energy and be great fun – as well as being invaluable for heavy work such as breaking concrete. 'Mini' machines, including diggers,

A dry stone wall in harmony with its surroundings and an invaluable habitat for plants and wildlife.

dumpers, tractors and their accessories, are perfect for small-scale landscaping. Before hiring, check the width of the access to save embarrassment!

Find out the location and depth of services – gas, electricity and water – all of which may run across your garden (Bob has more to say about this on pages 97–98), and keep details of your findings. You can hire a tool designed for the purpose; it is called a CAT or Cscope (CAT stands for Cable Avoidance Tool) and should be used according to the manufacturer's instructions. If necessary, contact the relevant authorities to obtain a plan of the site. To avoid damage to other areas of the garden, mark the machines' route across the plot using brightly painted canes with rags attached to the top, or to the twine between them. Indicate the relevant depths of cables or pipes on temporary signs as a useful reminder. Beware of using large machinery under low power cables; if in doubt, hire an experienced operator to do the job for you, but make sure they know which features are to remain by marking them clearly. Once all the major ground clearance is complete, plough or rotavate the site to break up compacted soil, particularly on heavy ground, incorporating soil conditioners if necessary. Take care to avoid bringing any subsoil to the surface when digging or rotavating.

Removing rubbish

The cost of removing rubbish varies. To keep costs down, compare skip hire with the price of a grab loader. Obtain three quotes, ideally based on recommendations from friends or local builders who have already ensured the best deal! To use space efficiently, flatten old drums or fill them with debris; reduce materials with a sledgehammer before packing the skip to avoid paying for air space! Recycle materials whenever possible. Concrete and broken slabs provide useful hardcore for foundations, flints can be incorporated into walls or garden features and organic material stacked for composting, rotting down or wood piles. When finalising levels, try to 'lose' as much rubbish as possible on site; landfill sites are filling rapidly. If you're really unsure of what to do with anything, send it round to Bob's!

Dealing with unwanted plants

Annual and perennial weeds can be sprayed with glyphosate (see page 112). This treatment is particularly effective in spring when they are growing rapidly; even better when perennials are flowering or just as they begin to die down in autumn. Brambles and other woody weeds are better cut down and the re-growth sprayed in early summer. Gardeners who prefer to get to know the site before changing the landscape or who garden organically should dig out woody weeds, cut back excess vegetation and cover the site with black polythene, old hessian-backed carpet or corrugated cardboard for at least a year.

Glyphosate kills unwanted turf too. Alternatively, you can remove it with a turf cutter and stack the turves upside down to rot for compost, or chop and bury them upside down if they are weed free. Dig out unwanted trees and shrubs from borders. If they are well established, and you don't have a mechanical digger, hire a winch to lever them out (see opposite), or pull them out with a length of rope, making optimum use of angles for leverage. Always keep an old saw and mattock handy to break and dig out the roots. If you are left with masses of stumps of different shapes and sizes, consider creating a 'stumpery' and filling the gaps with ferns. Remove as many roots as possible from the ground.

A good time to clear the garden is just before 5 November when you can be excused a bonfire in smokeless zones – but take care not to ignite your fence or hedge (unless it's not required for your new design!). You can use the wood ash from the bonfire as fertiliser around flowering and fruiting plants. Finally, why not make your own 'time capsule' to bury in the garden. Don't forget to include a copy of your plans, a photo of the original garden, yourself, a current gardening magazine – and a CD of *Gardeners' Question Time*!

using a winch to dig out an old apple tree

Hiring a winch is a useful option for removing trees that would take time to dig out using hand tools, making it easier to remove larger trees and speeding up the removal of smaller specimens. Always follow the manufacturer's instructions for operation and if you have soft hands, wear stout gloves!

1 Anchor the winch in a secure position, such as to an unwanted tree.

2 Choose a strong vertical trunk to act as a lever (easy if it's a tree).

3 Cut back any side branches that might impede the cable.

4 Cut a notch in the trunk of the tree you are removing to stop the cable from slipping.

5 Attach the cable as high as possible on the tree to be removed for maximum leverage.

6 Winch the plant out carefully, following the safety instructions on the winch.

paths & patios

Matt: Once you have worked out where your mains services are, drawn up your site plan, and cleared the garden of debris and weeds, you are ready to get stuck into the hard landscaping. Paths and patios are a good place to start and you should begin by marking where they are to go using canes and garden string or twine.

Paths

There are two types of path in the garden: those forming a framework, allowing you to stroll around the garden and view the flower borders whatever the weather; and access paths, such as the one to your front door or garage, that usually follow 'desire lines' – that is, the most direct route from A to B. Access paths are used regularly and should be made from hard-wearing materials such as concrete or natural stone slabs.

Paths should always be wide enough for their intended purpose. An access path should be wider than, say, a secret path leading into a woodland garden, which can deliberately be kept narrow to create an air of mystery. A minimum width of 90cm (36in) usually provides enough space for two people to walk side by side, or for one person carrying two shopping bags, or to turn a wheelbarrow at a junction. However, do make allowances for plant growth – there should be enough space for plants to billow over the path and soften the edges without impeding access.

The design of a path has a subconscious effect on the speed at which you walk. You will notice that people walk more slowly around curves than they do in a straight line, so curved paths are desirable where you want to encourage people to stop and look at the flowers. The tighter the curve, the slower the walk. Curves also disappear behind plants and round corners, enticing the visitor further into the garden. There is an interesting psychological impact: a brick or stone path with the mortar joints running along the path makes you walk faster than one with joints running crossways.

Judas trees (*Cercis siliquastrum*) create a shady pergola in summer and display artistic tracery in winter.

Stepping stones and loose surfaces such as broken slate or gravel slow down walking speed. Ensure that stepping stones are spaced the correct distance apart so they can be walked across comfortably. They are generally better for meandering paths or to reduce wear on grass than for covering distances. The impact of slowing down walking speed and creating 'disappearing' paths combines to make a garden appear larger.

Hard surfaces for paths

Hard surfaces should reflect the style of your garden – tiles with barley-twist edging suit a Victorian or Edwardian house, granite setts have a rustic look and are ideal for established gardens, while decking paths are suitable for contemporary designs. Bricks can be laid in different patterns and are useful for linking the garden to the house; make sure they are frost-proof engineering bricks or they will eventually crumble.

Slabs need proper foundations (see page 59) and are available in a range of colours, textures and materials, usually concrete, reconstituted or natural stone. In my garden, they are Indian sandstone in a colour called 'Desert Sand'. It is a delightful material, with a range of tints from pink to honey, with fossil imprints to add a touch of style. Despite advances in concrete products, there's nothing like the real thing! Recycled natural stone is also available, the disadvantage being that some types have only one level surface, making them difficult to lay.

Some surfaces tend to become slippery when wet, particularly in shaded areas such as under trees or in a small, north-facing garden. Timber, unless it is grooved to reduce the problem, slate and smoothed tiles should all be avoided if the path is going to be used when wet. Concrete manufacturers now produce high-quality imitation terracotta and slate tiles that are less slippery than the natural material.

Paths don't have to be constructed out of orthodox materials. The only limit is your imagination! In Hildegard Holt's garden in Dulwich, south London, for example, a long path, gradually narrowing towards the end to create the illusion of length, incorporates a fabulous underwater scene. Colourful fish and starfish swim among the tentacles of a giant octopus

With imagination, even the humble path can become an attractive garden feature, like this one in Hildegard Holt's garden.

that stretch almost the whole length of the path. When it is finished, they will reach a giant crocodile, made from glass beads. A rough design was drawn on paper and the path laid with the help of a friend, Memeth Hassan. It was cut out without the aid of lines or string and the soil removed to a depth of 15cm (6in). Rubble, begged from skips, was then laid along the trench and compacted.

The cement was mixed by hand and the path laid in sections so the patterns could be created while it was still wet. Most of the materials used to create the path were recycled – slate tiles, removed when the house was being re-roofed, are set vertically and are the outline for fish filled with glass beads. Ceramic tiles, scavenged from skips or donated by her son when his kitchen was being redone, fill gaps or cover the bricks, edging the path in a pattern of blue and white. An

elegant blue and white fish is recycled from the remains of a ceramic seat. Only the sand, cement, pebbles and glass beads were bought. Hildegard, a potter, made some small fish, which are set on tiles buried just below the surface of the concrete to increase the surface area so that they didn't sink in the wet concrete when laid. The path is very easy to maintain, the texture of the mosaic means that it does not become slippery in the rain and it is easy to brush the leaves away in autumn using a 'rice' brush. Paths like this are ideal for moderate use but less so as a main route with regular foot and wheelbarrow traffic.

Bark or loose gravel paths

The path to our front door runs through the rough grass of an orchard of cordon fruit trees and is used only by the children going to and from school, the postman and occasional visitors. Because it's rarely used, it wasn't worth investing in a formal path and yet the style needed to be rustic and semi-formal to blend with the surroundings. It also needed to be soft in case the children fell on it. The solution was simple: we have a bark path. Bark chips are better than partially rotted forest bark because they drain more freely. The only problem we experienced was the difficulty in pushing a pushchair along the path until the bark was sufficiently compacted. Once they have rotted down, bark chips can be topped up or replaced and used as a soil conditioner. They are inexpensive and easy to lay, but there are plenty of other surfaces you can use if you prefer, from slate or stone chippings to gravel, at least 20mm (¾in) in diameter. Gravel and stone chippings come in a range of colours to match your local stone or the surrounding plants. Weeds root in loose surfaces, but they are easy to control by hand weeding and hoeing. 'If you hoe when there are no weeds, you won't get any' is an old gardening saying and it's true. The action of hoeing disrupts germinating seeds and prevents them from growing. Loose surfaces tend to be difficult for wheelbarrows and especially wheelchairs, but it is marginally easier if they are pulled rather than pushed. It is also easy to change the type of surface if you get bored!

A stone chipping path, the edges softened by foliage, lends a relaxed informality to a garden.

making a bark or loose gravel path

Loose gravel and stone chippings make ideal surfaces for informal paths. Allowing the chippings or gravel to overflow onto the border and create an informal edge that plants can spill over.

1 Mark out the lines with site pegs and string.

2 Remove vegetation and soil to a depth of 4cm (1½in), or 5cm (2in) if the path runs through grass, reducing the need to edge the lawn.

3 Dig out any soft or muddy patches and backfill with crushed stone or sandy subsoil, then walk over the area on your heels until it is firmed, or tamp it down with the base of a fence post. Hammer the site pegs vertically into the ground every 60–75cm (24–30in). The pegs should be at least 20cm (10in) long, longer in soft soil. (If you intend to stain the timber, paint it beforehand.) Hold a piece of off-cut timber horizontally across the top of the peg to prevent it splitting or splaying when you are hammering it in.

4 For a semi-formal path, attach strips of pressure-treated 100mm x 25mm (4 x 1in) timber to the pegs to act as a restraint. Drill pilot holes, two per peg, slightly smaller than the rust-resistant screws. Alternatively, use galvanised nails. The timbers can be fixed to either the path or the soil side of the pegs, although if they are on the inside and the path is narrow, you are more likely to stub your toe! If the end timbers butt up against a brick post or path, leave a small, vertical gap between the two to allow for expansion, particularly on a sunny site.

5 Cover the base of the path with landscape fabric, ensuring the edges overlap the timber edging to prevent weed growth from the sides.

6 Lay a 7.5cm (3in) layer of bark over the surface, rake it level and firm it with your feet.

laying a path

It is worth hiring a concrete mixer for projects like paths. Stack the bags of cement in a dry place, raised above ground on a pallet or similar. Cover with polythene if necessary; if cement becomes damp it is useless. Find the dimensions of the slabs to be used and draw a plan on graph paper, adjusting the size of the slabs to avoid having to cut them. Some landscaping suppliers will do this for you on computer. Alternatively, make your path the same width as the slabs.

1 Mark out the area with pegs and string, using a builder's square to check the right angles. If the path is by a building, the surface should be at least two brick courses lower than the damp course. Dig out the topsoil or turf and stack for re-use or disposal. It should be to a depth of 25cm (10in) over the whole area. Then compact the soil with a tamper or garden roller.

2 Lay a sub-base of 'scalpings' at least 8cm (3in) deep, Different suppliers have different names: it is often called MOT type one. Compact with a vibrating plate compactor or roller, rented from a hire shop.

3 Stack the slabs at convenient locations around the site. When laying a path, allow for a fall of 1:75 for drainage. i.e. for every 75mm along the horizontal you drop 1mm (or for every 75in you drop 1in). If your straight edge is 3m (10ft) long, put a 40mm (1½in) piece of wood on top of the peg and tap the peg level; that gives a 1:75 fall. Put a level line along the back of the path

4 Natural stone should be laid on a slightly wet bed of mortar made from five parts sharp sand to one of cement; concrete slabs only need a dab of concrete at each corner and one in the centre. Tap each slab down gently with a rubber or lump hammer on a piece of wood. Make minor adjustments using the handle. Do not tap the edges, as they may break. Keep the fall constant with string lines and keep the joint sizes constant. Cover the newly laid slabs with polythene to protect from inclement weather; in summer use damp hessian.

5 Once the bedding has set, mortar the joints with a moist, crumbly mix of 3:1:1 sharp sand, soft sand (bricklaying sand) and cement. Keep a note of the mix – if you need to mortar the joints in the future, the colour will then stay the same. If mortar spills onto the slabs, wipe it off with a damp sponge. Smooth the joints with the edge of a wet trowel or 'bucket handle' from the builder's merchants.

Laying a patio

Patios are traditionally used for relaxation and dining and are sited by the house to be near the kitchen, but there's no reason why they shouldn't be elsewhere in the garden in sun or shade; just beware of shady, humid corners that attract midges in summer. Patios should be an integral part of the garden design and should complement or contrast with surrounding shapes. Squares and circles of slabs or bricks are traditional, but contemporary shapes such as triangles work well, too, in the right context. There should be enough space on the patio to walk round the table without bumping into chairs, and room to store hoses when watering in summer.

Choose a surface that complements the location. Stone or concrete slabs, pavers and bricks are all suitable; cobbles can make an uneven surface for seating, unless they are bedded well. Because of their shape, slabs are better for square patios; bricks and especially cobbles fit into circles. Contemporary shapes are better in concrete, or timber decking cut to shape with a jig-saw. Designs can incorporate more than one surface, perhaps pebbles set in a dry cement mix and then watered in to fill any gaps. Alternatively plant thymes, chamomile and other carpeting plants by lifting a slab or two, breaking up the sub-base and forking in gritty compost. Avoid gravel; furniture will sink and wobble. If you can't do without it, make the patio of concrete and press gravel into the wet surface, though it tends to come loose. Buy furniture and cushions that suit the style of the house and garden. Using the same style of furniture throughout the garden makes the design more cohesive.

Choose plants that create the desired atmosphere around the patio and survive happily in the growing conditions; include some evergreens for all-year interest. You may want a barbecue on New Year's Eve just to remind you of summer as we did one year, in the snow – they're great fun! The number of containers should reflect the time you have for watering; installing automatic watering systems or planting in raised beds (see page 68) will save time. If you intend to have lighting, get professional advice: it is generally better to lay the cables before the patio is installed.

A shady patio – the perfect place for al fresco dining.

This circular patio comes in a kit of specific dimensions. Follow the procedure for laying a path on page 59. If this is your first patio, lay out the slabs first to ensure that the spacing is correct.

1 Mark out the circumference using a peg, line and spray paint or a line of sand.

2 When measuring the fall for drainage over a long distance, use a straight edge; these can be rented from a hire shop.

3 When laying a circular patio, work from the centre outwards.

concreting posts

This is a useful technique for a number of the projects in this chapter. As with laying a path, it is worth hiring a concrete mixer to help you with the job.

1 Dig a hole to the required depth and about 10cm (4in) all round wider than the post. For most situations, a 1.8m (6ft) fence panel needs a hole 60cm (24in) deep with a 15cm (6in) layer of hardcore in the base; a 1.2m (4ft) fence needs a hole 45cm (18in) deep, also with 15cm (6in) of hardcore in the base. This is particularly important if the fence is to be covered in climbers or is on an exposed site.

2 Break up the base with a fork and scoop out the soil with a post hole borer or shove holers. These are like a pair of sugar tongs and make picking up the soil easier; they are inexpensive to hire. If you have a lot of posts to erect, you might like to hire a powered auger, but take care when using it and make sure you wear gloves and protective clothing. Augers can be designed for one or two people or attached to a mini tractor.

3 There are two options when securing posts – you can either fill the holes with concrete, using a mix of one part cement to four parts all-in aggregate or fence-post concrete, or you can pack the hole with compacted rubble to about 15cm (6in) below ground level, then top it off with a stiff mix of concrete that is firmed in layers to remove the air and smoothed at an angle with a wet bricklayer's trowel. If you are using concrete, mix it on a board nearby.

4 Add the concrete in layers, tamping it firmly around the post with a timber offcut or similar.

5 Raise and slope the concrete to allow for rainwater run-off, smoothing the surface with a bricklayer's trowel.

Woven hazel stems create living archways over a woodland path.

arches

Matt: Arches are a useful way to divide gardens and create height without the need for width, which makes them ideal in smaller plots. They can also be erected against hedges or walls to make an arbour.

The easiest way to make an arch is to buy a kit made from timber that has been 'tanalised' – that is, pressure treated with preservative to increase its longevity. These usually have trellis panels in the sides to support plants. It takes about half a day to erect an arch, longer if the posts are set in concrete because it will need time to set. As only a small amount of

concrete is required, buy a bag of specially formulated fence-post mix from the builder's merchant or DIY store. Ideally, there should be 30cm (12in) of timber buried in the ground, more on exposed sites. If using fencing spikes, check the location of underground services before use.

Alternatively, you can create your own rustic arch. These are normally made from stripped or bark-covered poles 7.5–10cm (3–4in) in diameter, with smaller poles in diagonal or horizontal patterns to create the decorative design. Rustic arches are perfect for a cottage-style garden and can be bought as kits from garden centres or wood yards, or made to your own design.

making an arch

This arch is made from two pairs of vertical posts concreted into the ground, with horizontal rails providing rigid support at the base and tops of the poles, and thinner poles for ornamentation. Ideally, the main framework should be screwed together for strength, although galvanised nails will suffice. Arches should be robust enough to support climbers such as roses, clematis or honeysuckle – or whatever cultivars suit the size of the arch or can be easily controlled by pruning. To ensure the framework fits together securely, cut v-shaped notches in the top end of each upright or make an L-shaped cut 2.5cm (1in) deep on the vertical and horizontal pieces so the two flat faces slot together. Treat all cuts with wood preservative before constructing the arch.

1 Lay the sides of the arch on the ground and put the cross timbers in place; as the arch is 'rustic', you can do this by eye. Use a drill to make pilot holes for the screws.

2 As the base of the poles will be buried or bedded in concrete, remove any loose bark and stand them upright in a bucket of timber preservative overnight to soak up as much of the liquid as possible, or scorch the ends with a blow torch to seal, but not burn, the wood.

3 After assembling the sides, dig four holes in the ground, making sure they are spaced correctly for the posts. Shovel a layer of hardcore in the base of each hole.

Opposite: *Clematis montana* var. *wilsonii* softens the lines of this rustic arch.

4 Use a spirit level to check that the side pieces are both at the same height, and that they are vertical and at right angles. Nail temporary battens to the uprights at the correct spacing to hold them in place while the concrete hardens. Buy a bag of dry mix, fence-post concrete, mix with water and tip it into the holes, packing the concrete round the poles with a stick to force out the air bubbles. Form a slightly domed top to the concrete using a trowel to encourage rainwater to run off (see page 62). Leave the concrete to 'cure' for 24 hours and check it is completely hard before fixing the top of the arch in place.

5 Assemble the arch section at ground level, then lift it into position on the top of the side frames and secure with screws.

6 The finished arch.

pergolas

A familiar feature in tavernas and sun-steeped Mediterranean gardens, pergolas add an air of expectation to a garden. They are a statement of belief, even in mid-winter, that one day there will be sunshine! Because most pergola designs are formal, they tend to blend better with straight-sided features such as garden walls or buildings; they are perfect for shading indoor rooms from the summer sun. Think carefully before deciding where to site your pergola – it should be in proportion to the surrounding buildings and provide a pleasing view from all overlooking windows. Placed in the centre of a garden, as they so often are, pergolas can look like stranded spaceships

and easily dominate the landscape, particularly if painted in dark colours. Gertrude Jekyll's fine solution was to create pergola 'corridors' as bold landscape features to link several areas of the garden together. Remember that rain drips from foliage, so beware if you are planning to use your pergola for covering a path or sitting area – you may end up being wetter than you would in the open! Pergolas should be a minimum of 2.4m (8ft) high to allow for hanging vegetation, but should be easy to reach from the top of a ladder for painting, pruning and tying in. Note that it is easier to cut and paint the parts before construction, although in only a few years you will have the laborious task of repainting them while balancing on a ladder! Alternatively, go for the 'natural' look.

Pergolas bring a touch of the exotic to a small urban garden.

constructing a pergola

Pergola kits make construction easier but if you decide to design your own, don't be too ambitious. Draw accurate plans on graph paper with accompanying measurements for reference; never rely on memory! If you are looking for inspiration, there are some attractive designs on the Internet. Calculate the length of material needed in multiples of the size of standard floor joists – either 10 x 5cm (4 x 2in) or 15 x 5cm (6 x 2in) – or the size of timber you are going to use. Secondhand timber is cheaper, but needs treating with preservative and nails removing from the wood. Cedar weathers attractively but is expensive; oak is heavy too and generally needs brick piers. Most domestic pergolas are constructed from treated softwood.

If you are going to attach trellis panels between some of the uprights, the interior measurements between the posts should be 1.8m (6ft). Level the site if the ground is uneven and make a detailed materials list.

There are two options for linking the pergola together. Either cut joints in the timber or use U-shaped galvanised brackets to support the timbers on top of one another; the latter is a simple, less time-consuming option. However, the overall design is less streamlined unless the pergola is small and narrower timbers are used. Paint all cut surfaces with wood preservative.

1 Mark out the shape of the pergola, then lay out the timbers to check that they are correctly spaced.

4 When the spikes have been hammered into the ground, lay the timbers between them to check they are horizontal.

2 Double check to ensure that the fencing spike is at right angles to the timbers.

5 Insert the post into the sockets and check they are vertical before tightening the securing bolts.

3 Hammer in the fencing spikes, constantly checking they are vertical using a spirit level.

6 Attach all timbers using screws, making a smaller pilot hole first.

a note about 3-4-5 triangles

As you may remember from school, a triangle with these dimensions creates a right angle, so whenever you need one in the garden, use these measurements, or multiples thereof. For example, if you want to ensure that a fence is at right angles to the house, measure a distance of 3m (or 3ft or 3 anything else that is convenient to the plot) along the side of the house, and a distance of 4m (or 4 whatever) away from it where the fence is going to be. You have got a right angle when the line that links the ends of these first two lines to form a triangle measures precisely 5. And if it is more convenient to start with 6m (2 x 3), your second measurement needs to be 8m (2 x 4) and your third 10m (2 x5).

You can take these measurements using a tape measure, string and canes, a builder's square or make your own triangle from offcuts of timber. The pictures on pages 67 and 94 show this handy trick in practice.

Steps

Although steps may generally be regarded as functional, the great garden designers have transformed them over the years into stylish features that blend perfectly with their surroundings and are an integral part of the design.

Edwin Lutyens used layers of elegant semicircles in natural stone in his 'Arts and Crafts' creations; Antonio Gaudí lavished them with mosaic-decorated balustrades and lizards at Parc Guell in Barcelona. But imaginative steps don't just rest with the great and the good. In Karla Newell's tiny courtyard garden in 'frost-free' Brighton, there is a run of small steps, the risers ornamented with Mexican tiles and the treads with pebbles set in concrete.

Like garden paths, the style of a flight of steps dictates their use. Vertical steps with narrow treads encourage a quick uphill sprint, while wide steps and treads slow the pace, encouraging you to stop and look – perfect for longer slopes, ideally with terrace-like 'pauses' so you can rest and view the garden. Rather than a straightforward flight of steps, think about constructing something more interesting. A series of 'dog legs' creates interest in smaller spaces, adding further mystery when the steps disappear round a hidden corner. For safety, each step should be of equal height and evenly spaced to create a natural rhythm. Ideally, you should be able to walk up them without looking where you are going. Irregular spacing breaks that rhythm, is dangerous and is best avoided.

The ideal step for most gardens has treads 45cm (18in) wide, with 15cm (6in) risers and the correct gradient for wheelbarrows and lawnmowers to be moved up and down the steps easily (although a ramp is useful for machinery access where space allows). There should always be a handrail at adult and child level and it should be checked regularly to ensure it is safe.

The two low steps into my back door have treads of Indian sandstone, laid with a one in fifty gradient so water runs off. I think natural stone is beautifully elegant and formal. New bricks sit happily in urban gardens, while old, recycled ones blend well into cottage or Victorian gardens. Always check the bricks are frostproof before buying and that they don't become slippery when wet, something to consider with slate or ceramic tiles. Concrete manufacturers now make quite attractive imitation stone, slate and terracotta tiles that are less expensive, almost identical and non-slip compared to natural materials.

In the informal setting of a woodland garden or in a rural setting, log roll steps are a simple yet stylish solution. Cut out the shape of the steps in the bank, anchor the sawn logs with treated timber site pegs, fill the risers with compacted sub-base or hardcore and top with a 7.5cm (3in) layer of gravel, stone or bark chips.

raised beds

Raised beds have many advantages. Some are slightly raised, improving drainage, so that the soil warms more rapidly in spring and the top few inches develop a good structure. They can also be reached easily from the path, so the soil doesn't become compacted by your walking all over it. Taller raised beds may reach 30–60cm (12–24in) high or more, depending on what your ideal height is, making them easy to get to without bending or from a wheelchair.

Raised beds are ideal places to grow ornamental plants that do not naturally flourish in local soil, like acid-loving plants in

Steps as an ornamental feature – you could do it too!

making steps in a bank

To work out the number of steps you need, start by measuring the height of the slope. Drive a cane into the ground at the base of the slope and a peg at the top, then put a string line between the two and use a spirit level to ensure it is horizontal. Measure the length of the string, divide it by the depth of a tread – 45cm (18in) – and you will have the number of steps needed; a comfortable ratio is 45cm (18in) tread to 15cm (6in) riser. If the number of steps does not divide exactly into the height of the bank, set the bottom step a little lower.

The foundations should be cast in concrete to support the steps above. Subject to ground conditions they should be about 10cm (4in) wider than the finished step and the same depth; in light soils they need to be wider to provide a more substantial foundation.

1 Mark out the area to be covered by the steps with pegs and string. It should be a multiple of the width of the slabs.

2 Excavate the topsoil and compact the subsoil with a plant vibrator, garden roller or sledgehammer, depending on the size of the steps (wear gloves to avoid blisters). Hammer 2.5cm (1in) site pegs vertically into the ground – you will need two or more, again depending on the size of the steps.

3 The pegs should finish slightly proud of the soil so they are level with the top of the concrete. Check the levels with a spirit level; the steps should be level from side to side, but falling slightly towards the front for drainage.

4 Pour in the concrete (six parts all-in ballast to one part cement) so it is level with the top of the guide pegs and tamp the surface, leaving it textured so that the first course (of bricks, stone or other chosen material) will bond.

5 Lay the first riser, two courses high. Check that the courses are horizontal, using a spirit level. If you are laying slab or stone steps, allow for a 3.5cm (1⅜in) overlap beyond any brickwork.

8 Lay the next riser...

6 When the mortar is dry, ram hardcore in the gap behind the stonework and, if necessary, top up with concrete level with the top of the stone. Allow to set.

9 ...and the next slab in the same way, and the next.

7 Lay the slab on a line of mortar round the perimeter or dab five spots of mortar at the corners and centre of the concrete slabs, with a slight fall for drainage. The necessary fall can be achieved by putting a small piece of wood under the downward end of the spirit level and setting the bubble to horizontal so the fall remains constant. Alternatively, the level can be with the bubble touching the line at the shallow end.

10 Cover the newly laid slabs with polythene to protect them from inclement weather; in summer, use damp hessian. Once the mortar bedding has set, if you are using bricks, mortar the joints with a moist, crumbly mix of three parts sharp sand to one part soft sand (bricklaying sand) and one part cement. Keep a note of this mix in case you need to mortar the joints in the future so the colour of the mortar will stay the same. Avoid spilling mortar on the slabs. If this happens, wipe it off with a damp sponge. Smooth the joints with a wet trowel or bucket handle.

alkaline areas. They can also be turned into seats if the edges are wide enough and topped with timber or brick. Most are constructed in rectangles or squares, but they can also be built in tiers to form terracing. Enlist the help of a professional for more complicated schemes or for walls over 90cm (36in) tall. Brick planters should be painted with bitumen or lined with waterproofing membrane, and they should also have weep holes at the base so that water drains from the soil behind, reducing the pressure of the soil on the wall.

Raised beds for vegetables are usually constructed in 'strips' for easy access and should be a maximum of 3m (10ft) long to discourage people from cutting corners and narrow enough to enable you to reach the centre without stretching. They are dug only once and perennial weeds are removed when the bed is constructed, so the soil structure is allowed to develop. Vegetable beds can be raised just above soil level, to a height of your choice – 23cm (9in) is good for most purposes – using tanalised timbers painted with wood preservative if you want to make them more ornamental. Make pilot holes and screw the timber into site pegs at the four corners and at intervals of 60cm (24in) along the edges. The frames of taller beds should be made of 10 x 5cm (4 x 2in) tanalised timber, screwed to 10 x 10cm (4 x 4in) posts,

Raised beds bring high levels of productivity to the small garden.

buried by one third or secured with concrete or fencing spikes, depending on the type of soil. Space the posts every 1.2m (4ft) and paint the timber with preservative before construction to improve their appearance.

Raised beds are an easy way to keep the garden neat and prevent soil spilling over on to the paths.

Mark out the shape of the bed using a 3-4- 5 triangle (see page 68) and string. Dig out the base to one spade's depth, add a layer of rubble for drainage, then cover with landscape fabric that overlaps up the sides. On lighter soils, fork lightly over the base and cover with landscape fabric that overlaps the sides, leaving a small gap at the base of the timber to allow for drainage.

Fill the bed in layers with your chosen compost, allowing it to settle before planting.

Crops are normally sown close together in blocks, rather than rows, or in diagonal patterns. This uses space efficiently and reduces the need for weeding at later stages as the canopy of leaves keeps weed germination down. Pathways between the beds should be wide enough to push a wheelbarrow along and there should be enough space to turn at the corners.

rock gardens

Matt: Save us from plum puddings, currant buns, dogs' graves and other calamities of construction masquerading as rock gardens. Too many are made from a pile of soil with small rocks scattered over the surface; the noble Alps would laugh to see such mimicry. Rock gardens don't have to be designed on a grand scale with pools, paths, screes and streams. They are ideal where space is limited, because the compact nature of the plants means that plenty can be packed into a small space, and the raised construction is ideal for close viewing.

The key to success is the design. Try to make rockeries look as natural as possible, mimicking the way the rock strata project at angles from the ground. If possible, visit the mountainous areas of the world to see what nature's own rock gardens look like in the Lake District, Alps and Dolomites; take photographs and modify their magnificence to suit your own back garden. There's great inspiration too in visiting the rock gardens at Edinburgh's Royal Botanic Gardens, Duffryn Gardens in South Wales or the legendary Schynige Platte Alpine Botanic Garden near Interlaken in Switzerland, at 2,000m (6,500ft) altitude with views of the Bernese Alps and over 600 species!

Rock gardens should be in a sheltered, open, sunny site, away from overhanging trees. Sloping sites have a distinct advantage because it is easier to make the rocks appear as though they are naturally projecting from the ground.

One of the great bonuses of a rock garden is that the planting 'pockets' can be filled with different types of compost to accommodate a wide range of plants. Most alpines flourish in a gritty, free-draining medium with some organic matter. Those eking out an existence on screes will need added sharp sand and grit. Some species prefer limy conditions, others grow only in acid soil, so the composts can reflect these needs. Many will thrive on a mix of one part peat substitute to one or two parts horticultural grit or sharp sand and one part sterilised loam. Scree-dwelling plants need three to four parts grit to one part good loamy soil. Acid-loving plants need four parts peat substitute, rotted forest bark or similar, to one part sharp sand.

On alkaline soils, planting pockets for lime-hating plants should be sited towards the top of the rock garden because alkaline water draining down will eventually make the compost at the base of the rock garden alkaline. Lining the planting pockets with butyl liner or polythene with drainage holes in the base helps to contain the different soil types.

A rock garden is an opportunity to add colour, character and some magical plants such as these daphnes.

Matt's top ten alpines

Gentiana sino-ornata forms carpets of rich green leaves with exquisitely marked azure-blue flowers from early autumn to early winter. It's pointless trying to resist their beauty. Humus-rich, moist, acid soil.

Pulsatilla rubra is the red form of the Pasque flower, and to my mind it is one of the most wonderful plants in the garden. With its exquisite spring flowers and swirling seed heads, its presence soothes the soul. Neutral to alkaline, free draining.

Pulsatilla rubra

Hacquetia epipactis has a tiny mound of lime-green flower heads, which catches the eye in spring. This weird and wonderful relative of celery is perfect in dappled shade on moist, humus-rich, neutral to acid soil.

Ramonda myconi is a tiny plant with clusters of lavender flowers on straight stiff stems that dance above a rosette of puckered leaves in late spring. Moist, humus-rich, well-drained soil in shade.

Saxifraga 'Tumbling Waters' has a frosted rosette, which, after several years' anticipation, explodes into a disproportionately large flower spike up to 60cm (24in) long – amazing! Free-draining, gritty, alkaline, soil.

Soldanella montana is delicate, delightful, delicious! A plant whose style demands superlatives with finely fringed lavender flowers in an art-deco style. Moist, acid soil, in an open position with indirect shade.

Dryas octopetala forms a creeping carpet of tiny leaves that is cloaked with simple white flowers with stamens dipped in gold, followed by fluffy seedheads. Perfect for well-drained, humus-rich, neutral or alkaline soil.

Daphne cneorum 'Eximia' has wreaths of serpentine stems that sprout shimmering red buds, bursting to pink-star like flowers in late spring. Gritty, neutral to alkaline, free-draining soil.

Corydalis flexuosa and its enticing cultivars have flowers of turquoise blue set against delicate pale green foliage, a 'must-have' plant for moist, free-draining soil.

Cyclamen coum has prettily patterned leaves, which, in late winter, become encrusted with jewels ranging from pretty pink to gleaming white; the perfect ground cover for moist, free-draining soil.

There are superb alpine plant nurseries worldwide. See the Internet for details, visit them and spend, spend, spend!

Saxifraga 'Tumbling Waters'

Cyclamen coum

making a rock garden

Choose your rocks carefully – your local stone in a range of sizes, including the largest stones possible, creates the most natural-looking rockery. Granite is hard and unattractive; shales soon disintegrate. The best materials, including sandstone, have obvious strata or natural lines. Garden centres and building suppliers generally have smaller pieces, so a better source is your nearest quarry. Don't buy weathered or river-washed limestone – it may come from a conservation area; if in doubt, ask.

Take care when moving rocks – wear gloves, a safety helmet and safety footwear, lift correctly, bending your knees not your back, work slowly and stop if you feel overtired. Beware of crushing fingers!

Most rocks can be moved using a trolley or sack barrow, preferably one with pneumatic tyres; take care if using a wheelbarrow, in case it tips. Large rocks should be moved using a block and tackle. An alternative is to put the stone on a board and roll it over scaffolding boards using sections of scaffolding poles, replacing the rear pole at the front as it rolls out from the back. This worked for Stonehenge and the pyramids and should be fine in your garden too! Ensure that equipment does not sink into soft ground by laying scaffolding planks and boards over the lawn or other even surfaces.

Rocks should be buried by about one third, tilting slightly backwards. The finished result must look natural – the key is to ensure the natural strata are aligned or parallel. Choose each rock carefully, building by size in tiers so that each one appears to emerge from the soil at an angle. Place the larger rocks first, filling in with smaller rocks behind. Stand back and view the overall effect regularly as you work; it is much easier to make changes while work is in progress.

Once in place, make the final adjustments with a crowbar, using smaller rocks as a pivot, wedging rocks securely with smaller pieces. For safety reasons, everything should be absolutely secure.

1 Clear all perennial weeds from the site by hand using a garden fork, working methodically through the area, or spray with glyphosate in spring when weeds are growing rapidly, when they are flowering or dying down in autumn for the greatest impact. On lawn areas, lift and stack turf.

2 Improve drainage by installing a soakaway – this is particularly important on heavier soils such as clay. Dig out the soil to a spade's depth, fill the hole with brick rubble...

3 ...and cover with landscape fabric, or invert the turves from the lawn.

4 Import and stack the topsoil to the required height and allow to settle.

5 Sketch out a plan or make a model from stones or polystyrene pieces to finalise the basic layout.

6 Outline the rock outcrop with a garden line and pegs...

7 ...including the location of larger rocks or 'keystones' at prominent points.

8 Move rocks carefully with crowbars and build up the tiers.

9 Tip them back slightly, burying about one third of their bulk for the 'natural look'.

10 Fill the planting 'pockets' with compost and plot the position of your plants before you plant them.

11 Once you are satisfied with the layout, put in the plants, adding shale screes and stone chippings for a realistic finish.

water features

Matt: You may not be standing in the corner of your garden like Lancelot Brown declaring 'it has capabilities' and, with a regal waft of the hand, submerging acres of countryside for your latest grand scheme; most gardeners have more modest projects in mind!

The cooling, relaxing presence of water is always desirable in the garden, whatever the scale. Pond building was my first contribution to the garden at home and it is a great way to encourage a childhood interest in natural history and gardening. A plastic pond only 120 x 60cm (4 x 2ft) nestling in the corner by the shed was later replaced by a more sophisticated kidney-shaped design, but both provided hours of enjoyment.

Choosing a style of pond

Ponds are available pre-formed from fibreglass or plastic (see pages 82–83), or you can create your own design using a flexible liner (see pages 84–85). Pre-formed ponds are available in formal and informal designs. Fibreglass is more expensive than plastic, but it is tougher and has a lifespan of ten years or more. Flexible liners are ideal for informal ponds and can be cut to fit any shape or size. Butyl rubber is hard wearing and long lasting with a life expectancy of up to 50 years. It is expensive, but worth the investment. PVC, available in a range of dark colours, is of moderate strength and longevity; it is usually guaranteed for ten years. Polythene should be avoided; it cracks and perishes in sunlight and is better suited to bog gardens.

At the time of writing there is growing interest in creating swimming ponds, where human and aquatic life share a habitat filtered by marginal plants that absorb the nitrogen and grow in sediment-free and nutrient-free substrate. They have appeared at the Hampton Court Flower Show, and the Swiss and Austrians have been indulging in them for decades. It sounds like a wonderful idea – perhaps there's a little of Capability Brown in everyone after all!

Pond or rill? Try unorthodox shapes for your water features.

John's tips on siting a pond

Depending on the type and size of the water feature, positioning can be critical. Here is a list of things to avoid for all but the smallest of features.

● Don't excavate for a pond where there is a naturally high water table because the pressure from below will push the liner up, forcing the pond water out. You can work out the level of your water table is by excavating a hole until you see water. It is best to do this in winter, when any water table will be higher than in summer.

● Don't position the pond under or close to deciduous trees. Autumn leaves will be a problem over a four to six week period.

● Don't site a large pond in full sun because it will attract green algae (which respond to sunlight). If there is no alternative site, in the northern hemisphere, you should plant a selection of bulky shrubs on the south side to cast shade over part of the surface of the water.

● Don't forget that for moving water, the pump will be powered by electricity. Consider access to mains services and make sure you employ a qualified electrician.

● Don't construct the pond on sloping ground. The water surface will always be level, leaving the liner exposed at the highest end.

● Don't undertake too major a job. Employ a contractor to do the heavy work.

● Safety: remember that all electrical work must be undertaken by a qualified electrician. Water and electricity don't mix well. Always switch the power supply off at the mains before repairing or cleaning the pond, or servicing the pump.

● Where there is concern for young children and the risk of accidents, cover the pond with galvanised wire mesh. This in turn may, for aesthetic reasons, be covered with water-worn, smooth river stones. Fencing the pond is a practical, if unattractive, alternative.

John's tips on water pumps

● Keeping water moving helps to keep it clear and prevent it from becoming stagnant. It also produces that lovely, soothing, bubbling sound. For this, you need a pump, which can supply water to a fountain or via a hose to feed a waterfall. I would always choose an electrically powered pump – there are small, solar-powered water features on the market, but for my money they deliver a piddling amount of water and tend to make you want to do the same!

● In order to choose the right pumping system for your garden, you need to estimate the flow of water required. Obviously if water has to be pumped uphill, the flow will be less powerful than if it is to be pumped downhill or at the same level.

● Pumps come with a chart showing the outflow at a given outlet height, so check this before you buy. A 35-gallon (150-litre)-a-minute pump would be too much for a small fountain, but would provide the right flow for a cascade and waterfall 27–30cm (9–10in) wide and about 3m (10ft) high. It is a good idea to buy spare capacity – i.e. choose a pump that is more powerful than your immediate needs – in case you want add another water feature at a later date. You will still be able to run both without the hassle of installing another pump and electrical connection.

● Where water is being pumped to an upper pond, use top-quality, flexible hosepipe and bury it below spade and garden fork depth to avoid puncturing it. To obtain maximum flow, always use as large a diameter of hose as possible. Don't forget to leave an outlet under the paved edging of the pond to feed the electricity cable and hose through. Leave sufficient spare pump cable in the pond to enable you to lift it out of the water onto the surrounding area for servicing.

● If you want a fountain, make sure your pond is big enough to catch the falling drops. It is surprising how far water droplets can be blown to one side on a windy day. Where water loss occurs, you may need to reduce the height of the water display. You can either turn down the water pressure on the pump itself or buy a connection that allows you to do this. Where the pump is feeding water to both a waterfall and a fountain, it is usual to divert most of the flow to the waterfall. Pumps with one outlet will need to be fitted with a Y-shaped junction to connect two hoses, one for each feature.

● Clean the filters of submersible pumps on a regular basis. During winter, if there is a risk of the water freezing, the pump can be removed, cleaned and stored in a frostproof cupboard until spring.

Aquatic plants

Plants are essential to the success of your pond, as a wildlife habitat, to oxygenate the water and discourage algae and, if you are operating on a larger scale, to provide a hiding place for voracious herons! Plants also ensure that the pond harmonises with the surrounding garden. As far as colour is concerned, bog gardens should be considered as an essential element of your garden design and the gardening year. Pond plants fall into four main categories: marsh and bog plants flourishing in the wet ground beside a pond; marginals growing in shallow water 15cm (6in) deep or more; plants for deeper water with leaves that float, like water lilies (the depth of water each tolerates varies and will be shown on the plant label); and those that simply float. Ensure that there are adequate planting ledges around your pond for a decent display; you have more control when creating a pond to your own design using a flexible liner.

Matt's top ten plants for ponds & surrounds

Gunnera manicata

Gunnera manicata, the mighty, magnificent giant rhubarb from Chile. Not for the faint-hearted or for most small gardens; the emerging and adult leaves and Jurassic flowers are a perfect portrayal of the prehistoric. Bog plant, needing a 'bog depth' of 3m (10ft) plus.

Aponogeton distachyos, the water hawthorn, from South Africa, was one of the first plants introduced to my watery world. A sweetly scented delight, whose flowers and cigar-shaped leaves float elegantly on the surface of the water. Floating leaved; water depth 12–62.5cm (5–25in).

Caltha palustris, the common kingcup, has cheery, glossy, golden flowers against a backcloth of mid-green rounded leaves. Superb in spring alongside its white-flowered cousin, **Caltha palustris** var. **alba**, which boasts a golden central boss of stamens. Bog or shallow marginal; water depth 0–15cm (0–6in).

Schizostylis coccinea is not your archetypal aquatic, yet it flourishes in moist soil or shallow water. Spikes of sword-like leaves are topped with goblets of coral red, opening to become elegant stars; perfect for a late summer/early autumn display. Bog or shallow marginal; water depth 0–10cm (0–4in).

Zantedeschia aethopica 'Crowborough' – architectural leaves the shape of arrow heads and pure white, ethereal flowers in summer are the reward for providing copious moisture. Bog or marginal; water depth 0–30cm (0–12in).

Schizostylis coccinea

Nelumbo nucifera – only for those blessed with tropical climes. Glorious rounded parasol-like leaves and the straightest stems topped with white flowers with blush-pink tints make this majestic, revered plant the source of many legends. Floating leaved – and beyond; water depth 15–90cm (6–36in).

Nymphaea 'Marliacea Chromatella' – pretty primrose flowers with a golden boss of stamens and attractively marked copper young leaves with purple streaks; the leaf undersides are speckled with purple. Reliable, lovable, easy to grow and value for money. Floating leaved; water depth 45–90cm (18–36in).

Stratiotes aloides looks like the top of a pineapple; in warm weather it floats on the surface basking in sunshine, then spends winter submerged, well below Jack Frost's icy glaze. A fun plant for children of all ages. Floating.

Hottonia palustris – an elegant beauty that emerges from the depths in spring, creating a cloud of lavender-tinted flowers that hover above the pond. Not to be confused with that gaudy thug *Houttunyia cordata*. Marginal; water depth 30–90cm (12–36in).

Pontederia cordata – spiky, lance-shaped leaves direct the eye to compact clusters of rich blue flowers, ornamenting the plant from late summer to autumn. Marginal; water depth 10–20cm (4–8in).

Nymphaea 'Marliacea Chromatella'

John's tips on keeping the water clear & weed-free

Once the pond has settled down and there is a balance between aquatic insect life, plants and oxygen levels, the water should become clear and clean. If it doesn't, try immersing barley straw into the water, which should clear the water after about six weeks and help keep it free of algae for the rest of the summer. You can buy sachets of barley straw that will give some idea of the quantity you need; alternatively for a pool 3m (10ft) in diameter and 60cm (24in) deep, an old pair of tights packed with straw will be adequate and entertaining. Introducing water snails and oxygenating plants such as *Ceratophyllum demersum* or *Lagarosiphon major* will also help. Water lilies and other leafy aquatics provide shade and reduce the risk of green water.

Thick strands of dark green blanket weed are best removed by hand or with a net, or by twisting them around a brush shaft. Never use a rake, fork or other sharp tool in the pond; the liner is tough but not immune to being punctured.

Oxygenating plants quickly form a mass of foliage. In summer, this carpet should be thinned to prevent it choking the pond. In autumn, remove dying foliage before it sinks to the bottom as the gases that are released when it rots may be harmful to fish and other pond life.

Any weeds, plants, debris or bottom mud that is removed from the water should be left beside the pond overnight to give insects a chance to return to the water, before it is dumped or put on the compost heap.

installing a pre-formed pond

Ponds should be in an open site, with at least six hours of sunlight a day, away from trees where you are less likely to hit tree roots while digging. and near a water source for easy 'topping up' in summer.

Ponds should be at least 60cm (24in) deep if you intend to keep fish. Sunken ponds look more natural and should be sited in the lowest part of the garden, but beware of fertiliser run off if you feed your lawn regularly. A photograph was sent into a GQT correspondence programme where this had happened and the pond was choked with algae caused by the fertiliser seeping into the pond.

3 Dig out the shape of the pond, taking into account the depth and width of each shelf and allowing for a 2.5cm (1in) barrier layer of protective underlay (available from garden centres or water-garden specialists), rubberised carpet underlay or builder's sand on the horizontal surfaces of the pond. Remove sharp stones and roots. If necessary, put the pond back into the hole and press it down to leave an imprint of the shape in the soil. Follow this shape as you dig.

1 Level and clear the site. If the pond is formal and symmetrical, invert the mould, mark out the shape with pegs and string or cut carefully round the shape with a half moon or edging iron. If it has an informal shape, stand the pond the right way up and use canes to mark out the shape before joining them together with string.

2 Cut around the shape with a spade or half moon and remove the turf. If the pond is being edged with slabs, cut another strip 15cm (6in) wider than the outline of the pond and the same depth as the paving slabs so they sit level with the soil. Alternatively, raise the pond just above soil level to prevent fertilisers from the surrounding land from being washed into the water.

4 Check the surface is level using a straight edge and spirit level.

5 Firm the soil, then line the base with builder's sand or underlay (see step 3 above).

6 Lower the pond liner into the hole.

7 Fill the pond with about 10cm (4in) of water so it beds down. Check the levels again and fill in any gaps around the sides with sifted soil or builder's sand. Continue the process of adding water, filling around the sides and checking the level until the pond is full. If you have difficulty forcing sand down into the gaps, wash some down with a hosepipe. Continue filling the pond until the water is about 5cm (2in) from the top.

8 Pack sand under the marginal shelves for added support.

9 Cover the edges of the pond with slates or stones.

10 Surround the edges with soil, levelling and filling the gaps between the stones and grass.

11 Re-seed or turf the area to blend the pond with the surrounding lawn.

installing a pond with a flexible liner

To estimate the amount of flexible liner needed, first measure the maximum width, depth and length of your pond. The width of the liner should equal the pond's width plus two times the depth, plus 30cm (12in) overhang. To calculate the length of the liner, add the pond's length to two times the depth, plus 30cm (12in) overhang.

1 Mark out the shape of the pool with a hosepipe or pegs and string. Live with it for a few days to check that you're happy with the shape. Make any modifications necessary.

2 Cut carefully round the shape with a half moon.

3 Dig out your pond. Shelves for marginals should be at least 25cm (10in) wide and deep and slightly angled so the sides won't collapse; these too can be marked out with a hosepipe or string. The deepest point for most garden ponds is 60cm (24in).

4 Remove roots, stones and debris, then line the base either with a layer of protective underlay (available from garden centres or water garden specialists), rubberised carpet underlay or 2cm (½in) of builder's sand. Firm damp sand carefully by hand.

7 Fill the pond slowly with water. As the liner becomes taut, fold the creases neatly into place, preferably on the ledges where they will be hidden from view. Avoid weighing the liner down around the sides with heavy weights because this creates tension, which in turn could stretch or weaken it.

5 Check that the surface of the pond is level using a spirit level placed on a straight-edged piece of timber.

8 Fill the pool to within 5cm (2in) of the rim, then trim off any excess liner, leaving a 15cm (6in) overlap on all sides to be buried by soil or edging slabs. If using edging slabs, position them so they project over the edge of the pond by about 5cm (2in). This will conceal the liner and protect it from sunlight, which may cause it to perish.

6 Spread the flexible liner in the sun to warm it and make it supple, then lay it over the hole so the centre of the liner is in the centre of the pond.

9 Plant up with marginals, floating-leaved plants and oxygenators (see pages 80–81). Be different and try *Zantesdeschia elliottiana* and other frost-tender plants, though these will be only temporary plantings in much of the UK.

Foliage-covered boundaries provide a tantalising glimpse of what's beyond. This backdrop is a blend of *Clematis* 'Madame Julia Correvon' and *Vitis coignetiae* 'Claret Cloak'.

boundaries

Matt: There are two types of garden boundaries: those marking the perimeter of a garden, which usually provide security and privacy; and those within the garden, which generally demarcate different areas, screen storage areas or just add character to your creation. Boundaries are also used to provide habitats for plants, giving them shelter, shade or vertical spaces to climb up.

Most gardeners are happy to erect a few trellis or fence panels, but many regard extensive fencing or wall projects as jobs for the contractors. Before accepting larger challenges, compare the time and effort it will take with the money you will save by doing the job yourself. Check with your local planning authority for information regarding the height of fences: in most areas you can build up to 6ft 6in (2m) before planning permission is required.

Fencing

Fence panels are made of tanalised softwood (see page 00). Panels should last up to 20 years or more depending on the location, but as an added protection should be painted regularly with wood preservative. I once met someone who painted their fence with a 50:50 mix of creosote and old sump oil; the fence was 50 years old and still standing. Although I've never tried them, some wood preservatives can be sprayed on – having endured years of laboriously painting fences, this has to be a tempting option!

When erecting a fence, make sure you treat all sawn surfaces with wood preservative, 'cap' the posts and install 15cm (6in) strips of timber (gravel boards) to protect the base of the panels from water splash and rotting.

Posts

Timber posts are usually made of tanalised softwood. Hardwoods such as green oak are available, but they are expensive, heavy to lift and can twist and split if they are not cured properly. However, they are highly resistant to rot, long lasting and have an attractive grain. When buying posts, check they are suitable for the panels you have chosen – heavy-duty panels need large posts. It is very important to check the length of your posts before buying. For most purposes, 60cm (24in) of the post is buried below ground level. If the ground is uneven or slightly sloping, or if you are on an exposed site, the posts need to be longer. Always buy posts that are longer than you think you need, particularly if the ground is sloping; it is easier to cut off extra length than to add to posts that are too short!

In heavier soils, tanalised softwood posts supporting a low wooden or wire fence will last about 15 years when knocked straight into the ground. Concrete posts look harsh and utilitarian. However, they can be painted and will last indefinitely. Climbers that are naturally self-clinging will attach themselves to fence panels, but be prepared to drill supports for others into the concrete posts. A system of concrete posts and gravel boards, with fencing panels slotted into pre-formed grooves in the posts, is easy to manage and will last for years, but it is somewhat municipal. When removing old panels and slotting in the new ones, make sure you ask your neighbours to remove their climbers first!

securing posts

Setting posts in concrete provides stability, particularly in lighter soils, but there is a tendency for timber to rot at the junction between post and concrete unless it is thoroughly treated with preservative beforehand; removing a lump of concrete to replace the post is a nightmare! A good alternative is to raise the concrete a few inches above ground level and slope it away from the post to encourage water to drain away and reduce the likelihood of this happening. Ready-mixed fence-post concrete is available from building suppliers or DIY stores and is an excellent, if somewhat expensive, small-scale option. For instructions on setting posts in concrete, see page 62.

Fencing spikes are useful in heavier soils and can be fixed in concrete for added stability in light soils. The posts are fitted into sockets, making them easy to replace.

1 Before doing any digging or hammering, check the location of services such as gas, electricity and water using a CAT (see page 52).

2 Make a pilot hole with a crowbar or metal spike and sledgehammer, This is particularly important on stony soil as the spikes twist if they hit large stones or flints.

3 Insert the driving tool designed by the manufacturers to avoid damaging the socket. If you hit the spike itself, the sides of the socket will splay.

4 Use a sledgehammer to drive the spike into the ground with vertical blows. Check with a spirit level every few strikes to make sure the spike stays vertical.

5 Stop when the 'box' is just above the ground and screw in the post.

Gravel boards

A gravel board is the horizontal strip of treated timber at the base of the fence that prevents the fence panels from touching the soil and rotting. It is cheaper, more durable, easier to replace and quicker to paint than a panel. The alternative to using gravel boards is to put the fence panels above ground level so that they don't touch the soil; this will prevent them rotting, but it does leave a gap at the base of the fence.

Styles of panel

Close board is constructed of vertical boards attached to two 'arris' rails and nailed together, the thick edges overlapping the thin edges; it is also known as feather-edge fencing.

Close-board fencing can be bought in panels, with the wooden coping strip already fitted – something that it is usually forgotten if you fit your own. Although it is not the most rigid style of fencing panel, it makes a robust fence that is ideal for boundaries.

Wavy edged is one of the most common styles of panel. It is visually attractive and constructed of overlapping horizontal strips in a softwood frame. It is moderately secure.

Basket-weave panels have thin woven slats in a light frame. They are useful for screening, but are flimsy and tend to buckle, bow and finally collapse, particularly when exposed to direct sunlight. If using basket-weave or wavy-edged panels and you have the 'fair face', think of your neighbours. Don't plant shrubs too closely to a basket-weave fence because the branches have a tendency to squeeze through the gaps between the strips of timber in the panel, damaging the fence. Where climbers or shrubs are planted against a fence, check and prune them regularly to prevent any problems.

Trellis that is lightly covered with plants filters rather than blocks the wind, reducing the eddying effect and damage to plants on the other side of the fence that is caused by solid barriers. A good way to deter burglars is to place trellis on top of a fence (see page 225).

Wattle hurdles and other ornamental fencing, such as framed willow screens or split bamboo, make excellent screens within gardens. They are not as long lasting as other designs and are difficult to treat with preservatives, but a coat of matt yacht varnish should help – just make sure it is forced into all the cracks and crevices. Informal willow hurdles, 1.8m (6ft) tall, should be anchored to rustic posts with 60cm (24in) buried in the ground and concreted in position in exposed areas. The best way to attach the hurdles to the poles is using galvanised wire at three equidistant points along the post; don't use nails, which may split the pole. If willow hurdles are left untreated, stand them on pressure-treated gravel boards, painted with timber preservative, for increased longevity.

Low-level picket and ranch fencing is only suitable as boundary markers within the garden or perimeter fencing in open-plan estates. Spiked chain fencing is purely aesthetic; it doesn't stop the local dogs from watering your plants and is irresistible to schoolchildren of all ages, particularly those coming back from the pub at night who find it difficult to resist swinging on or jumping over the chains!

Clockwise from top left: *Jasminum nudiflorum* brings welcome colour in winter when trained up wire or trellis; woven cedar panels can be a striking garden feature; trellis atop informal fencing makes an ideal home for a rambling rose; post-and-rail fencing is simple yet effective; honeysuckle and hurdles harmonise to create a cottage-garden style.

erecting trellis

4 Erect concreted posts as shown on page 62.

1 Mark out the line where the trellising is to go.

5 Use a spirit level to check that the fence and posts are vertical.

2 Lie the trellising on the ground and mark the centre of the holes that take the fence posts with canes.

6 Attach the trellising to the posts using galvanised nails or brackets. Put a line along the base to ensure that they are at the same height.

3 Cut out the shape of the hole round the cane.

7 The finished fence – stand back and admire your handiwork!

Matt's tips for erecting a fence

● Before buying panels and posts, mark out the position of the fence with a garden line and check it is straight using a 3-4-5 triangle (see page 68). Measure the length of the fence, work out the number of panels, gravel boards and posts required, not forgetting to add the two end posts, and making allowances for the height of the gravel boards.

● The 'base' line for each panel is along the top of the posts rather than at ground level, so that the tops remain level whatever the slight irregularities in the ground. The tops of the posts are cut to length and treated with preservative once the fencing is completed. Avoid cutting the base of the posts because these have already been treated.

● If the ground is steeply sloping, your fencing needs to be stepped. Work out the height difference between the highest and lowest panel and ensure the 'steps' are equally spaced. Do this by securing a taut horizontal line from the top of the slope to the bottom, attach it to a cane and measure the change in depth. Measure the horizontal line to work out how many panels and posts fit in that length. When making important mathematical calculations, it is worth getting somebody else to check them for you; answers may have to be modified! The most important factor is that the fence looks level to the eye, even if it isn't.

● If you are using concrete to secure the posts, erect a run of panels first, holding them upright with hardcore and supporting them with battens, then make any final adjustments before adding the concrete – rather than making up the concrete in small batches.

● It is vital that the posts are vertical; check them constantly, holding a spirit level against each face in turn and adjusting as necessary while packing rubble around the post to hold it upright. It is possible to buy spirit levels specially designed for checking posts, with both vertical and horizontal levels, which are attached to the post with rubber bands. Make sure the string marking the fence line is level with the centre of the each post and work out whether the boundary lies in front of or behind the line, otherwise life might get rather interesting!

● If the first post of your run of fencing is attached to a house wall or outbuilding, secure it with 7mm (1/4in) diameter expanding coach bolts. Drill the central hole first and the two other holes equidistant from that. Check that the post is vertical using a spirit level, then make pilot holes at the relevant points with a masonry bit, marking the brickwork below. Drill the holes of the correct size through the timber and fit coach bolts into the wall. The bolt head must be countersunk into the timber so the first fence panel lies flush against the side of the post. If there is a gap between the wall and the timber, because the wall or timber are not vertical, pack it with wedges cut from slivers of timber that have been treated with preservative, or use plastic wedges. It can be a nuisance trying to get the positioning right, but it is vital that the first post is vertical otherwise there will be gaps in the fence.

Fixing pre-fabricated panels

There are several methods of fixing panels to posts. One method is to nail them using galvanised nails through the outer frame of the panel and into the posts. If you are not using gravel boards, prop the panel up on bricks and check the level before nailing. Alternatively, you can use L- and U-shaped brackets with pre-drilled fixing holes. These should be fixed in the centre of the post and attached with 5cm (2in) galvanised nails. Make a T-shaped gauge with two off-cuts: the vertical one aligns with the edge of the post and the horizontal one marks the centre of the post.

Shortening a panel

If the fence does not finish with an exact panel width, it is easy to shorten a panel. Measure the distance between the penultimate and final post, scribe a vertical line down the panel, then carefully remove the upright batten at the end and re-position it on the inside edge of the scribed guideline. Hammer galvanised nails through the batten; putting a brick underneath turns the ends of the nail for added security. Then support the batten on a workbench or table and carefully saw off the protruding ends with a panel or jig-saw using a blade with fine teeth; work slowly and carefully to prevent the timber being split or damaged, cutting as close as possible to the outer edge of the newly repositioned batten. Paint the cut ends with wood preservative.

gates

Go through any gate and there is a sense of expectation. A gate may offer you an enticing glimpse of what's beyond, or it might be solid to provide privacy and security – and maybe an even greater sense of anticipation, particularly if it is marked 'private'! Gates should blend with the surrounding design. Keep the top of the gate at a similar height to the adjacent wall or fence to create a sense of balance; ideally the width of the gate should relate to the path that follows. Gates should suit the style of the entrance. A dramatic, ornamental gate becomes a feature in its own right. Even the door furniture should relate to its surroundings. If you have a large

entrance gate across the drive into the front garden, it's easier for pedestrians if a side gate is installed as well. Pedestrian gates should be at least 90cm (36in) wide, wider if you have to fit ride-on mowers or other equipment through. Gates for vehicles should be at least 2.4m (8ft) wide.

Metal gates

Metal gates are usually made of wrought iron. Choose one that is not too flimsy, particularly if it is the garden gate. They may be ornamental or security gates, but the overall impact is formal. An architectural blacksmith can help you with your own design. I once saw a fabulous gate decorated with old garden tools. Whatever you choose, make sure it blends with the surroundings and is not too ostentatious; it should not be noticed for the wrong reasons! Wrought iron combines well with brick walls. Always hang gates so that they are high enough and don't scrape on the ground when opened. Metal gates need regular painting, particularly on the underside, to ensure they don't rust. Be bold and paint them in a bright colour.

Wooden gates

Wooden gates can be traditional or contemporary, using the same material as the fence to create a sense of uniformity. Keep the design simple. A carpenter can help you realise your dreams!

walls

A brick or mortared stone wall blends perfectly with a house wall in the same material, creating cohesion of design. Brick walls should be the length of one brick wide – horrible half-brick walls are as flimsy as they look, fall over easily and need buttresses or piers at regular intervals. If a low boundary wall ends at the drive, plant something tall at the end that is clearly visible to prevent the wall from being hit by reversing drivers!

There are many patterns for brickwork, including the English garden wall bond with one course of 'headers' (with the end of the brick facing you) to three or four of stretchers (showing the long side). Scottish bond has five courses. Flemish garden wall bond has one to one or three to one stretchers to headers in each course; it is very decorative. English bond has one row of headers to one of stretchers and is one of the strongest. For a tidy finish, make sure the courses are level and avoid getting mortar on the bricks.

This beautiful gate provides a barrier while framing a view of the garden.

Slate walls create a pleasing texture and home for plants such as hostas.

93

A greenhouse enables you to over-winter tender plants and raise seedlings and cuttings – plants for free!

greenhouses

Matt: Site your greenhouse in an open, sunny, sheltered position, away from frost pockets, chilling wind and shading trees. Ideally, the apex should run from north to south to make the most of summer sun, and east to west for over-wintering plants and raising seedlings. However, few gardens have perfect conditions and it's often a question of compromise. Take note of nearby trees. A walnut tree in my neighbour's garden is not so close that falling branches or leaves would crash through the roof or block the gutters. It doesn't come into leaf until late spring, so the greenhouse catches the spring sunshine. It is shaded from scorching summer sun at midday, but gets sunlight in late afternoon. The benching is erected along the north side of the greenhouse, so the tree doesn't cast a shadow over the south side that is dug as a border.

If space is limited, consider a 'lean to' against the wall of the house. You will find it is convenient for providing electricity and water, and in sunny situations the bricks will act as night storage heaters, absorbing heat during the day and releasing it at night. It also makes an impressive porch in a sheltered spot. Side louvres fit snugly and improve air circulation. Greenhouses are available in plastic, aluminium or timber. For more information on choosing one see Bob's chapter on Glass, pages 278–89.

erecting a greenhouse

After years of nomadic existence and working in other people's greenhouses, I'm so excited that at last I have my own! Before you start unpacking and assembling your greenhouse, make sure you read the instructions several times. Photocopy them so you have one working copy and another master copy filed away for future reference. Count all the parts against the manufacturer's parts identification list; label them and the packets clearly – it's even worth checking the number of screws!

1 Measure the outline of the greenhouse, hammer in the first site peg, checking the 3-4-5 triangle (see page 68), then lightly hammer in the other pegs.

2 Check the diagonals of the rectangle – they should be equal. When satisfied that all the measurements are correct, hammer the pegs firmly into the ground.

3 Mark the outline with nylon line.

4 Dig a trench one spade's depth (a bit deeper in lighter soils), ensuring that its sides overlap the edge of the greenhouse. Hammer site pegs approximately 1.8m (6ft) apart into the base of the trench, so that the tops are level with or just below the surrounding soil, checking the tops are horizontal with a spirit level. Install the electricity cables to save tunnelling under the foundations at a later date. They should be in armoured cable, at least a spade's depth and covered with a layer of sand or ducting and a warning tape. Leave enough spare cable to reach the switches at one end and the junction box at the other.

5 Pour in concrete at a mix of five parts all-in ballast to one part cement until it just covers the site pegs. Tamp the concrete to remove air bubbles, then cut the surface to the right level. Store the cement off the ground on an old pallet or similar and cover with polythene (it's useless if it gets wet).

6 Cover the concrete foundations with plastic sheeting or damp hessian until they are dry, then lay one course of bricks as a foundation, checking the diagonals. Engineering bricks last indefinitely, but are very hard to cut. The line marking the outline of the greenhouse should run down the outer edge of the bricks. Smaller greenhouses can be secured with ground anchors, which are like tent pegs that are set in concrete. The foundation course should be absolutely level to support the greenhouse. If there are gaps, the greenhouse is liable to bow and the glass may crack. Check using a spirit level, then check again!

7 Once the mortar is dry, lay the base rail along the length and put the end sills in place. Check they are square by measuring the diagonals; they should be equal. Lay the two end sections in place, ensuring the door is at the correct end. Drill a hole at the centre of the base rail, marking the depth on the bit with masking tape. If using a domestic electric drill, make a pilot hole first because the bricks are so hard; alternatively hire a heavy-duty drill. Loosely secure the bolt and tighten later.

8 Attach the spans and lower cross pieces.

9 Put the lower vertical panes of glass into the frame. The weight will cause the greenhouse to 'settle'.

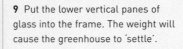

10 Remove individual panes as required to drill out the remaining basal fixings. Note how the glass slots into place and is edged with rubber, a useful safety feature (but it is better to err on the side of caution and always wear gloves).

11 Follow the remaining instructions, working slowly and methodically, slotting the panes of glass in place. Put water butts by the downpipes to collect rainwater for the greenhouse. Install power points with waterproof safety switches (attach these to pre-painted plywood) and install fluorescent strips or 'grow lamps' as required.

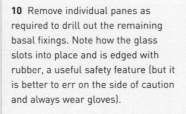

An old shed adds character to a garden.

sheds

Matt: When buying a shed, decide what size you want, then, if space allows, double it! Most sheds become untidy because there is insufficient room for all the equipment stored there. Before buying, think about how much kit you have and what you are likely to purchase in the future. Make sure there is enough hanging space for hooks to hang hand tools and ground space for mowers and barrows. Put a concrete ramp up to the door frame for barrows and mowers and, if there's space, down the other side.

Alternatively make a wooden wedge as a temporary ramp. Doors should be high enough so you can enter with ease and wide enough for equipment to pass through. You should be able to move around comfortably inside under the eaves. If the shed incorporates a floor, jump up and down to check its strength and check the doors and sides are strong enough – if they are too flimsy, don't buy it! Make sure the shed you buy is substantial and secure and buy the best you can afford. Metal sheds are a useful alternative to wooden ones and, because they have internal hinges, are more secure.

Security is paramount as you may have thousands of pounds' worth of equipment stored inside without realising. It is advisable to change the hinges on the door because most of them are too weak. If there is a lock, add a good quality padlock and a hasp and staple. Always fit bolts and screws to the frame. If internal hinges can be fitted, do so. Replace all small screws with longer ones and spoil the heads so they can't be unscrewed from the outside; alternatively, use 'coffin' screws, smear the heads with super glue or, best of all, use coach bolts. Bar the windows on the inside or fit curtains or blinds to obscure what's inside and fit toughened glass. Chain expensive equipment to a concrete floor and keep a note of the codes or mark with an ultraviolet pen somewhere that can't be worn off with use. Better still, engrave your postcode and fit security lighting outside and an alarm. Some sheds are designed with security in mind and only have small windows located under the eaves. If possible, anchor small sheds to the ground; they have been known to be lifted up and moved to get at what's inside, and they are particularly vulnerable on allotments. Thieves have also been known to remove the roof or the side of a shed.

A garden shed need not be an eyesore. Turn it into a feature to suit your taste. Use coloured wood stain, add window boxes, shutters, trellis and climbing plants such as roses and honeysuckle, decorate the eaves; even put up curtains!

services

Bob: Before embarking on any gardening work, and especially before making any changes, make sure you know exactly where your existing services are and where other hardware is positioned. Make a reference map to show where everything is and use it to mark any new features that turn up. Nail a copy somewhere permanent.

If you are adding new features, such as a water garden or greenhouse, bear in mind that the position or supply of some utilities will dictate much of the cost. Make sure that taps and so on are positioned conveniently; if it is physically hard to get to a tap or power point then it will not be used as often. A simple light will make a greenhouse much more useful, as will a tap, but the cost of getting them there may be exorbitant. Good planning is essential because it will be expensive to alter groundwork at a later date – particularly if areas of hard standing, patios or stone are to be laid in the path of future pipe runs. Installing pipes and electrics should be carried out by a qualified professional; do not try to do alterations or installations yourself unless you know what you are doing and are qualified to do so.

Gas, water and electricity

Gas, water and electricity have fixed points of entry into your property and you are responsible for what happens to them on your land. Make sure any pipes or wires are highlighted on your plan and avoid disturbing them. Plan well, so as not to have to move pipes in the future. Although your home's gas supply may have little relevance to the garden, a chimney or vent outlet does and care should always be taken so plants don't grow to block them. Water is, of course, most important and an outdoor tap is almost essential. A separate tap for the vegetable bed or greenhouse is useful, as is one near the car parking place for those who indulge in car washing.

Electricity is not necessary in the garden itself, but outdoor security lights are convenient. Power is almost essential if you are to get full use out of a greenhouse. If you are starting from scratch, it is a good idea to have proper outside sockets fitted with an appropriate safety device for power machinery, as well as for using household items on the patio or in a summerhouse or bower. Special damp-proof light fittings are available for the more rustic places.

Safety

It cannot be overemphasised how important proper installation and fail-safe isolating devices are, especially in a greenhouse, garden or by water. The power requirements for a greenhouse with soil-warming cables, fan heaters, lights and possibly pumps and grow lights are considerable, and require heavy cables and proper equipment. Likewise for large water features and three-phase garden machinery. You may not need mains for some tasks. Consult an expert about fitting isolating transformers and low-voltage systems, which are safer alternatives to mains electricity for many applications. At the moment solar-powered lights and accessories are pricey and not long-lived, but the newer versions available soon with white LEDs and longer-lasting storage batteries should be ideal.

An outdooor tap saves carrying muck into the house and water out. Hoses should be hung like this out of harm's way as they will trip you up if left lying around.

Utility poles and lines

Utility poles and lines may cross your property, even if they don't actually go to your house but to a neighbour's. It is important not to block access to these or interfere with them – by growing climbers that can attach themselves to them, for example. It may be possible to have them replaced by underground lines. If not, try screening them with a vertical tree such as *Juniperus scopulorum* 'Skyrocket' or the flowering cherry, *Prunus* ' Amanogawa'.

Manhole covers

Manhole covers and, in the country, septic tanks are another problem. In some cases, it is possible to have them lowered and made flush with ground level or to raise the surrounding ground, but in every case access must be maintained. Special hollowed-out planter lids are available, but I find a large but movable tub full of flowers placed on top a simpler solution for hiding them.

Oil and gas tanks

Oil tanks and lines or LPG gas tanks may well need screening. A separate free-standing trellis and posts are advisable rather than attaching anything to the tank itself. Any screen must be set away from the tank so as not to constitute a fire hazard and to allow air to circulate, since a damp atmosphere could rust the tank. Remember to mark on your plan the path of the oil line to the house, and to leave free access through your screening for the delivery driver.

Surface drainage, main drains and ditches

Rainwater run-off from patios, paths and drives should be planned for prior to installation and be linked to the correct main drain or to a proper soakaway a sufficient distance from the foundations. If flooding occurs, extra drains may be necessary. Aim to store as much rainwater as possible (see below) and divert any surplus to the correct main drain, and not to the sewer. Mark any such underground drains on your plan. The sewer dirt pipe can often be spotted after snow because it melts there first from the extra warmth. If you have a ditch at any side of your garden, you are usually obliged to keep it clear and free from blockage.

Water supplies

Mains water is obviously the first choice for simplicity, but it is not always the best. First, when you need water most, during a drought, they put a ban on using it! Secondly, it is expensive and demands either a fee or a metered fee for garden use. Thirdly, mains water is supplied under pressure and this can sometimes be too great for automatic irrigation systems, which may need a separate self-filling header tank (a toilet cistern will do). Pressure can vary by the hour in some areas – if you suffer from low pressure, try to water before everyone else gets up and see if this makes a difference. All mains supplies to a garden need to be fitted with a non-return valve to prevent contaminated water from being pushed back down the pipe. Large gardens probably need their own separate mains supply, especially if you have to fill a pool of any size. You may want to install computer-controlled automatic sprinklers, but make sure your water supply is large enough to cope to avoid having to upgrade it part way through.

Sprinklers use, and waste, a lot of water; mains water is not always the best source of supply.

Tap water brings its own set of problems. Although it is sterile and safe, the temperature is usually very chilly and it is full of chlorine. This may not pose a problem when it is sprayed or irrigated on hardy outdoor plants, but it can shock tender and greenhouse specimens and therefore should be allowed to warm up before application. If space allows, consider fitting a holding tank in the greenhouse, where the water can give off some of the chlorine; this can also be an opportunity to add some liquid feed to the water.

Hosepipes and taps

A proper tap and fitting make sense. If your garden is large, or if you have a greenhouse, you may need more than one. For spraying and watering plants, a rubber or plastic hosepipe will be necessary. Choose the best quality you can afford – the better ones kink less and last longer. A reel mounted on a wall is probably the best place to store a hosepipe when not in use. It is also worth investing in quick-release junctions, sprinklers and so on if you expect to water often.

Winter measures

When water freezes, it expands and this can cause pipes and hoses to break or crack. For this reason, all mains pipes must be well lagged and insulated. In very cold spells, it is also worth draining down watering systems for extra safety. Empty rubber and plastic hosepipes and store them in a frost-free shed. If they are accidentally left out in freezing weather, avoid moving them until after the water has thawed and warmed up to prevent them splitting. Be careful of dripping pipes, which can freeze drop by drop until the pipe blocks and the water backs up.

Wells, pools, ponds and ditches

To supplement your mains water supply, you may also wish to take water from wells, pools, ponds, ditches or water courses. This is usually warmer than mains water and free of chlorine, but it may be muddy or carry disease. If you have your own well, and it is fairly deep, it should contain fairly cold, cleanish water; however, if it is a shallow, ground-water sump-type well the water may be dirtier. In either case, make sure you stand the water in a settling tank to warm up before

This water butt will certainly collect rain water, but your recycling system would work even better if the roof was guttered.

giving it to tender or greenhouse plants. Water from pools, ponds and ditches is usually warmer, and even muddier. Such dirty water may be full of plant nutrients, diseases or even pollution, so make sure you use it with care. Simple electric pumps enable all these sources of water to be utilised. Keep in mind that in most areas, you will have to pay a fee for taking water from a water course.

Collecting and recycling water

At least they're not yet charging us for the rain! An amazing amount falls in a year and every effort should be made to collect and store it, especially as it is clean(ish) and not full of chlorine and salts. Rainwater is loved by house and pot plants and by acid lovers such as rhododendrons and camellias. To make the most of this precious resource, fit rainwater guttering to every roof and pipe it to storage butts. These can be linked together by overflow pipes or siphons to increase the holding capacity. Once a year, at least, empty the butts and clean them out, brush out the gutters and fit the downpipes with an old sock as a filter.

You may also wish to recycle greywater from sinks, showers and baths. This can, local bylaws permitting, simply be led away by hoses rammed up the outlets during times of drought and diverted to valued crops, or it can form part of a permanent set up. Reed beds and other similar ecological cleaners can be used to convert the house's greywater back into clean water for irrigation or pools. It is feasible, but beyond the realms of this book and most of us, to recycle the sewage, dishwasher and washing machine water into the garden. This is fraught with difficulties – better to stick to storing more rainwater.

Water can be stored in plastic water butts, metal water tanks, or, less often, hole-in-the-ground cisterns. Water is heavy, so make sure you stand butts and tanks on substantial foundations. All water containers need lids if children or pets are likely to climb in. To make drawing water from a butt or tank convenient, it should be raised up on substantial blocks and fitted with a tap near the base. This should be fixed just above the bottom, so as not to allow any sediment to come out, and high enough from the ground to allow a watering can to be stood underneath. Overflow pipes are necessary to prevent water running down the side, which could undermine the foundations and eventually cause the butt to fall over. Ideally, overflows should be diverted into extra butts. Water can be moved by gravity and if you arrange the overflow so it goes from one butt to the next it will do so. If, however, you join the two by siphons instead, then the flow will also reverse. In this way, you can not only fill many butts from just one downpipe but you can also draw from any one of them. (They must all be on the same level.)

Anne's treasured wooden wheelbarrow always looks the part.

tools

Anne: Every gardener needs a good set of basic gardening tools. These will become your trusty friends and allies in the garden, so choose carefully and look after them well. Before buying, always 'weigh' a new spade or fork in your hand. Work the blades of shears and move them from hand to hand. Grip the secateurs, play with the open and shut mechanism and try the handles. Only buy if the tool feels comfortable and you think it will easily become an extension of your body. I also feel it is important to surround yourself with items that please your eye. Kitting a tool shed from scratch is an expensive business, so it's worth asking around the relatives first, to see if they have any spares. Most towns have a second-hand shop where old gardening tools have been brought in, mended and sharpened for re-sale. They are often very well made, cheaper than new and good-looking.

Never put a tool under pressure by asking it to do more than the job for which it was intended. Many a shaft on fork or spade was broken because the tool was levered too hard. Chip away at the soil or reach for a stronger tool. The same goes for secateurs. If the wood is too thick for them, use loppers and if they won't cut the stem, use a pruning saw.

Basic kit (what you really need)

Spades

I always laugh when I watch television programmes and see someone misguidedly trying to dig with a shovel, or for that matter, shovel with a spade. These two tools look the same, but serve different purposes. A good spade has a neat, rectangular blade designed for digging. Use it to turn soil over and to dig holes for tree and shrub planting. You can also use it like a shovel, to move soil from one place to another and to lift loosened compost from the heap into a barrow. I like stainless-steel blades because they stay cleaner and slice beautifully through the soil. However, they are rarely sold with little shoulders or treads at the top of the blade and these are good to cushion your foot when you have a lot of digging to do. If you are frail for any reason, hunt around for a small-bladed border spade. Yes, digging will take longer but you won't be tempted to lift too much soil in one go. For the record, shovels have larger, usually thinner and slightly curved blades and are not essential items of kit. They are useless for digging, but good for moving piles of earth or coal.

Forks

Versatile and easy to use, every gardener should really have two. I would buy a smaller, border fork first. They are so useful for tickling up weeds and the soil between plants. Although small, they'll also lift leeks, or fill a wheelbarrow with manure. Later, invest in a full-sized fork, useful for loosening solid, stony soil and levering up large clumps of perennials. Then, when you have two forks, they can be used, back to back, to split clumps of perennials into smaller pieces. A hand fork is not essential, but is useful for fiddly weeding jobs. A flat-tine potato fork is a luxury.

Choose a trowel that feels comfortable in your hand.

Wheelbarrow

In a garden of any size, a wheelbarrow is essential, though in a small plot you might be able to make do with a bucket. I use mine for wheeling compost between heap and borders. I use it to collect weeds and prunings and to move heavy items such as bags of potting compost from the car to the greenhouse or shed. Sometimes one job will take me a week or two to complete and I can keep all the tools I need in the barrow, wheeling them into the shed overnight and bringing them out again when needed. I use a small galvanised metal model, because I'll always stuff my barrow full and pushing the larger ones is hard work. Pile the weight towards the front, over the wheel, to make life easier. I also have a beautiful wooden wheelbarrow. It is heavy and harder to push, but it lifts my heart just to look at it!

Trowel

The indispensable trowel is needed to dig holes for small plants and bulbs. Buy one with a blade of average width, as this is versatile enough for all jobs. Make sure the handle is comfortable and wear gloves when carrying out mass plantings; it is easy to get a blister.

A spring-tine rake enables you to tidy the leaves without damaging the lawn.

Buckets and trugs

You can never have too many buckets. I use two when weeding (one for compostable weeds and one for perennial roots). Always keep a bucket of water with you when planting, to give each plant a good drink before it goes in the soil. Trugs are brilliant for transporting small potted plants, freshly lifted perennials, bulbs and so on, and for collecting flowers or vegetables.

Spring-tine rake and broom

Keeping the garden tidy is important and to rake up leaves and other rubbish from lawns, a spring-tine rake can be used lightly. If you press harder and dig deeper, a spring-tine rake is useful for scarifying the turf and removing dead grass and weeds. A broom with medium bristles sweeps most paths and hard areas.

Knife

Buy a general-purpose, straight-bladed knife for taking cuttings, trimming the ends of string and so on. You'll also need a sharpening stone and oil to keep the blade sharp.

Pruning tools

Buy the most expensive pair of secateurs you can afford – using them will be a joy and they'll last well. You will need long-handled pruners (I call them loppers) for thicker stems. A folding pruning saw takes care of most small branches.

Watering cans

To keep a garden healthy, you will need a couple of large watering cans with roses (sprinklers) on the end. Use them for watering in plants that are newly planted, feeding plants, watering plants in containers and to keep seedlings moist.

Long-handled 'loppers' are ideal for pruning thick stems and tall plants like this eucalyptus.

Edging shears take the back-breaking effort out of trimming lawn edges.

Shears

For a lawn of any size, edging shears are a must. These allow you to trim the grass edge while standing comfortably. Ordinary hand shears are just right for trimming small hedges regularly (most gardeners opt for mechanical shears for long, tall hedges). They will also take care of small areas of long grass, say at the base of a tree where bulbs are naturalised.

Hoes

Those with small or average-sized gardens can probably survive quite well without a hoe, although they are always useful to have. But those with kitchen gardens will find them indispensable. The most useful is a push-pull Dutch hoe. The blade severs weeds from their roots and you can clear an area of weeds in no time, as long as the blade is sharp. Regular use of a sharpening stone is important.

When not in use for carrying small plants from one part of the garden to another, a trug is an ideal storage container for garden paraphernalia.

Other tools

Having started with a basic set of tools, you can gradually add more as and when required. There are many different kinds of hoe and for the kitchen garden, a draw hoe is useful for chopping at weeds and also for drawing long drills in the ground. An onion hoe is similar in use and shape, but has a shorter handle.

A metal garden rake for drawing to and fro to level soil is useful for creating seedbeds and for raking gravel. Where weeds come up between cracks in paving stones, a great alternative to weedkiller is to dig them out using a specially designed hand-weeder. There are many types on the market, all designed to wiggle out tap roots and dig into a variety of nooks and crannies.

For straightening lawn edges and any other job where cutting turf is involved, a half moon iron is brilliant. But on a small scale, some gardeners will use an old, long-bladed kitchen knife for cutting turf.

Besoms are excellent for sweeping lawns. Use them to distribute worm casts or to brush top dressing into holes. There is a vast array of irrigation equipment on the market. Larger gardens will benefit from a long hosepipe kept on a reel. Personally, I can live without sprinklers and watering nozzles, but I know some people like to have them.

Chapter 3

weeds & weed control

Anne: Weeds are essentially plants growing in the wrong place. All of our gardens are potentially full of them and even if at some point we succeed in eradicating every weed from our plot, they will reappear as if from nowhere. Light seeds fly in on the wind (thistles and rosebay willowherb), birds drop seeds from berries they have eaten (bramble and elder) and perennials like bindweed, ground elder, brambles and ivy creep insidiously through boundaries from neighbouring gardens and fields. Weeds can even hitch a lift with new plants – many a garden has been infested with bittercress whose seeds and seedlings were inadvertently planted along with a new shrub or herbaceous perennial. This annual weed matures rapidly and soon fires its seed out of taut pods, colonising around new plants.

Keeping our gardens as clear of weeds as we can is important not just from an aesthetic point of view, but also because weeds tangle themselves up with our cultivated plants, competing for space, light, air, water and nutrients. Their eradication and control may seem like a chore, but weeding can be surprisingly satisfying and is best tackled little and often. Clearing an area of weeds also brings us into close proximity with our plants. Enjoying the peppery fragrance of lupins, the textural buds on moss roses and the mouth-watering aromas from aniseed-scented agastache or rosemary are some of the side-benefits of weeding.

Even if we can't prevent weeds appearing, there are plenty of ways to control them and make life as difficult as possible for them.

Nigella damascena 'Deep Blue', a delicate love-in-a-mist, is one of the many 'free' plants which may self-seed into bare patches of soil in the garden. Learn to recognise its feathery seedlings and you won't mistake it for a weed.

light weeding

The first lesson in weeding is how to tackle an ordinary border where weeds are starting to colonise the spaces between plants. While shrubs are still knitting together and herbaceous perennials are making spring growth, there are gaps where seeds can land and pernicious (perennial) roots can creep. Controlling these is routine maintenance and the time to step in is while the weeds are still small but large enough to handle; all you need is a wheelbarrow, two buckets and a small border fork.

1 Work systematically through the border from side to side and from back to front, weeding small sections at a time. This is the sort of job you can come and go at, loading the equipment back into the barrow and storing it until the next opportunity arises. Using the fork, loosen the soil carefully between your plants before pulling the weeds out.

2 What you have at your fingertips is a fascinating mixture of plants, and the novice weeder would do well to pause and consider what these are. The usual mixture consists of common annual weeds like fat hen, chickweed and speedwell (shown here), with some useful seedlings of garden plants that you want to keep (Bob will have more to say about these on page 119). If you are unable to identify some plants, leave a few in position and wait to see what they grow into. If they prove to be weeds, identify them (see pages 116–19) and pull them up. But you are just as likely to find seedlings of columbines (*Aquilegia vulgaris*), honesty, sweet rocket, poppies, love-in-a-mist or dusty miller (*Lychnis coronarius*). The beauty of slow, steady hand weeding is being able to leave these 'free' plants where they come up naturally.

3 Mixed in with annual weeds, you will almost certainly find some perennial ones growing either from seed or from small portions of underground stem left behind from previous weeding sessions. Most perennial weeds give themselves away by their roots. Even on young plants they look as though they want to travel and they tend to be thicker, longer and paler than the more innocent, darker, fibrous roots of annual weeds. Winkle these perennial weeds out first, putting them in their own bucket to be disposed of separately. Annual weeds, unless they are seeding, can go on the compost heap if it is hot enough throughout to be sure of killing them. Perennials must be disposed of elsewhere. Either burn them, or put them in the rubbish. If neither is possible, leave the roots on a hard surface to wither in the sun and, when they are completely dried out, add to the compost heap.

routine weed control

Weeding is an on-going task in the garden. The least complicated and most obvious method is to loosen the roots from the ground and pull them out by hand. Weeds can be cut from the ground using a hoe (see page 110) or levered out from cracks and crevices with specially adapted hand tools.

Digging in

Where a weedy patch of soil is free of plants and needs to be cultivated, digging and weeding can be carried out simultaneously. All you need to do is skim the weeds from the top of the soil using a sharp spade and bury them at the bottom of each trench as you dig. They will rot down to feed the soil and any re-growth can be hoed off quickly. For more information on digging, see pages 139–42.

Cracks and crevices

Weeds will grow even in the most inhospitable of places, including the cracks between paving stones, especially where these have been laid directly on the ground or on a bed of sand rather than concrete. There are plenty of hand tools with sharp blades specially designed to cut weeds out of narrow gaps, but the ultimate solution is either to fill the gaps with plants like creeping thyme (*Thymus serpyllum*), chamomile (*Chamaemelum nobile* 'Treneague') or Corsican mint (*Mentha requienii*), or point the gaps neatly with cement.

Dandelions are common weeds in lawns and at the edges of paths. Fortunately, their tap roots are fairly easy to dig out. Never let them seed.

Winkling out patches of weed is an easy task in a small lawn.

Lawns

Hand weeding is only feasible for small lawns, but it can be surprisingly effective on new or clean lawns if it is carried out regularly. Carefully lift patches of creeping weeds using a handfork and winkle out the long tap roots of dandelions with a screwdriver. You can fill any holes from a bucket of proprietary top-dressing compost or good garden soil mixed 3:1 with sand. Grasses will soon recolonise the patches.

eradicating problem perennial weeds

We have talked about ordinary weeding to maintain a garden in good order, but when perennial weeds have run out of control, a more radical approach is needed. This mainly applies to nuisance weeds like ground elder, couch, horsetail and bindweed, whose roots are thick and spaghetti-like underground. Ordinary hand weeding will be impossible, so continue to maintain edges, pull out any annual weeds you can see and start planning an eradication strategy.

hoeing

The secret of hoeing is to have a really sharp blade; ideally you should keep a sharpening stone nearby as a reminder.

There are several different kinds of hoe, but the flat-bladed Dutch sort is most commonly used for weeding.

Standing straight and with the blade virtually flat to the ground, use a push-pull action to slice the weeds from their roots.

I use the hoe extensively in areas like the kitchen garden when I want to keep unoccupied soil free from weeds. Take great care not to slice into crops or disturb the roots of soft fruit.

Some gardeners like to switch to a draw hoe for more controlled hoeing near plants. The blade is carried on a curved neck at right angles to the handle, making it ideal for chopping into weeds growing in more restricted spaces.

Although hoeing is usually used to control annual weeds, it can be amazingly effective at preventing the regrowth of some perennial types, although only if it is carried out regularly. I once cleared some ground of the persistent, tuberous pink-flowered *Oxalis corymbosa* by digging out the established plants as best I could and then hoeing up the regrowth weekly during the first year and fortnightly during the second year.

1 The flat-bladed **Dutch hoe** is the best general-purpose version for weeding. To make life easier, try to hoe weeds off while they are still seedlings – slicing through larger weeds like these is harder work.

2 A **draw hoe**, with the blade at right angles to the shaft, is useful for removing isolated clumps of weed. You can use a more forceful chopping action than you would with a Dutch hoe.

3 An **onion hoe** has a much shorter handle than a conventional hoe and is good if you need to get close to the plants and work in restricted spaces.

Many gardeners use a glyphosate-based weedkiller (see page 112) to control large, dense areas of difficult, deep-rooting perennial weeds, but repeated digging (see pages 139–42), perhaps in conjunction with smothering (see opposite), can work with the likes of nettles, ground elder, couch and bindweed. The key to success is regularity. However hard you try to dig out all the little pieces of root, they will re-grow and must be weeded again so that they barely see the light of day. Without light, the weeds cannot photosynthesise (obtain energy using sunlight) and will eventually weaken and die, although this can take a couple of years or more.

Couch grass, one of the nightmares of the weeding world.

I shall never forget the sad story of a friend who became totally demoralised with her gardening. Her plot was overgrown and she was very busy, but every few months she spent a weekend skirmishing around to clear a patch of soil. However, by the time she got out there again, the area had closed over once more with weeds and grasses. If only she had smothered that cleared soil with old carpets, black polythene or a proprietary weed-suppressing fabric, she would have saved herself so much work and eventually would have created beds and lawn. Soil should never be left open, because weeds will colonise with surprising speed. Either plant the area quickly and go back regularly to weed around the new plants until they become established, or smother the soil.

clearing the ground

1 To control a bad infestation of perennial weeds, you first need to clear the ground of everything except the weeds. Leave established shrubs with woody stems...

2 ...but remove perennials around whose roots the weeds will be tangled. Don't replant them in other areas of the garden, as this will spread the weeds. Instead, if you want to save the plants, wait until spring to clear the ground and take basal stem cuttings of the young shoots arising from the plants' crowns. These cuttings can then be rooted (see page 236) without the danger of weed material hitching a ride. Once the ground is clear, you can then dig, smother or resort to using weedkillers.

Smothering the soil with a piece of old carpet (left) or a weed-killing fabric (right) is an efficient but long-term approach to weed eradication.

Smothering

A non-chemical method of eradicating perennial weeds is to smother the area using carpet or black polythene weighted down with bricks. The idea is to exclude light so that the weed eventually gives up, which could take 18 months to two years. Make sure portions of weed are not creeping up around the smothered area. You can put the barrier straight on top of the weeds, but some determined gardeners physically dig out as much weed as they can and then smother the re-growth. Others apply one dose of a glyphosate-based weedkiller and smother what comes through afterwards.

Killing problem weeds

Having cleared the border of desirable plants (see box, left), use a glyphosate-based weedkiller (see page 112) to eradicate persistent weeds. Horsetail (*Equisetum arvense*) is extremely difficult to kill, as its leaves deflect water and spray and its roots travel deep into the soil. Crushing and stamping on the foliage prior to spraying helps the take-up of the chemical. Use brushwood killers for tangles of woody weeds like brambles.

weedkillers

Like many gardeners I prefer to use a minimal amount of chemicals and will always look for an alternative. But I share the garden with my husband who, when we are taming weed-infested areas of the plot, chooses to use a glyphosate-based weedkiller on swathes of nettles or ground elder. Our compromise allows this initial use of glyphosate, but once the area is cleared, we rely on hand weeding for maintenance. Think hard about whether you really need to use chemicals in the garden, or whether there is some other way of tackling the problem.

using weedkillers

● **Read the instructions through beforehand and make notes of key points. Some will deal with safety precautions and others are to make sure the product works properly.**

● **Timing and weather are often crucial to success.**

● **Safety is paramount. Never cut corners on precautions such as gloves and other suggested protective clothing.**

● **Be organised and uncluttered when mixing chemicals. Put lids straight back onto the bottle of concentrate after use. Don't exceed the recommended rate.**

● **Never spray weedkillers in windy conditions, as the drift may kill cultivated plants and lawns.**

● **Store chemicals carefully out of reach of children and animals, preferably in a locked area.**

Many sorts of weedkillers appear on the shelves, but on close inspection they often prove to be different brands using the same active ingredients. When choosing a product, check to see when you can plant after use. Some residual weedkillers can persist in the soil for up to two years (mainly those used for clearing paths and drives), and replanting is not recommended during this period.

Glyphosate

This useful weedkiller is foliage-acting, being translocated or taken up by the green parts of the plant and moving down to the roots. It does not persist in the soil and biodegrades, so planting can take place as soon as the weeds have died off. It is not selective, and therefore should be kept away from plants you wish to keep. You can spray while the weeds are in growth during summer, but autumn applications are surprisingly successful, as the chemical is drawn down into the roots. We have successfully treated a bed riddled with ground elder by clearing it of all but the major shrubs, and then spraying twice during the course of the growing season, waiting for re-growth and spraying again. We were then able to dig the bed and replant. There were a few sprigs of re-growth during the second summer, but they were weak and we could easily weed them out by hand.

special situations

Brushwood, stumps and suckers

Woody perennial weeds such as brambles and saplings often require more than one approach to control them. First dig or hack as much of the stump as possible out of the soil, clearing small areas at a time and returning regularly to deal with re-growth. Then use a combination of smothering (see page 111)

Brambles colonise gardens by arching out of hedges and rooting at their tips.

and digging techniques to keep the areas free of weeds while you continue. There are weedkillers specially formulated for brushwood, including glyphosate and a chemical called ammonium sulphamate. The latter is foliage and soil acting, meaning that it acts through the foliage and also vertically through the soil. It biodegrades first to sulphate of ammonia, which on releasing nitrogen, turns into plant food. Because it is soil-acting, be careful with surrounding plants and don't replant for eight to twelve weeks.

Paths, patios and drives

Try to plan these hard surfaces so that weeds cannot grow and take hold in the first place (see pages 55–61). Gravel, shingle or stone chippings are hard to keep free of weeds because dirt settles among the stones, allowing weed seeds to germinate. You can run a hoe through fine gravel to stop the weeds, especially grasses, from colonising, or weed small areas by hand. However, large expanses can be challenging. If you want to use a weedkiller, glyphosate-based types work well on drives. Sodium chlorate is good for treating both annual and perennial weeds, providing you apply it before too much growth takes place, but it persists in the soil and treated areas can not be planted for six months. Some products contain cocktails of chemicals that combine a translocated weedkiller to reach down into the roots of weeds with a residual weedkiller to prevent growth and sometimes a pre-emergent type to prevent the germination of annual weed seeds. All of this will be explained on the label.

Lawns

Personally, I'll settle for a more or less flat green surface for my lawn and actually welcome clover, daisies and selfheal. But for those who demand a perfect sward, or whose lawn has other problems (bad drainage or poor soil), causing weeds to thrive at the expense of the turf, there are selective weedkillers which from one treatment will control the likes of white clover, black medick, trefoil, daisies and dandelions from mid-spring to early autumn. Most say that children and pets can be allowed back on the lawn almost immediately, but do check the label. I would not allow my guinea pigs to eat the grass. Check the instructions for advice on what to do

with treated grass clippings, as the first cut may have to be kept away from plants and the compost heap. There may also be a minimum recommended composting time for subsequent mowings to make sure there is no chemical left when the compost is added to garden plants. Many a mystery death in the border could be attributed to using polluted clippings as a mulch.

Japanese knotweed – even more of a nightmare than couch grass and ground elder.

dealing with Japanese knotweed

This is one of our worst and most thuggish garden weeds and has become a big problem in the countryside – so much so that there are laws dictating how it should be disposed of. Knotweed (*Fallopia japonica* syn. *Polygonum cuspidatum*) has been the subject of many trials and investigations, yielding knowledge to help the gardener. One of its mysteries is that it appears to be capable of going into periods of dormancy for as long as 20 years, so we can never really talk about eradication, only control. Never cut or chop it, as pieces weighing as little as 0.2g, about the size of your thumbnail, are capable of regenerating themselves. Attempts to destroy a vigorous clump by digging it out or by cutting and smothering it are doomed to failure, because underground stems can travel horizontally for up to 7m (23ft) and will pop up again in other parts of the garden where they will be even bigger pests. Shoots are adept at finding holes in buildings and have even been known to invade houses.

To control knotweed without using weedkiller, you will need to debilitate the clump over a long period by cutting its canes off without disturbing the crown. Dispose of the canes in your garden by laying the fresh stems out on polythene to dry. Once thoroughly dry, they can safely be burned or composted. Never compost pulled stems, as they will contain a portion of crown at the base.

The weedkiller solution is to apply a glyphosate-based product in late summer and autumn. Because knotweed dies back to survive winter as an underground rhizome, it draws plant foods from the dying leaves and canes into the heart of the plant. A translocated herbicide travels down with the plant food where it can cause most havoc to the plant.

Treating a clump of large-leaved stems reaching 2.5m (8ft) in this way is not practical on a domestic scale. Instead, I would suggest clearing the dead debris away in spring, allowing the stems to grow back and spraying again when they reach about 1m (3ft). They will re-grow, but hopefully this new growth will be weaker and ready to spray in late summer. Expect the battle to continue for three to five years.

keeping weeds at bay

Having successfully cleared an area of weeds, the next challenge is to keep them out. The obvious solution is to cover the soil in one way or another, so that there is no room for weeds to grow. The best way of doing this is to fill beds and borders with cultivated plants. While they are growing, there will be bare patches, but these can be covered by mulches. In the kitchen garden, use green manures to cover and protect as well as nourish soil (see page 133).

Ground cover

Some cultivated plants are particularly good at knitting together above and below the soil to form a thick, weed-suppressing cover. A border planted with shrubs and trees, with the spaces in between filled with ground-covering plants, will be virtually maintenance free after the first year. Ground cover works best in swathes and carpets of similar plants, so use three, five, seven or more young plants of one type.

Mulching

Covering the soil with a mulch spread at least 8cm (3in) thick will help keep the soil between plants weed free. Some mulches feed the soil and all will help with moisture retention. For keeping weeds down, shingle and coarse bark mulches are probably the best, though these are the least good for feeding soil. You still have to pull weeds out, but they are weakened by having to grow through the mulch.

The ultimate mulch is a special membrane laid over the soil. Water and air can penetrate this, but weeds cannot. You fit it like a carpet to your prepared soil, cut crosses in the surface through which to plant and cover the surface with a thick mulch to conceal the fabric used. Polythene (usually black)

tips on controlling perennial weeds

● Keen gardeners in search of a new property should vet a prospective garden carefully, checking for aspect, soil and traces of invasive perennial weeds such as Japanese knotweed, horsetail and bindweed. A serious infestation could affect your enjoyment of the new garden. If you have to search in winter, ask the owners and take a look around to see what is beyond the garden fence.

● If you need to control knotweed but are daunted by the prospect of spraying, hire a qualified gardener and check they have an NPTC (National Proficiency Tests Council Certificate of Competence) for the use of pesticides.

Anne's top ground-cover plants

Japanese rush (*Acorus gramineus* 'Variegatus') (sun)

Lady's mantle (*Alchemilla mollis*) (sun/shade)

Elephant's ears (*Bergenia* 'Morgenröte') (sun/shade)

Winter-flowering heathers, such as *Erica* x *darleyensis* 'White Perfection' (sun)

Beach asters, such as *Erigeron glaucus* 'Elstead Pink' (sun)

Sweet woodruff (*Galium odoratum*) (shade)

Hardy cranesbills, such as *Geranium macrorrhizum* , *G.* x *cantabrigiense* 'Biokovo', *G. nodosum* and *G. endressii* (sun/shade)

Nepeta faasenii (sun)

Golden marjoram (*Origanum vulgare* 'Aureum') (sun)

Cotton lavender (*Santolina chamaecyparissus*) (sun)

Ice plant (*Sedum spectabile*) (sun)

Lambs lugs (*Stachys byzantina*) (sun)

Stachys macrantha 'Superba' (sun/shade)

Common thyme (*Thymus vulgaris*) (sun)

Tulbaghia violacea (sun)

Viburnum davidii (sun/shade)

A mixture of heathers (*Erica* spp.) makes a handsome ground-covering carpet. Some need an acid soil, but the winter-flowering heathers tolerate lime.

tips on ground-covering plants

● When choosing ground-cover plants, look for large perennials to divide straight away into two or three. Failing this, save money by planting one, mulch around it to keep the soil covered, wait a couple of years for it to bulk up and then split the plant into several divisions to make a wider group. Set them approximately 30cm (12in) apart.

● Some ground-cover plants can be clipped into attractive hummocks. Cotton lavender is best cut in spring and common thyme in summer after flowering.

can be used as a short-term covering, say in the vegetable plot, but there is no exchange of air or moisture to the soil beneath. These are good tools for those trying to reduce their garden work to a minimum, but personally I hate to be cut off from my soil. I would rather struggle with weeds, rejoice in the free seedlings of cultivated plants and have unrestricted access to my beds and borders.

Oxalis is another of those plants that can look lovely in the right place but become a tiresome weed in the wrong one.

identifying common weeds

Bob: As Anne has said, the classic, and true, definition of a weed is a plant in the wrong place. Every plant has its use and place, but in our gardens we want only our chosen ones to prosper – not those that just appear on their own. A weed may be any plant at all. So a lovely ground-cover plant such as oxalis, so suited to shady woodlands, becomes a weed when it gets among our vegetables, herbaceous borders or greenhouses. Some grasses might be fine in the lawn, but not in the flowerbed next to them. Flowering plants become weeds if they self-seed everywhere or run and spread wildly, or outgrow or out-compete the more choice plants around them. In many ways even a big tree or climber, or a *Leylandii* or privet hedge (especially if it belongs to a neighbour!) is a potential weed problem.

Of course, not all weeds are a problem. If, for example, you want to encourage wildlife in your garden, then you may find that many weeds are beneficial in some way. However, they should still be controlled in most parts of the garden, since they can harbour diseases and pests. Any weed carrying a pest or disease may potentially spread it to our garden plants, especially if it is closely related to them. They also compete too well with our chosen plants for air, light, water and nutrients. In order to control weeds, it really helps to know and recognise the different common types, where they occur and how they behave, so that you can deal with them most effectively.

What grows where naturally

Nature soon fills any bit of empty ground. Weeds, probably blown in by seed, will eventually grow in a pile of builder's rubble and within a few years it will be covered. First it might be stinging nettles (*Urtica dioica*), then brambles (*Rubus* spp.) and finally weedy tree saplings, such as sycamore or elder. Your lawn can go the same way. If you stop mowing, it will become a scrub and then a wood. And every plant on the way will be self-sown. Old and neglected gardens are therefore not full of just cultivated plants, but all sorts of weeds too. The type of soil and the degree of shade and moisture will

Ground elder leaves emerge from early spring. Eradicate completely at least once a week!

some ways, seedlings do not need to be identified (except by their habit of springing from seed and their being vulnerable), but it is easier to get rid of them if you can recognise the different types from an early stage. A good idea is to put some garden soil in a tray on the windowsill and watch the seedlings come up. Remove any duplicates, leaving one of each sort to grow on until you can identify what it is. This soon gets your eye in and will simplify weeding out the commonest offenders earlier on.

Established weeds are a different matter. They are much more difficult to control because their reserves allow them to survive many weeding attempts and to grow through mulches. The worst are the spreaders, which root and run everywhere, such as mints, stinging nettles and bindweeds. It is essential that you recognise these early on so you can deal with them promptly. Tap-rooted weeds, such as docks and thistles, also

determine which seeds will germinate. If the soil is poor and acid, it will have one set of weeds or wild flowers; if it is wet, rich or chalky, then others will flourish. So a good sign of a rich, moist soil in a prospective garden is a really lush, thick stand of stinging nettles! Newly turned bare soil will grow a flush of poppies (*Papaver rhoeas*) and nightshade (*Solanum nigrum*), if its seeds have long been buried. Soil that was once a horse meadow will produce docks (*Rumex* spp.). Rich topsoil, freshly uncovered, as in a vegetable bed, will probably become covered with chickweed (*Stellaria media*) and *Cerastium* spp., groundsel (*Senecio vulgaris*) and goosefoot (*Chenopodium* spp.).

Seedlings or established plants?

The biggest factor in deciding how to deal with weeds is whether they are small seedlings or established plants. The latter are far harder to control and survive more brutal attacks than seedlings, which succumb to almost any weeding regime. To put it another way, those common weeds of bare, well-cultivated soil may be legion but are all relatively easy to deal with and pose no problem for the diligent gardener. In

Dock is a common and familiar weed of all sorts of waste spaces, often found growing near nettles.

'Free' plants such as these slender speedwell (*Veronica filiformis*) often crop up in unkempt patches.

recover from light weeding and need several attempts to clear them. These are often a problem in lawns.

Common lawn weeds

Most lawn weeds are easy to spot – they are not grass. Others might be grass, but not the right grass! Common and unwanted lawn weed grasses are the tussock-forming rough grasses, running, spreading knotgrasses and the annual seeding grasses. The first and second sorts are usually found in neglected lawns and annual seeding grasses in well-maintained but heavily cut and worn lawns, where they appear in the worn patches. Mosses are only usually a problem if a lawn has poor drainage or shade, or the turf is not healthy enough to out-compete it. They are easy to spot as they look like shreds of wool.

In very wet and acid soils, rushes (*Luzula campestris*), with their round, grass-like stems, move in. Clovers (*Trifolium* spp.), with their distinctive three-lobed leaves and pompom flowers loved by bumble bees, are common lawn weeds. They can be spotted easily when the grass browns because patches of clover stay green. Similar are the trefoils and

yarrow (*Achillea millefolium*), with its silvery leaves. Then there are the tap-rooted and rosette-forming weeds, such as docks, dandelions (*Taraxacum officinale*), plantains (*Plantago* spp.) and thistles (*Cirsium* or *Sonchus* spp.). Regular cutting often fails to remove them from closely cropped lawns.

Lawns on acid soils with fine-bladed grasses often get speedwell (*Veronica filiformis*) infestations, which, although their little flowers are pretty, are hard to treat. Wetter acid soils may be choked with buttercups (*Ranunculus* spp.) and if a lawn is too closely cut it will tend to have a lot of daisies (*Bellis perennis*).

Common 'woody' weeds

A garden that is neglected often accumulates 'woody' weeds that go long unnoticed. Sycamores are very common, elders likewise. Oaks, ashes, hollies, chestnuts, yews and cotoneasters appear as if by magic, and even non-descript apple trees can spring up from nowhere. Brambles are a real nuisance, especially in gardens near woodland, as the birds drop the seeds. In acid, wet regions, *Rhododendron ponticum* is a very serious problem. Even attractive climbers such as Russian vines, Virginia creepers and rambler roses, such as *Rosa* 'Kiftsgate', climbing hydrangeas, jasmines, honeysuckles, montana clematis and especially ivies, can become a real pest if given half a chance.

Common herbaceous weeds

The hardest to get rid of are the spreaders, such as *Equisetum* spp., known as mare- or horsetail, with its distinctive prehistoric form which can infest large areas. If it's in your garden, then it's probably in all your neighbours' too, and you all need to work together if you are to eradicate it. Be careful to ensure that climbers such as hedge bindweed (*Calystegea sepium*) and field bindweed (*Convolvulus arvensis*) never become established. The white-trumpeted hedge bindweed is a wide-ranging thug.

Japanese knotweed (see pages 113–14) is another horror, at its worst on wet ground where it forms thickets. The rosebay willowherb (*Chaemaenerion angustifolium*) is similar, but on a slightly smaller scale. Ground elder (*Aegopodium podagraria*), creeping thistle (*Cirsium arvense*), dead-nettle (*Lamium* spp.) and stinging nettles can become all too common in damp, rich soils, although they will succumb eventually to good weeding regimes. Lesser celandine (*Ranunculus ficaria*) and winter heliotrope (*Petasites fragrans*) may seem pretty, even useful at first, but they soon prove to be the weeds they are.

Many vigorous herbaceous garden plants are nearly as bad if not controlled, as they will soon outgrow their position. These include lemon balm (*Melissa officinalis*), any of the mints (*Mentha* spp.), comfrey (*Symphytum* spp.), lamiums, ajugas and alstroemerias, which, despite their prettiness, are wide-ranging spreaders. In the vegetable garden, watch out for Jerusalem artichokes and horseradish (*Cochlearia armoracia*), which, once in, are hard to eradicate.

Cleavers or goosegrass will self-seed rapidly if you let it.

Common seed weeds

Weeds that spread mostly by seed, including many of the above, pose a different problem. Flushes of seedling weeds appear wherever there is a patch of bare soil with some moisture and at least some light (but bear in mind that any place that grows no weeds at all will grow nothing else either!). Since most seeds need to be in the topmost soil to germinate, a thick mulch will usually stop any weed seedlings from emerging (see pages 114–16). Then it doesn't matter much what they are, even if they would eventually become perennials.

Certainly the most common weeds to spread by seed are grasses, especially *Poa* species and couch grass (*Elymus repens*), and floating seeds, such as dandelions, groundsels and thistles. Canadian fleabane (*Conyza canadensis*) can be really troublesome – like a groundsel on steroids. Shepherd's purse (*Capsella bursa pastoris*) and hairy bittercress (*Cardamine hirsute*), which, although small, is a vicious seeder, are also quite common. And, of course, who could forget the poppy? Among the bigger plants are goosegrass or cleavers (*Galium aparine*), with its twining sticky stems and seeds. Even many of our cultivated plants are notorious seeders, unless dead-headed, such as golden and ordinary feverfew, honesty, chives, Himalayan balsam (*Impatiens glandulifera*), bluebells, forget-me-nots, foxgloves, pot marigolds, lady's mantle, goldenrod, Shasta daisies and sisyrinchiums.

Uncommon weeds that you might want to know about

It is worth getting to know your regular weeds, so that you can spot any unusual ones. However, in some areas, with many enthusiastic gardeners about, you might come across a whole store of interesting 'weeds' that can make good garden plants. Beware brambles and strawberries, the 'wild' versions of which are always inferior to garden varieties, although raspberry seedlings are worth growing on, as are blackcurrants and redcurrants. Forget cultivating trees that spring up from seed – they take too long to get established and yield poor results. Rose seedlings will also probably be wild and grow into nasty specimens. Holly, yew, laurel, honeysuckle and cotoneaster are good finds, but also look out for those choice oddities – I've discovered several nice daphnes in this way.

Chapter 4
soil

Anne: Soil is taken for granted, yet the dark, crumbly substance most of us find in our gardens is fascinating. Imagine bedrock, then a layer above that where the rock has weathered into smaller portions, or perhaps been deposited by water or glacier. The surface layer closest to the air has been weathered further, so the mineral particles are much smaller. Plants probe this upper layer with their roots and when they die, various organisms consume their remains, creating organic matter or humus. This wonderful mixture of inorganic and organic particles making up the loose surface layer of our planet is soil.

Gardeners will hear and read about topsoil and subsoil. If you dig a hole and look at the vertical wall you've made, there are usually two distinct layers. The lower layer, or subsoil, is usually of finer texture, lighter in colour and more compacted. The upper layer, or topsoil, contains much more organic matter and is the part of the soil we work regularly. When garden soil is described as 'good', this usually means it has a thick layer of fertile, workable topsoil. The average topsoil is made up of half solids and half gaps or pores between the solid particles. When in a good state for plant growth, pore spaces will be roughly half filled with air and half water, while the solids will be about 90 per cent mineral in nature and 10 per cent organic or humus.

The aim of soil management is to create a deep, rich topsoil ideal for the nourishment and growth of plants. Whatever type of soil we happen to have in our gardens, we can manipulate it by adding grit or sand to improve drainage, or more organic matter and fertilizers. We often also need to guard against erosion by making sure the surface is covered and protected by plants, mulches or green manures. Then our precious topsoil cannot be washed away by rain.

Soil life

Healthy soils are teeming with life, much of it too small to be seen with the naked eye. Between them, soil organisms break down organic matter, releasing plant nutrients and mixing the soil. When a dead leaf falls to the ground, it is chewed into smaller pieces by larger organisms, such as mites, beetles, millipedes and woodlice, creating a greater surface area for the smaller fungi and bacteria to work on. In one gram of soil there are between 100,000 and several billion bacteria. Earthworms pass soil through their bodies and are effective mixers. Their casts are higher in bacteria and organic matter and plant nutrients than the surrounding soil.

To help the soil organisms help us, we can do a lot to improve their well-being. Most soil organisms work best in a well-aerated, warm soil, so paying attention to soil structure and applying mulches to conserve warmth are both good tactics. Rather than waiting for nature to take its course, gardeners can speed up their soil improvement by rotting down their garden waste and organic matter in compost heaps and using well-rotted compost, animal manure, leaf mould or other humus-rich material to improve texture.

Soil, dug over and left for the elements to break down during winter, will make a fine tilth for plants by spring.

worm facts

Known as 'nature's gardeners', earthworms are fascinating creatures.

● In laboratory conditions, the common earthworm (*Lumbricus terrestris*) will live for seven years, though in the wild they probably die sooner.

● The numbers of earthworms per square metre of soil varies considerably. In Britain, one test yielded 40 from pine woodland, 79 from manured arable land and an amazing 848 from a grassy orchard.

● Earthworms have an oxygen circulatory system driven by five pairs of pseudo-hearts. They are hermaphrodites and mate by exchanging sperm with each other.

analysing your soil

Anne: The soils found in established gardens are usually good because they've been cultivated over a long period. I have a fairly large plot and up by the house, where the land is more or less level and previous owners have done their best to keep flower beds and raise a few crops, the ground is workable and easy to dig. By contrast, soil in the further reaches of the garden is an unimproved clay with flints. This is sticky, solid and difficult to dig. The gardens of brand new houses, where soil has been disturbed, often end up with subsoil at the surface and either a thin layer of topsoil or none at all. Hard work and patience will be needed before the soil becomes workable and pleasant.

Depending on the geology of your area, you could end up with a garden on well-drained but poor sand, or rich but sticky clay. Some soils are acidic and others chalky or alkaline, and this will affect the way they behave and the plants that can be grown. If you don't know much about your soil, take a good look at it before choosing plants. Life for a gardener is much easier if you garden in harmony with your soil and climate rather than fighting against it. Decide what your soil has to offer, choose the plants to suit it and you'll avoid a lot of unnecessary struggle. Knowing more about your soil will also help decide how best to make improvements.

soil maps

● Buy a soil map of your area. These fascinating, beautiful maps detail exactly which soils there are and their perimeters. Display your map on the wall and everyone will be able to consult it.

Soil structure

Soil structure is a fascinating subject and the chemistry of the way soil particles behave, how they stick together and generally relate to one another, and to water and nutrients, is complex. Clay and humus are central to the dynamic nature of soil, because it is over their surface areas that chemical reactions and nutrient exchanges occur. Ions (electrically charged atoms or groups of atoms) are attracted to their surfaces and nutrients are held safely, to be released slowly for plants. Bridges are built between particles too, helping the soil maintain a granular structure.

a simple way to test your soil

● You can learn a lot just by looking hard at the consistency of your soil. A basic test is to take a handful of damp soil, squeeze it together and attempt to throw it up and down gently like a ball. Sandy soil won't ball together much at all and falls apart at the first attempt, feeling gritty to the touch. A good, balanced loam (what we all want) will form a ball and will break apart after the second or third throw. A sticky, solid clay forms a solid ball you could throw up and down forever.

Sandy soils

The large particles making up sandy soils refuse to bond together into a good crumb structure, and this means they lose water quickly and don't hold on to nutrients well. But gardening on a light, sandy soil is not all bad. These soils warm up quickly in spring and you can tread, fork and dig them on virtually any day of the year. Improvements include adding lots of organic matter, but you'll find this disappears quickly. There are plenty of plants more than happy to grow on well-drained soils, including many of Mediterranean origin. Herbs such as lavender, thyme and rosemary will be much happier on sand than a sticky clay. Plants of dubious hardiness will come through hard winters much better with drier roots and survive on sands when they would have rotted away on damp clays.

> ## tips for gardening on sandy soil
>
> ● A good way of conserving water in sandy areas is to mulch beds with a layer of shingly stones. Start by digging and enriching your flower bed with plenty of humus. Choose a good range of drought-tolerant plants and plant them slightly proud of the soil. Water thoroughly and mulch with an 8–10cm (3–4in) layer of shingly stones (not too fine). The stones will help to keep out the weeds and protect the soil from evaporation.

Loam soils

Midway between sand and clay, loam is our ideal soil as it combines the workability of sands with the moisture-holding and nutritious value of clay. We try to make our sandy soils more loamy by adding well-rotted matter and we attempt to make our clay soils more loamy by adding sharp sand or grit to introduce larger particles with more air spaces for improved drainage.

Clay soils

Individual clay particles are so small they are visible only under a microscope and clay soil is made up of more than 25 per cent of them. Mixed with water, they can be sticky and cement-like. Where there are less than 8 per cent clay particles, yet the soil is still heavy, there could be silt mixed with the clay. Silt compacts easily but is less sticky. Tiny particles mean tiny pores and a clay or silt soil is less well aerated and dries much more slowly than a sandy soil. Although sticky clay soils can drive you mad when they bake hard in summer and are too wet to work during winter, the very nature of those tiny particles means they can hold onto water and nutrients, and are great for plant growth. A wide range of plants, including roses, relish improved, fertile clay soils and if you switch, as I have, from an impoverished sand to silty clay, you will certainly see a difference in growth rates.

> ## tips for gardening on clay
>
> ● If you need to access heavy clay soil, or are standing on a lawn edge, use boards to spread the weight.
>
> ● Improve drainage for crops like garlic by planting into ridges made above soil level. This is especially useful for winter crops and early plantings, because the roots are raised out of the coldest, soggiest part of the soil.
>
> ● To dry a cold, wet, heavy soil early in the year prior to planting and sowing, cover with polythene. Alkathene piping fixed over beds in hoops will raise the polythene off the soil to keep rain off but will allow air in to dry and warm the soil.
>
> ● Drying soil by covering is easier when the beds are only 1.2m (4ft) or so wide and slightly raised above the surrounding level.

Acidity and alkalinity

Gardeners worry a lot about the acidity and alkalinity of their soil, measured using a pH scale of hydrogen-ion activity, running from 0–14. A neutral soil is 7, while anything lower is acid and higher is alkaline. Most plants like to grow in soils with a pH of 6.5–7 but some are more tolerant of chalky or alkaline soils, while others, including rhododendrons, pieris, fothergilla and blueberries are lime-haters and thrive best when the pH is around 5.5.

When soils start to veer away from neutral in either direction, certain minerals needed for plant growth are likely to be in short supply. Soils over chalk or limestone are alkaline and contain plenty of calcium, though they may lack manganese, boron or phosphorus. Acid soils often contain too much manganese and aluminium. Neutral soils offer the best environment for bacteria, meaning decomposition is speeded up and more nutrients are available for plants.

Altering the pH of an alkaline soil

On the whole, it is best to work with the environment of your garden and plant according to the type and pH of the soil. For some reason, chalk (alkaline) soils are often perceived as something of a problem, yet there are plenty of plants more than happy to grow on alkaline soils, which, if they are well-drained, open up plenty of opportunities because you can

testing for acidity or alkalinity (pH)

● You can learn a lot about pH by taking a look at neighbouring gardens. If there are plenty of glossy, green, healthy-looking rhododendrons, then you can safely assume your soil is acid. But if there is a suspicious absence of any acid-loving plants and everyone's hydrangea flowers are turning from pink to blue, then it could be alkaline. Lumps of chalk turning up in soil are another giveaway sign.

● The only way to be sure about whether your soil is acid or alkaline is to carry out a pH test. Small kits are available from garden centres and shops and, for very little outlay, you can test several samples from different parts of the garden and potentially save a fortune by not wasting money on the wrong plants. I strongly advise more than one test per plot, because not only do soils vary naturally from place to place, but previous owners may have worked to change the pH in certain areas.

Like the rest of its family, this *Rhododendron* Cilipinense Group prefers lime-free conditions, so growing it in a pot is an option if you have alkaline soil.

choose plants that don't thrive with wet roots. Thin soil over chalk is ideal for a wildflower meadow. Perversely, though, owners of alkaline plots often gaze wistfully at acid-loving plants, especially camellias and rhododendrons. The best way of satisfying this urge is to grow these plants in containers of ericaceous (acid) compost. Camellias and rhododendrons are of woodland origin, so stand the containers where they will not be cooked by harsh sunlight. You can create a small, raised bed of acid soil by buying in a neutral or acid topsoil and enriching and further acidifying it by the addition of well-rotted garden compost, leaf mould or pine needle mould. It is possible to lower pH and raise acidity slightly by adding sulphur to soil, but I have never resorted to this.

Liming an acid soil

Those with acid soils are not always content, especially when they are vegetable growers. Most crops grow best in neutral soils and brassicas (the cabbage family) prefer a slightly alkaline soil.

Once you have carried out a test to determine pH, an acid soil can be gradually neutralised by adding crushed limestone, but not quicklime, as this is too caustic and could scorch plants. Liming can be done at any time, except when manure is being added. This is because lime reacts with nitrogen in the manure, releasing ammonia, which could damage plants. Most gardeners build additions of lime into their crop rotation programme, spreading it during winter digging, so it can be well incorporated and will have time to take effect before brassica crops are sown or planted. You should be scientific about lime application. To a pH of 5.5, add 130g lime per square metre on sandy soil, 190g on loam and 260g on clay. To a pH of 6, add 118g on sand, 155g on loam and 215g on clay. In reality, most gardeners use guesswork and simply sprinkle a dressing of lime on the soil they are digging, or fork lime into the surface. Regular pH checks to assess the outcome are important. Wood ash will also increase pH.

When adding lime, as with any fertiliser, keep an old pair of scales for weighing, use gloves and apply on a still day, using goggles to protect your eyes.

plants for acid soils

These plants need an acid soil to thrive. Where a soil is not quite acid enough, plants may show signs of iron deficiency (see page 277), including yellowing leaves. Regular feeding using a special formulation for ericaceous plants will help, but nothing compensates for the acid soil they need.

Camellia
Enkianthus
Fothergilla
Heaths and heathers (*Erica* and *Calluna*)
Kalmia
Leucothoe
Magnolia
Pieris
Rhododendron
Skimmia

Kalmia latifolia 'Myrtifolia'

plants for chalky soils

These plants are all tolerant of chalky (alkaline) soils. Although the flamboyant, large-flowered rhododendrons, camellias and most magnolias don't thrive here, there are plenty of alternatives. For early flowers on shady walls, train Japanese quince (**Chaenomeles**) as a fan. For big, spectacular blooms, choose summer-flowering peonies (**Paeonia**), **Eucryphia, Carpenteria californica** and the Californian tree poppy (**Romneya coulteri**).

Apples and crab apples (*Malus*)
Ash (*Fraxinus excelsior*)
Birch (*Betula*)
Box (*Buxus*)
Butterfly bush (*Buddleja*)
Californian lilacs (*Ceanothus*)
Californian tree poppy (*Romneya coulteri*)
Carpenteria californica
Clerodendrum trichotomum

Daisy bush (*Olearia* x *haastii*)
Deutzia
Elaeagnus
Escallonia
Eucryphia
False castor oil plant (*Fatsia japonica*)
Firethorn (*Pyracantha*)
Fuchsia
Honeysuckles (*Lonicera*)
Hydrangea
Japanese quince (*Chaenomeles*)
Lilac (*Syringa*)
Lime (*Tilia*)
Magnolia x *loebneri* and cultivars
Myrtle (*Myrtus communis*)
Osmanthus
Peony (*Paeonia*)
Pittosporum
Pocket handkerchief tree (*Davidia involucrata*)
Rock roses (*Cistus*)
Rosemary (*Rosmarinus*)
Rowan (*Sorbus*)
Stachyurus
Viburnum

Paeonia suffruticosa 'Alice Palmer'

soil improvements

The soil you inherit with your garden is only the starting point, as improvements to structure and fertility will be made as soon as you start adding well-rotted organic matter by digging and mulching. The difference will be obvious even after a couple of years of good cultivation. To make our kitchen garden, we had to dig out an old tarmac driveway and, inevitably, the soil structure across the whole plot was poor. But by digging in plenty of compost and manure we grew good crops right from year one. Sowing fine seed direct into the soil was impossible in some areas, because there were too many sticky lumps. But we worked around this by planting seed potatoes in the worst parts, and by raising crops like lettuce, runner beans and sweetcorn under glass and planting out from pots.

improving your soil

The old adage 'feed the soil, not the plant' is a good one, because adding organic matter to soil improves it in so many different ways. Light soils are given much-needed fibrous bulk and body. They will hold more water and hold on to nutrients better, while heavy soils are broken up and become less sticky. In nature, soil is nourished by the rotted remains of plants, from their stems and leaves to their roots. This encourages animal life, which provides a secondary source of organic matter. In the garden, we tend to remove dead plant tissue, so if we insist on tidying away all this natural goodness, it makes sense to pile it on a compost heap or into compost bins, create crumbly, well-rotted compost and return it to our soil in this more attractive and ready-rotted form.

As much as 75 per cent of plant matter that falls to the soil is likely to be made up of water. The rest will be composed mainly of carbon, with oxygen, hydrogen and inorganic materials also present, together with nitrogen, phosphorus, potassium, sulphur, calcium, magnesium and trace elements or 'micronutrients', all of which will be released during decomposition. Once the organic remains hit the warm soil, a veritable army of soil organisms attack them. As gardeners, we usually wait until our compost has finished, or nearly finished, decaying and has turned into dark, crumbly humus. Adding well-rotted organic matter to soil literally brings it to life.

Organic material
There are plenty of organic materials available to add to your soil and the choice of what to use will have more to do with where you live and what is available, rather than what might be best.

The right time to add organic materials is whenever you can get at the soil. On preparing a new or renovated border for planting, take advantage of the opportunity to dig in plenty of humus before filling the ground with plants again. In an ideal world, it is good to rest the soil after digging, to enable it to settle and to hoe off annual weeds brought to the surface. In practice, planting often has to start straight away. In this case, always tread fluffed up soil down first, to avoid sinkage later. As long as all organic material, especially manures, are well rotted, there should be no harm done to the plants. Where just a few new plants are being added, clear as large an area as possible, fork over to break up compaction and then fork in well-rotted matter.

For vegetables, digging and conditioning usually takes place during the preceding autumn and winter. The advantage of making 1.2-m (4-ft) wide deep beds is that an initial digging is often enough for several years. As long as you never tread on the soil, you can top dress with organic matter every year instead.

Where plants are established, add 8cm (3in) deep organic matter as a mulch spread over the soil and around the plants . But brush the mulch away from the woody bases of trees, shrubs and some herbaceous perennials, to avoid it piling up and rotting the stem.

Animal manure
Never use fresh manure, because it gives off ammonia harmful to roots. The ammonia and other soluble nitrogen

compounds are used by bacteria and stored in their bodies to be released when the bacteria die. Spreading rotted manure is also more efficient, because one ton of fresh manure will lose half its weight in the rotting process. Horse manure is the richest (especially when the animals have been bedded on straw or shredded hemp), followed by pig, cow and poultry manure. A light covering of the soil or trench with manure is all you need and I often apply manure 50:50 with well-rotted garden compost. Poultry manure is caustic to plant roots and I never add this directly to the soil. Instead, I add chicken manure to the compost heap and let it work in there as an accelerator, finally adding it in well-rotted and mixed form. Horse manure is available in most areas, but you usually have to forage for it yourself. In rural areas, arrange with a local farmer to deliver cow muck. Be fussy about the origin of manure, especially if you garden organically. Avoid manures from intensive production systems because they could contain contaminants. Most horses and ponies are wormed regularly, but chemical residues should dissipate during decomposition.

Garden compost

Conditioning your soil using garden compost produced and rotted down on-site is the most efficient way of disposing of household and garden waste and nourishing your soil at the same time. In this environmentally sound approach, no fossil fuels are burnt in the process and little energy is used other than your own. The rich, nutritious compost that results can be used to dig in or as a mulch (see page 132 for advice on how to assemble your own compost heap).

Leaf mould

Well-rotted autumn leaves provide a fabulous soil conditioner, particularly good for your woodland plants, as this is what they would grow in naturally. Instead of layering collected leaves into the compost heap or bin, stack them separately, allow them to break down to a crumbly dark mass and add to the soil the following year. You can even break leaves down by bagging them up, adding a microbial compost activator, making a few air holes in the bag and sealing it up.

Twin compost bins mean you can start piling fresh material into one, while the other is almost ready for use.

Peat

Bags of moss peat (from sphagnum-rich moorland bogs) or sedge peat (from sedge and reed-rich lowland marshes) used to be a popular soil conditioner years ago, especially when gardeners wanted to acidify their soil. Nowadays, its widespread use has been curbed by environmental concerns. Worried about the long-term effects of commercial peat extraction, many gardeners have stopped using peat products and search for alternatives. Coir or coconut fibre has been widely embraced as a peat replacement.

Spent mushroom compost

This by-product of the mushroom-growing industry used to be more widely available than it is now and was much-favoured by landscapers. A mixture of animal manure, loam and chalk, this used to provide a cheap source of bulky organic matter to dig in or spread over soil as long as lime-hating plants like rhododendrons were not present. Organic gardeners should only take compost from organic mushroom production units. One would usually order a small lorry load for the garden from local suppliers, but it is scarcer and being superseded by waste from municipal compost recycling schemes.

Municipal compost

Under initiatives to reduce landfill, local authorities are embracing their own composting schemes. Green waste is collected from households and composted on an industrial scale. The results are sold to golf courses as top dressing for greens (the finest grade), bagged and sold through garden centres as soil conditioner and sold by the lorry load to landscapers and those with larger gardens. The compost is thoroughly rotted and the temperature of the heaps is tested regularly throughout the process and is high enough to kill the roots of pernicious weeds and weed seeds.

Composted bark

Bark is widely used in horticulture, but only well-composted bark should be dug into the soil. This is potentially an expensive way of conditioning soil, but bags of bark are widely available at garden centres and are an easy means of improving small areas of ground.

Pulverised bark and shredded prunings

Both these materials are routinely spread over soil as a mulch to conserve moisture and suppress weeds, but as they are not yet decomposed, they have the potential to rob the soil of nitrogen while rotting down, because the bacteria involved will use up nitrogen. Don't dig these mulches in and, if you use them, add a fertiliser to the soil under the mulch. Heavy mulches like these discourage self-seeding and are perhaps not a good idea in cottage gardens where one would like aquilegias, forget-me-nots, foxgloves, honesty and other plants to self-sow.

Cocoa shell

Many gardeners looking for mulching materials favour this product, which is made from the outer husk of the cocoa bean. It makes a good weed-inhibiting mulch, is said to repel slugs and will acidify soil. Cocoa mulch can be harmful to dogs and some are tempted to eat it. At one stage in its decomposition, a mould grows over the mulch, but this is quite natural.

Seaweed

Seaweed contains a lot of potash and an alginate that helps bind soil particles together. Either dig straight into empty ground when wet, or add to the compost heap. I used to worry about the salt content, but some gardens have been treated with seaweed over a long period with no unwanted side effects. Dried seaweed meal is a good soil improver and calcified seaweed seems to benefit both light and heavy soils, improving structure and helping plant growth.

drainage

Although conditioning the soil with well-rotted organic matter improves its structure and helps drainage, there are extra methods to help with waterlogged soils, caused by tightly packed particles of silt and clay, or a high water table.

The red stems of *Salix alba* subsp. *vitellina* 'Britzensis' glow throughout the winter in this boggy pond-side site.

Where wet soil is a problem, analyse the symptoms and causes carefully and decide on a plan of action. Winter wetness resulting from badly cultivated, heavy clay soils can sometimes be alleviated with good cultivation and the addition of coarse sand or grit (not fine sand, which can further clog the soil). Try digging a hole. If this fills with water, then the water table is high and artificial drainage will be needed. Sometimes there is a hard layer or pan lying 30–45cm (12–18in) under the surface. Pans are often found where soils are rich in iron and aluminium and this thick, impenetrable layer stops water from draining away from the top layers of soil. Deep digging to break up the pan (a mattock or crowbar might be needed in the process) is the long-term solution.

Gardening in wet or boggy areas

A small wet area at the bottom of a garden can sometimes be an asset. Instead of trying to cure the problem, exploit the situation by choosing plants happy to grow in wet soils. Plants gradually dry soils out and will certainly bind the soil together with their roots and penetrate down into the lower layers.

Trees happy to grow on damp soils include the silvery, black-stemmed coyote willow (*Salix exigua*), height 4m (13ft) and spread 5m (16ft), and *Salix gracilistyla* 'Melanostachys', grown for its black catkins, height 3m (10ft) and spread 4m (13ft).

If you put plants that don't enjoy damp soils on a site like this they will simply drown for lack of oxygen.

Cultivars of white willow (*Salix alba*) grown for their stems include *Salix alba* subsp. *vitellina* 'Britzensis', stooled (coppiced) height and spread 1.5m (5ft). Alders tolerate damp soils and, for a colourful tree, the yellow-leaved grey alder (*Alnus incana* 'Aurea') has orange stems and catkins, with yellow leaves turning pale green in summer, height 10m (32ft) and spread 5m (16ft). A useful tall, slender tree is the swamp cypress (*Taxodium distichum* var. *imbricatum* 'Nutans'). This deciduous conifer reaches a height of 10–20m (32–65ft) but a spread of only 1.2–1.5m (4–5ft). Interesting smaller plants include arum lilies (*Zantedeschia aethiopica*), pink loosestrife (*Lythrum virgatum* 'Rose Queen') and bulbous summer snowflake (*Leucojum aestivum*).

Providing artificial drainage

Where a whole garden is badly drained, investing in a proper drainage system will carry water away and make gardening possible and enjoyable. The most common system is land drains, generally laid in a herringbone pattern to collect the water and discharge it either to a ditch or, if there is no accessible ditch, to a soakaway. Lay the main drains to run parallel with the slope of the ground, making trenches 60–90cm (2–3ft) deep and 30cm (12in) wide. In most heavy soils, a mini-digger could be used to excavate the ditches. Do this when the ground is dry and avoid criss-crossing the site to minimise soil compaction. You would generally space the side-drains coming off at angles from the main drain, 4.5m (15ft) apart on clay and 7.5m (25ft) apart on loam.

The central drain pipe (usually perforated plastic these days but they used to be clay lengths butted up to each other) should be 10cm (4in) wide and the side-drains 8cm (3in) wide. Lay the pipes on a good 5cm (2in) layer of shingle and cover with more shingle before the soil is replaced. When excavating, make every effort to separate subsoil and topsoil, so the topsoil can go back in at the top. Sometimes a French drain or rubble drain is sufficient to drain a small area. Dig a 60–90-cm (2–3-ft) trench at the same spacing as land drains, but instead of laying a pipe, simply fill with broken bricks, flints or similar rubble, top with shingle and cover with soil. On flat land, the trench and pipes must slope down into the ditch so the water can run off. Soakaways should be dug 1.8m (6ft) deep and wide. They should be lined with dry brick walls, filled with rubble and topped off.

fertilisers

As long as plants are doing well, there is an argument for leaving well alone. Overfeeding is counter-productive, because sappy plants cannot support themselves properly, are more prone to frost damage in winter and are more likely to be attacked by pests attracted to their soft, succulent growth.

However, a plant showing deficiency symptoms is in need of help. Symptoms to look out for are yellowing leaves and poor growth, indicating lack of nitrogen. Brownish-purple markings and scorched leaf edges suggest potassium deficiency, especially if they are combined with a reluctance to flower and fruit well. Yellowing between the veins is the classic symptom of magnesium deficiency (also see page 276). Some plants are particularly hungry feeders and common sense should tell us when to intervene with a feed. There is usually most benefit to be had by applying fertiliser at the start of the growing season, or during spring and early summer when most growth is being made.

Sick plants cannot usually make use of fertilisers, because they need healthy root systems to absorb them. Nurse the plant back to health before feeding, otherwise the salts will build up in the pot or soil and damage a weak root system even further.

The major nutrients (or 'macronutrients') include nitrogen (N) for leafy growth, phosphorus (P) for strong roots and potassium (K) to encourage flower and fruit production. The big three are always listed in this order on packets and bottles of fertiliser, along with a ratio to indicate the proportions of each. Other macronutrients are magnesium (Mg), calcium (Ca) and sulphur (S). Micronutrients or trace elements are important too and include iron (Fe), manganese (Mn), copper (Cu), zinc (Zn), boron (B) and molybdenum (Mo).

miracle cure

● One year, a Tibetan cherry (*Prunus serrula*) became sickly, with leaves turning yellow and falling as though autumn had come in late spring. One application of Epsom salts at 200g (7oz) in 10 litres (2 gall) of water as a foliar and root feed was enough to perk the tree up. It had been suffering from magnesium deficiency, probably caused by heavy rain on light soil.

Types of fertiliser

There is a mind-boggling array of fertilisers on the shelves of garden centres, but they fall into just a few basic categories.

Straight fertiliser

A straight fertiliser adds only one compound to the soil. Inorganic sulphate of ammonia supplies only nitrogen, superphosphate is an artificial straight fertiliser supplying only phosphorus (natural rock phosphate would be an alternative for organic gardeners). Inorganic sulphate of potash or (for organic gardeners) rock potash adds only potassium.

Compound fertiliser

These fertilisers are added to the soil at a rate recommended on the packet, usually before sowing or planting crops or bedding plants. Organic examples are fish, blood and bone meal (nitrogen, phosphates and potash), fish meals (nitrogen) and seaweed meal (nitrogen, potash and trace elements). An inorganic example would be Growmore (nitrogen, phosphates and potash), but there are many other proprietary types aimed at feeding particular types of plants.

Slow-release fertiliser

These complex fertilisers release their nutrients slowly and are usually applied in late winter or early spring to trees, shrubs and herbaceous perennials in one dose to last a whole season. Some slowly degrade in the soil, while others are encased in a membrane that degrades with moisture and warmth over time. You would also use these in containers of bedding plants to avoid having to feed them regularly with a liquid fertiliser throughout the growing season.

using green manures

1 Sow your green manure (in this case, crimson clover, see opposite) onto a bare patch of soil.

2 Once it has grown to a cuttable height, shear off the top to put on the compost heap.

3 Turn the remainder into the soil, then wait 2–3 weeks before planting or sowing your crops.

tip

Having dug in your green manure, it may be difficult to produce a tilth ready for sowing seed. Some green manures even release germination-inhibiting compounds as they decay. Either delay sowing for a month or so or, better still, use the ground for young plants or sets rather than seeds.

Liquid fertiliser

There are plenty of proprietary brands of fertiliser to dilute into water and apply to plants through a watering can or hose. These are of most benefit to plants growing in pots both indoors and out, but can also be applied to plants growing in the ground. Both inorganic and organic examples are available. Many organic gardeners make their own brews by steeping nettles, Russian comfrey or sheep dung in water and diluting this to feed their plants. Never feed a dry or saturated plant.

Foliar feed

Some liquid fertilisers can also be applied by spraying them onto leaves. Foliar feeds are particularly good for epiphytes (plants with small root systems, whose natural growing habitat is up in the branches of trees) and plants whose roots are feeble.

green manure

Many gardeners want to enrich their soil with organic matter, yet may not be able to make their own garden compost. New gardeners will not have had time, there may not be room for a compost heap or bin and bringing in bulky humus will be costly in terms of money, effort or both. The answer lies in green manures, sown onto empty soil, grown and then dug into the ground two to three weeks before the area is to be

advantages of green manures

● Covering otherwise empty soil with growth helps prevent weeds and protects the soil from erosion. Sticky, badly drained soils are loosened up by the plants' roots and nutrients are drawn up into the plants from lower layers. Green manures provide a haven for beneficial insects, such as slug-eating frogs and beetles, as well as shielding the countless invisible soil organisms from extremes of weather. Green manures of the pea family have a unique ability to fix nitrogen from the air. A group of bacteria called rhizobium move into the root hairs of leguminous plants, such as clover, and form swellings or nodules where they live. In exchange for converting nitrogen gas to plant food, they are allowed to live with the plant and tap into its sugar. Dig up a pea or bean plant and you'll notice the root nodules.

sown or planted. You carry something as light and cheap as a packet of seeds into the garden and yet can glean so much organic matter from it, on site.

Choices of green manure

The only way to learn about green manures is to have a go at growing some. Notice how fast they grow and how soon after sowing they can be dug in (usually just before they flower) and these observations will help you choose the right type for each particular situation. In general, those that stand during winter are of most use to gardeners, because we tend to fill our ground with crops during the growing season and need cover mainly during the winter. Nitrogen-fixing leguminous types are especially good if you are planning to grow leafy crops next.

Anne's recommended plants for green manures

Alfalfa (*Medicago sativa*)
This perennial, leguminous nitrogen-fixer produces deep, penetrating roots and is good for breaking up solid soil. It likes to start off on rich soil, dislikes wet soils, and is extremely drought tolerant. Sown from spring to summer, it can be dug in during autumn or left through winter or longer. Rich in major elements and calcium.

Buckwheat (*Fagopyrum esculentum*)
This fast-growing, deep-rooting annual has a long history of use as a green manure and does well on poor soils, including acid ones. Sow during the summer and let it stand for one to three months. A good source of calcium. Flowers attract beneficial hoverflies, whose larvae eat greenfly.

Crimson clover (*Trifolium incarnatum*)
A trendy green manure whose flowers are so pretty most gardeners can't bear to dig it in until after the soft buds have opened. Bees love it. Sow from spring to summer and leave for two to three months, or over-winter in milder climates if needed. Prefers a light soil.

Red clover (*Trifolium pratense*)
Sow this perennial clover from spring to late summer and let it stand from three to eighteen months. Does well on good loam.

Fenugreek (*Trigonella foenum-graecum*)
A half-hardy annual, nitrogen-fixing legume related to clover. Sow from spring to autumn, when it will make prolific growth, and allow to stand for two to three months. Prefers a well-drained soil.

Field beans (*Vicia faba*)
These hardy annual, nitrogen-fixing beans look like broad beans and are great for over-wintering from an autumn sowing. They thrive in heavy soil and should be dug in just prior to spring planting and sowing.

Hungarian grazing rye (*Secale cereale*)
Some gardeners don't like this because it looks as though they've allowed grass to grow over their plot. Yet this is a good manure for improving the structure of heavy soil and is winter hardy. Sow in late summer or early autumn and dig in during spring before it flowers. Annual ryegrass is a less bulky alternative.

Lupins (*Lupinus angustifolius*)
A nitrogen-fixing legume with deep roots great for aerating soil and bringing nutrients up from lower layers. Sow in spring to dig in during autumn. Will grow on acid soil.

Mustard (*Sinapsis alba*)
Sow this fast-growing, half-hardy annual thickly in spring or summer to last for two to three months before digging it in, at or before flowering. Likes a well-drained soil and is said to deter wireworms.

Phacelia (*Phacelia tanacetifolia*)
Another green manure that is so pretty most gardeners let it open its blue flowers, beloved of bees. Sow this hardy annual from spring to early autumn and dig in after one to three months.

Trefoil (*Medicago lupulina*)
Sow this biennial, nitrogen-fixing legume from spring to summer and let it stand through winter. Dislikes acid soil, but is usefully shade tolerant.

Winter tares (*Vicia sativa*)
Sow these nitrogen-fixing vetches from spring to early autumn for an abundance of leafy matter. Turn in during spring. These are especially good at providing nitrogen for leafy brassica (cabbage family) crops.

Bob also recommends

Miner's lettuce (*Claytonia perfoliata*) and **Corn salad** (*Valerianella*)
Two salad crops unrelated to most vegetables that can be grown overwinter, producing masses of succulent growth that can be eaten, fed to hens, easily stripped and composted or sheet mulched in situ – much better than most farm-derived choices.

Poached egg plant (*Limnanthes douglasii*)
Hardy over winter, very good at excluding other plants and easy to incorporate afterwards. If you leave some plants to flower and seed they will be beneficial to insects, too. Especially useful under soft fruit and shrubs.

Planting several kinds of lettuce together makes the bed more colourful as well as giving you more interesting salads at harvest time.

crop rotation

Anne: A lot is said about the importance of rotating your crops from one piece of ground to another, so that the same family of vegetables – whether it's the onions, cabbages or potatoes – is not grown in the same patch of soil year after year. The principle is that this prevents pests and diseases from building up and nutrient levels from becoming imbalanced, because the soil gets a rest when playing host to a crop from a different plant family. In practice, crop rotation works less well in a tiny garden, where small growing beds are right next door to one another, than on a field scale. But it is still well worth carrying out, especially if you have a neat, tidy garden, perhaps with contained, slightly raised beds. By rotating crops, not treading soil from one bed to another on your boots and keeping tools clean between use, you are going a long way to safeguarding your crops and keeping the soil healthy.

four-year rotation

Rotating your crops is a good way of forcing you to plan and organise which ones are to go where. For best results (and if you have the space), divide your plot into four separate sections and operate a four-year rotation on each. This is what might happen to one section of vegetable plot over a four-year period.

Year one: before planting the legumes (group 1), add manure and a little fertiliser to the soil. When the legumes are gone, dig in manure and add fertiliser.

Year two: Sow or plant the onion tribe (group 2). When they've finished, add well-rotted compost and fertiliser for the potatoes.

Year three: plant the potatoes and any other root crops (group 3). When they're over, manure the soil and leave it for an interval before liming and adding fertiliser.

Year four: Plant the brassicas (group 4).

If you don't have enough ground for a four-year rotation, amalgamate the onion tribe (group 2) with the potatoes (group 3) and rotate over three years.

Group 1 legumes (peas and beans)	Group 2 Onion family	Group 3 Roots and tubers	Group 4 Brassicas (cabbage family)
Broad beans	Garlic	Beetroot	Brussels sprouts
French beans	Leeks	Carrots	Cabbages
Peas	Onions	Celeriac	Calabrese
Runner beans	Spring onions	Celery	Cauliflowers
	Shallots	Parsnips	Chinese greens
		Potatoes	Kales
		Salsify	Kohlrabi
		Scorzonera	Pak choi
		Tomatoes	Purple-sprouting broccoli
			Radish
			Swedes
			Turnips

dealing with permanent crops

● Some gardeners have a separate bed or area for permanent crops, such as asparagus and globe artichokes, but I prefer to slot them in wherever I want them (I do the same with fruit bushes). Then I just work around them.

tips for other crops, such as salads, pumpkins or sweetcorn

● Squeeze quick-growing crops of lettuce and other leafy saladings wherever they will fit, quite often as a catch crop between slower-growing types, such as sweetcorn or winter brassicas. Pumpkins take up a lot of space and can either have their own area to be rotated, or slot the odd one or two in with the potato group. I tend to plant sweetcorn wherever it will fit, but many gardeners put it with the pea and bean group.

Raised beds are an effective way of keeping your various vegetable crops separate and lessening the risk of spreading disease.

composts and manures

Bob: Any pile of garden waste will eventually rot down and, in time, will almost disappear. However, if it is kept warm and wet, it will rot more quickly, especially if everything is chopped up into small bits and many different materials are mixed together. The rich, well-rotted 'earth' that results is what we call 'garden compost'. It can be used as a potting compost, but is more often used as a soil enricher.

When making your own garden compost, it is important to include a good range of different materials, confined in a bin. If you have a lot of waste and layer it up carefully, there should be enough heat inside the bin to 'cook' the compost, making it even more valuable. However, you can still make a good mix with a small amount of waste, you will just have to re-mix it and re-pack it when the container is full (see opposite).

Making or choosing a bin or container

First you need a compost bin to contain the heap. On a large scale, four pallets tied at the corners is inexpensive and effective, but you could make an equally good bin using netting supported by posts and lined with cardboard. Smaller bins made of wood or plastic are available, but the drawback here is that the smaller the bin the more quickly it fills and

Four pallets tied at the corners make a good large compost bin for a substantial garden or allotment.

the less well it 'cooks'. If this is all you have space for, insulation is very important (see opposite). Rotating composters are a good idea in theory, but they don't perform well in practice; likewise those with flaps that allow the removal of the base material from underneath.

Whatever style of container you choose, you will need a lid to keep rain out because rainwater will chill the heap and leach out nutrients. Even a partly matured compost will still need a small roof to throw the rain off. For best results, try to construct some kind of cover that still lets in air at the sides to help the heap mature and dry out.

Choosing materials for the compost heap

In theory, almost anything that has ever lived can go on the heap, from kitchen and some household wastes to plant matter from the garden. Large quantities of any material, especially grass clippings, need to be mixed with other materials such as shredded newspaper or leaves. Evergreen and coniferous leaves are generally slow composting, and are probably better used as woodland mulches. Leaves, if in any great quantity, should be composted separately in plastic bags to make leaf mould (see page 127). Sawdust should only be added in small quantities and mixed in well.

It is best to leave out thorny wastes and burn or dump diseased or infected prunings, unless you are a very skilled composter. Likewise, avoid putting tough weed roots onto the heap unless they have been killed by desiccation or by immersing them under water for a month first. Bones, fats and meats should be given to friends with pets. Pet manures should probably be disposed of according to local regulations (though I compost the lot, litter and all). Cotton, wool, newspaper and cardboard, preferably shredded first, will all compost if wetted well. Feathers, hair and toenail clippings all add value!

Adding the materials

Try to assemble as wide a range of compostable materials as possible, because the more you put in, the more you get out in terms of quality. You can either add your material to the heap in thin layers as it becomes available, or store it temporarily in bin bags before mixing it all together.

Whatever you do, it is best to regard the accumulation and initial filling of the bin as just the first stage. Once the bin is full, you can either leave the ingredients to rot down slowly and dig it out the following year for use, or dig it out, re-mix it and re-pack it a week or two after the initial filling to speed up 'cooking' and create a really good compost.

Whether you layer up ingredients as you go, or re-mix and re-pack, make sure you do not pack the materials down too heavily or you will exclude air. For best results, alternate dry (straw, hay or shredded paper) with wet (fresh grass clippings) material and sprinkle soil or compost sievings on everything as it goes in (and activators, if using, see below). Re-mixing generally works best with two bins, so you can dig from one bin to the other – alternatively, shovel everything out onto a plastic sheet and then re-pack. When re-filling the bin, put the less well composted outer layer back in first, followed by the well composted core around the edges and top. Add more wet or dry material if needed. Top off with a thick layer of compost from a mature heap, as this will help keep in the heat and trap any beneficial vapours coming off.

Other ingredients

Water is almost always necessary, unless you have included a lot of fresh green wastes. Add plenty of water initially, and more again when the heap is re-mixed. It is better to use water from a ditch or pond than from the tap. If your heap has white fungus, known as firefang fungus, running though it (usually found on re-mixing) it makes for a poorer compost, unless treated with the addition of even more water with urine in it when re-mixing.

Activators always help, although if you have a good mix with plenty of fresh material in it they are not really necessary. Commercial activators are often little more than expensive fertilisers. The best activators are animal or poultry manure, urine, or blood, fish and bonemeal. Grass clippings and stinging nettles work well, making heaps 'cook' if mixed in

Not only garden waste but kitchen waste, cotton and wool clothes and shredded paper can all be composted.

thoroughly. Including compost from a previous good heap is an excellent way of achieving the right activating organisms.

Soil is beneficial to introduce organisms that help with composting. It also provides minerals and particles, which help to nourish your compost and keep it open and aerated. Most soils also contain lime, which 'sweetens' the compost by combining with vapours coming off. Lime or chalk absorbs the fertility that would otherwise be lost as ammonia when the heap ferments. Unless you want your compost for acid-loving plants, it is probably a good idea to add extra lime in addition to that in the soil. Wood ash works in the same way as lime or chalk and also supplies the compost with valuable potash (potassium).

Insulation is always beneficial, especially with small bins, but not underneath or it will stop the worms from getting in and out. Insulate the sides with bubble plastic or cardboard and, most importantly, insulate the top as well. Bubble plastic or bags filled with screwed-up balls of newspaper make good 'duvets' for the top. Any cover or insulation must be easy to remove to enable you to add extra layers to the heap.

Assessing when compost is ready

You can remove and sieve the compost at almost any time. A well-made heap that has been built and then re-mixed and re-packed after a fortnight, could be ready in another fortnight. However, it usually takes longer and six months to a year is often better as it allows the heap to mature and dry out – a drier heap is much easier to process and handle! Wet, claggy masses can be moved and used, but they are not easy or pleasant to work with. Usually it is better to mix them into the heap or use them as a topping for a re-mixed one. Compost that is nearly dry can be pushed through a coarse garden sieve before use – sieved compost is a delight to handle. Any dross that remains in the sieve should be sorted for plastic or stones and any partly composted material put aside for the next heap.

Worm composters

If you have little garden or kitchen waste and can collect no extras, a compost heap may be accumulated too slowly for it to work by itself. So let worms help you. You can either buy a proper wormery or make your own. Take a plastic dustbin, make a drainage hole with a spigot in the side close to the bottom and drill plenty of small air holes around the sides so the worms can breathe. Inside, lay three bricks and on these a strainer made of plastic or galvanised metal mesh. Put a generous layer of wet turves of grass and some old rich soil on top and then add your first few worms. Add your (chopped up) kitchen or garden waste little by little, sprinkling with soil and water after each addition. Once a week, give a sprinkling of lime or crushed baked eggshell.

When the bin is full, you can either start another one or re-use the same one, emptying the contents out first and putting the topmost layer in the base as the starter for the new one. Underneath the oldest material, you should find a layer of almost pure worm droppings. These can be mixed with potting compost to greatly enrich it. Drain off any liquid on a weekly basis to dilute as a feed for plants in pots. Worms can either be bought specially, or you can find similar ones available as fishing bait, or you can collect your own. Lay a wet piece of cardboard on the ground and pick up any of the small reddish worms that collect underneath after a day or so. A word of caution: always cover your wormery with a tight-fitting lid to prevent the worms getting out!

Snail composters

These work in the same way as worm composters, only snails are used instead. You can use a similar bin, but you will also need an old clay pot or jam jar as well for the snails to live in. This is placed inside the bin on top of a thin layer of turves and soil. It is important here to add the wastes bit by bit, so as not to bury the snails. They like more air than worms, so don't pack the materials down too tightly, and make sure you include a saucer of water for them to drink. Sprinkle the snailery daily with water and draw off the oozings to dilute as plant food. Snail droppings will fall to the bottom, where they soak in a sump to be drawn off as liquid feed. The solids can be cleaned out occasionally and the waste added to potting compost as an enricher. Snails are good for composting paper and many of the woodier materials that worms have trouble with, so you might like to run a snailery and wormery alongside each other.

Snail composter – make the blighters work for you!

digging

Bob: Digging is the breaking up of the ground to turn the soil into a better growing medium. This often involves removing debris, weeds and roots and incorporating compost or muck at the same time. It is done initially to prepare a bed or border for planting or sowing, and is often performed annually in the vegetable plot. The first case is obviously nearly always necessary for optimum results, but the benefit and sense of an annual dig is now contentious with 'no-diggers', who maintain that it's superfluous or even counter-productive to dig every year regardless.

Many, especially those with a heavy soil, believe a regular autumn dig helps to improve the texture. Those with a light soil, for whom ironically digging is much easier, apparently benefit from it far less, if at all. In either case, the use of fixed beds with permanent paths, or avoiding treading on the soil when it's wet to prevent compaction, reduces the need to dig more than once a year. In trials, a dig every five to seven years, mostly to break up mole runs and ant nests, seemed to be of optimum value. It seems that an annual dig will be a rather wasted effort, better employed turning the compost heap, collecting compost or hoeing weeds. This is even more the case with a vegetable bed where rotation is practised, since this ensures the soil is broken and mixed up anyway when harvesting the root and potato crops every fourth year or so.

Whether or not you want to dig annually is up to you and your choice of plants or soil, but bear in mind that it will become easier over succeeding years. I personally think that an initial dig of any patch is always crucial to success, if only to remove pernicious weeds and debris. Before starting, check there are no electric cables, drainage, oil or water pipes you may accidentally hit. Remove any top growth, saplings and surface junk and debris. Digging is usually easier if you first go over rough grass and growth with a tough rotary mower before trying to cut into an old turf sward.

There are several ways of dealing with the roughest topmost layer. You can simply invert each spit of soil as you dig, or skim and drop the skin in before covering it with a clean spit of soil. Or it may be skimmed off and stacked under an opaque plastic sheet to rot down into a useful loam for adding to potting composts. If it is full of pernicious, especially creeping, weeds, then this last option is the sensible one as it is foolish to bury them.

Those not wishing to be organic may want to kill off the weeds by applying a herbicide before digging (see page 112). These must be used according to the instructions and are most effective when properly applied by a trained operative. Some are available for home use, but ask your local supplier for advice according to your situation and intended planting. Bear in mind that herbicides must be applied at least several days, if not weeks, before you intend to dig and that some require the right weather after spraying to be thoroughly effective. Organic gardeners may wish to weaken or kill the weeds first with several treatments of flame gunning (the equipment is available from hire centres) or by covering the ground for a period of several months under an opaque plastic sheet.

If no prior treatment is undertaken, it is essential that weeds with strong root systems, such as brambles, thistles, docks and stinging nettles, are removed during digging or they will re-grow vigorously – even if buried a spit down. If the area is large enough to accommodate a mechanical rotary cultivator, an initial dig incorporating the weeds can be followed by regular digs until the weeds expire. However, even with power assistance this is still an arduous task unless the weeds are easy to kill. Less vigorous weeds such as fine lawn grasses, mosses, daisies, chickweeds and groundsels, green manures (see page 133) and most small weed seedlings may safely be dug under.

preparing a plot

1 Mark out the plot perimeter and divide the whole area into manageable chunks. Do not plan to do too much in one go, as this is a serious undertaking. Anyone who is unfit should consult a doctor first. Wear comfortable clothes, gloves to prevent blisters and tough protective boots. Warm up first with other light work so your muscles are warm and, as we say in Norfolk: 'Strip before you sweat and cover before you cool.'

2 Clear weeds from a patch of ground about 60–90cm (2–3ft) from the trench you are going to dig. This breaks both the digging and the clearing up into manageable chunks, making the task less boring and easier on the back. as you dig, and move your arms and bend your knees, not your back.

3 Whatever tool you choose to dig with, take small 'spits' or bites rather than huge ones.

4 Work methodically across the plot in strips, slicing first the edge and then the butt of each spit before lifting it up, inverting it and smashing it down again to shatter it into small clods. Clods can be broken up further with a slap from the back of the spade or a whack with the fork. Remove any roots or debris as you go along and throw into two buckets or barrows. Roots can then be burnt, or rotted under water and later composted. Debris such as stones, bricks, bottles etc. put to one side for using as hard core, post-hole filling or concrete mixing. Reserve plastic, wire and old batteries (surprisingly prolific in some gardens) to be safely disposed of.

5 To make the digging process easier, it helps if the first strip of soil spits are dug out onto a plastic sheet or into a wheelbarrow and put to one side.

6 For best results, break up the bottom of each trough before re-filling. You can use the spoil from the first strip to fill in the last strip (see step 9). Either wheel it in place or if the plot is to be worked in two halves, first one way then the other, the spoil will be close by the finish.

7 You may wish to incorporate muck or compost while digging. Fairly wet or claggy muck and compost may be forked into the bottom of each trough as it is broken up. Alternatively, you can spread it over the surface some weeks before digging to break it down further and then mix it in with the topmost layer when it is dug over. Other enhancements such as sand to improve drainage, burnt clay to improve fertility and water-holding, ground rock dusts, such as lime or rock phosphate, as well as wood ash or fertiliser may all be mixed in now. They are usually of most benefit when worked into the upper soil layer, rather than being buried deeply or inserted as a discreet layer. Dried sorts are most uniformly mixed in by spreading them on top of the ground before digging starts.

8 Skim off the surface from the next strip of spits and deposit in the first trough, then dig and turn as before.

9 When you reach the edge of the patch to be dug, wheel the topsoil saved from the first trench to fill the last.

10 The final result should ideally be reasonably flat, uniformly bare soil with few enormous clods or roots sticking up. It is important to give the soil time to consolidate again before introducing plants, as few like to encounter slumping soil or hollow air pockets. In the meantime, do not neglect weed control – weeds are likely to appear in multitudes (see pages 108–12).

when to dig

● Choose a sunny day with a light drying wind if possible. It is almost impossible to dig wet soil well, and bone dry soil can be too hard. Soak bone dry soil for a few days before you dig. The best, and easiest, time to dig is usually in autumn, when the soil has time to consolidate and form a good tilth ready for spring sowing or planting; lighter soils may just about be left until late winter or early spring. In most cases, it is not recommended to plant up immediately after digging. Worse still, never lay or sow a lawn on newly dug soil that has not been given sufficient time to consolidate or settle.

fork or spade?

● Some people prefer to dig with a fork, others with a spade. The latter, if well sharpened, is obviously more use for slicing off turf and cutting through roots. A fork kills fewer worms and helps to break up the soil more easily than a spade, making it easier to extract weed roots whole. In very stony soil a fork is almost obligatory. A small lady's 'border fork' is more manageable than a large wrought-iron 'navvy' sort! The same with a spade. Both are useful, but must be hard and sharp and have a long, tough handle.

how to dig – and how not to

1 If you aren't used to digging, you will probably find that your arms and legs are tired after a session in the garden, but this will soon ease.

However, with the wrong technique, shown here, you can do long-term damage to your back. Avoid this by choosing a spade to suit your height (the handle should reach waist height when you are standing up straight); keeping your back straight as you dig; and moving your arms and bending your knees, not your back.

2 Push the blade straight down into the ground.

If you hold it at an angle you will cultivate less depth of soil, so it will take more effort to reach the depth you want.

As with all cutting tools, keep the blade sharp so that the spade penetrates the soil easily.

Double-digging

Normal digging, even where the topmost layer is removed first and the bottom of each trough is broken up, only disturbs the upper layer of soil, the 'topsoil'. This is quite sufficient in most areas as it makes sufficient tilth for most of our plants to be sown or planted and for their initial roots to run in. However if the soil is dug even more deeply, using double or 'bastard' trenching, our plants' roots can penetrate down more easily, aiding their growth even more. This technique is often practised where the deeper or 'subsoil' is heavy, waterlogged or compacted.

How to double-dig

Start as before, but this time dig out three lots of soil. First, take the topsoil, and the next layer of subsoil (keeping these apart) from the first strip, and the topsoil from the second strip (which can be piled with the first strip's topsoil). Then break up the bottom of the deeper (two spits deep) trench you dug in the first strip. Place the subsoil from the second strip in the base of the first, deep trench, breaking it up with the back of the spade, and cover with the topsoil from the third strip. You can then break up the bottom of the second strip and put the subsoil from the third in the base, covering with the topsoil from the fourth strip. Carry on until you reach the last strip, which is filled with the retained subsoil and topsoil from the first trench.

Our garden at Sparsholt started life on such awful stony clay that we had to import better soil to dig in with it, but then it gave good results.

tips for double-digging

● Try to ensure that the subsoil is not mixed with the topsoil or brought to the surface, as it is usually poorer in both texture and fertility (it is also often a different colour). The topsoil is lighter in texture and is needed near the surface to keep all the air-breathing, fertility creating organisms alive. If your soil is especially waterlogged or compacted, the depth of the trenches can be increased further by digging yet another, deeper spit in the same manner. I'm not convinced of the benefit of this 'triple digging' on most soils, but don't let me stop you trying it – the Romans considered a depth of nearly 2m (6ft) sufficient, but they didn't do the digging themselves!

Chapter 5
lawns

Anne: Laying or sowing a new lawn will transform your garden and beautifully offset borders and paths, but before rushing out to buy seed or turf, think first about the look you want to achieve and whether you'll have time to maintain it. There are many different types of lawn grasses and the mix you opt for in seed or turf will determine the type of lawn you end up with.

Fine lawns

The beauty of a fine lawn, striped alternately deep and rich green by close cutting with a cylinder mower, is hard to deny. To achieve this effect, you need to set the lawn with specific fine lawn grasses such as bents and fescues, slow-growing types that demand a lot of pampering. Broad-leaved grasses and hard-wearing types, including perennial ryegrass, would spoil the effect.

You can try for the 'bowling green' look, but somebody in the family is going to have to make this lawn their priority throughout the year. This will start with immaculate preparation for the seed or turf, and what will have to amount to an obsession with weed and moss control, because these fine grasses don't take kindly to competition. Even with lots of effort, fine lawns will be doubly hard to maintain on poor, sandy soils with low nutrient content.

Good to look at, fine lawns are not designed for regular use by children, dogs or bicycles. Those old garden signs saying 'keep off the grass' meant what they said.

Left: The 'perfect' striped lawn.
Opposite: Slightly less perfect, but still a thing of great beauty.

For an area under trees and treehouse, choose a shade-tolerant mix of grasses.

Durable lawns

Most of us will opt for lawns that we can use as well as admire. Mixtures of grasses, including broad-leaved species and perennial ryegrass, stand up remarkably well to wear and tear. These are interesting lawns too, and the meadow grasses, crested dog's tail and Timothy often used in the mixes are pretty when they come up to flower, should a meadow area be left uncut. These are lawns you can walk on, lie on and let children and dogs play on. Our large durable lawn has to withstand badminton games, bicycles, scratching chickens and even the hooves of a Shetland pony.

Most lawn grasses need an open, light situation in which to thrive. If you are intending to start a lawn in a lightly shaded position, there are shade-tolerant lawn mixes to try. But in deep shade, where lawn grasses will always struggle, I would opt for a hard surface or shingle mulch.

Choose the right lawn for your household, and caring for it will be a pleasure rather than a horrible shock.

starting from scratch

Anne: The biggest question facing the gardener contemplating a new lawn is whether to seed or turf. In our last garden we had three small lawns, two of which were laid as turf and one sown. You really couldn't tell the difference between them, so the outcome can be the same and as good either way.

Sowing grass seed to make a lawn is cheaper than buying in turf. There is also something rather magical about carrying that box or packet of seed into your garden and creating an entire lawn out of it. By contrast, the volume of turf bought in for a similar area is huge. There is also a lot more choice when you go to buy lawn grass seed. You know exactly which grass species are in the box, and in what proportions. The disadvantage of seed is the anxious wait for it to germinate and the fact that you're at the mercy of the weather. Too much rain can wash the seed around, whereas too little sometimes forces you to water. On some soils, watering can make a 'cap' or crust over the soil, which the grass shoots then have difficulty penetrating. While seedling grasses are thickening up, weeds can encroach into the embryo lawn and these need to be removed so they don't compete with the grass at this crucial stage.

The main advantage of laying turf is the startlingly instant effect it creates. At the beginning of the day there is bare, brown earth and by the end of it, you have a green lawn. All the gaps are filled and there is no room for weeds to come creeping in. Buying turf, though, can often be a bit of a lottery. It's a good idea to see what you'll be getting, but more often than not, you order the turf and hope for the best. Most of the time it will be good, but I remember receiving one bad lot and having to insist that it was replaced. You should expect a good, uniform distribution of grasses with no or very few weeds. The grasses should be short and the colour rich and not yellowing. Expect the turf to be of reasonably even thickness and the grasses well rooted into good soil. The turves should hold together well and be easy to handle without tearing and falling apart.

Before ordering the turf, you need to be organised and have the site ready. Unlike a box of grass seed, turf will not store and should be laid as soon as it arrives. Each hour that it is stacked will see it deteriorate.

Preparing the site

Most lawn disasters can be traced back to bad initial preparation. Turf might look like a carpet, but the grasses are living plants and deserve the same care and attention as the flowering plants that you add to your beds and borders. Grass seed needs the same tilth of soil and moisture levels to germinate as seed yielding vegetables or flowers.

The first job is to clear the site thoroughly and methodically of any rubbish, including rubble, bricks and tree roots. Use a glyphosate-based weedkiller to eradicate perennial weeds. Alternatively, smother them or dig them out (see pages 110–11). Where trees are growing right next to the lawn, think carefully about the shade they will cast, as grass grows best in a bright, open position. You might want to take some trees out entirely or saw off some of the lower branches to raise the canopy.

If yours is a difficult site, now is the time to think about the gradient of the lawn and also consider drainage. Most sites are only going to require the minimum of levelling out and this can be carried out by digging first and then raking, but where there are deep holes and an uneven surface, you might need to shovel soil about and perhaps even buy in some extra topsoil. Where soils are badly waterlogged, proper drains or soakaways may be needed (see page 130).

Fortunately, the soil in most gardens will simply need digging (see below). For autumn action, dig over in early autumn, as soon as the soil is workable after summer's droughts, or during the autumn and winter to prepare for spring. Single dig the soil, so that the topsoil layer is loosened and turned over to a spade's depth (spit). Do this by removing a trench first, so that you can get at the subsoil underneath. Don't bring this up, but having turned over the top spit, fork into the bottom of the trench to loosen any hard pans of soil or solid clay, so that water can find its way through more easily.

digging and levelling

1 While digging, take the opportunity to improve the soil under the potential new lawn by adding well-rotted garden compost to light, sandy soil, or grit to open up thick clay. Remove all weeds and large flints or stones painstakingly as you go along.

Digging early allows time for the soil to settle naturally but, in reality, few gardeners work this far ahead. Some won't have time to dig and might use a mechanical cultivator instead. If so, allow for repeated treading and raking to make sure the surface is firm and flat before turfing or sowing. This is a fun job, but can only take place when the soil is dry enough – another good reason not to leave preparation until the last minute. Tread over the whole site, making small overlapping steps and digging your heels in.

2 Having done this, rake over the top. Repeat again and again until the surface is firm (though not rock hard) and the soil won't sink. This is a good time to grade the site and make small improvements to levels, using the eye as a guide. You might want the lawn to flow smoothly in a slight slope, following the lie of the land. What you don't want are bumps and hollows. I have always successfully used my eyes as a guide, but should you want to be sure of an absolutely flat lawn, use wooden pegs and a spirit level in much the same way as for laying concrete.

sowing a new lawn

Timing is critical, because grass seed needs the right amount of warmth and moisture to grow. For this reason, early autumn is generally considered the best time, followed by mid-spring. The disadvantage of spring is colder soil, or the risk of drought just when the grass starts to grow. Rake some general-purpose fertiliser into the soil a week or two before sowing. Buy in your preferred grass seed mix, allowing 30–40g per square metre (1–1½oz per square yard), then wait for a day when the soil has dried out enough on top for the rake to make a fine tilth, but with lower layers moist enough for the seeds to take up water and grow.

tip for sowing grass seed

● Shake or mix the grass seed before sowing, in case the different varieties have settled in the box. This ensures an even spread of types over the whole area.

sowing seed

1 The textbook method for sowing seed is to divide a large area into sections, weigh out the correct amount of seed for each and divide the seed for each section into two or even four batches. This is then sown from different directions (that is, by walking lengthways and crossways over the site, or up and down) to ensure an even distribution.

In practice, what I do is mark out a square metre on the ground, weigh the correct quantity of seed for that area and sow evenly into the space. I then take a careful note of the density, and replicate this over the entire area, sowing methodically and shaking the seed one way and then the other. Keep looking back at the original square occasionally to check density. For best results, sow 8–10cm (3–4in) over desired edges and cut or shape later (see page 157).

2 Having sown, rake lightly using a spring-tine rake to partially cover the seed. Where there are lots of birds or cats in the area, cover the area with netting to protect the seed from being eaten – and also from dust bathing, rolling and scratching.

Aftercare

Time seems to slow down just after sowing a new lawn. The gardener looks anxiously at the bare area day after day, until, after about two weeks, a haze of green appears almost overnight. During the wait, watch the weather carefully, because if there is no rain and lots of sun, the surface might dry out too much for the seeds to take up enough water and for the young seedlings to survive. Should this be the case, fix up a sprinkler and spray finely so as not to disturb the seeds. Deluges of rain are really unfortunate, as the seed will be

Water your grass seed only as a last resort, but the fine spray from a sprinkler will help it germinate during a dry period.

tip for re-seeding patches

● If, for one reason or another, germination is patchy, scratch the bare areas of soil lightly and incorporate a tiny quantity of multi-purpose compost before oversowing with more seed.

washed in all directions, leading to patchy germination. If this happens, wait for the surface to dry out, rake again (even if this damages any seedlings that have emerged) and re-sow.

Allow the seedling grasses to reach about 8cm (3in) high and then, if possible, roll them lightly. Few of us have light garden rollers in our sheds these days, so either hire one or use the roller on a cylinder mower, rocking it back to lift the blades clear. This will settle the soil and push any stones back in. In a couple of days, after the grass blades have sprung back up, mow to tip off the top third of growth (you might need to set the blades higher than usual). The best machine for the job is a sidewheel cylinder or rotary mower with no front rollers. If you have to use a mower with front rollers, lift or remove them beforehand. One cut will probably be enough for autumn-sown grass, but in spring continue to cut when needed, gradually reducing the height to normal.

Avoid using the new lawn as much as possible during its first season, but feed, weed and water as normal. When the grasses have knitted together, you can carry out the pleasurable task of cutting the edges. Use a garden line to mark out straight lines, then lay a wooden board along the edge and cut with a half moon iron using this as a guide. Mark curves with the blade of the iron first, before cutting. Fork up unwanted turf, fork up the border soil underneath and then flick the soil away from the edges to separate the lawn from the border.

creating a new lawn with turf

The best time to lay turf is in autumn (after this, the soil is likely to be too cold or too waterlogged by winter rain). If you miss the autumn slot, you can do it in spring, but be prepared to water regularly and thoroughly throughout spring and summer. The most difficult aspect of laying turf lies in predicting the weather and ordering turf to arrive when the prepared site is not too wet.

laying turf

The first job is to mark out the shape of the lawn, allowing for the fact that as turves are always laid in straight lines, you need to cover the areas where curves might eventually be cut.

1 Lay the first line of turves...

2 ...then put down the second so that the ends are staggered, rather like laying bricks. This means the ends won't make long lines which could split apart during a drought. Theoretically, turves should be cut to the same thickness, but sometimes you will need to excavate some soil to make the turf lay flat. Butt the edges up together and then press down, so they are as close as possible. I pat the turves down with my hand to push them into contact with the soil. In theory, one shouldn't bash turves with the back of a spade, but I have done this lightly with no ill effects. While working, lay the turves in front of you while standing on the soil.

3 The final job is to apply a sandy top dressing over the cracks and brush this in to really seal the edges together. To do this, stand on boards – never on the grass itself – and brush the dressing in with a besom (birch broom) or the back of a rake. Finally, cut any straights or curves into the turf. Some gardeners mark their curves with a hosepipe, but I prefer to draw mine on with the blade of a half moon, getting it just right before finally cutting. Mark straight edges with a line, place a long wooden board against the line and cut along the edge (see main text).

Aftercare

Avoid treading on the lawn until after the roots have started to penetrate into the soil and the turves have begun to knit together. The first time you tread on the lawn without boards is when it has begun to grow and needs its first mowing. Water, feed and control weeds as normal.

seedling turf

● Most gardeners lay conventional turves, but you might come across lightweight rolls of turf raised in specialist nurseries. These are much thinner than usual and need careful handling. Lay only when conditions are excellent, because the grasses will be more sensitive to cold and drying out. Some are supplied on a foam base, which disintegrates over time.

mending a bare patch

Bare patches are easy to seed over, but there's some work to do first. This method works for the middle of the lawn as well as for an informal edge.

1 Fork the bare patch thoroughly, using a border fork to work not only into the earth but also into the sparse grass around it. Continue until a good tilth has been made.

3 Sow over the surface with grass seed and cover lightly with top dressing or sifted soil, or rake very gently.

2 Add some top dressing to the area and tread and rake to make a firm surface. Top dressing is a mixture of loam and sand, sometimes with some organic matter. An example is 3 parts sandy loam, 6 parts garden sand and 1 part of fine, well-rotted garden compost. You can mix your own, but it is often easier to buy it in.

4 Peg a layer of polythene over small areas, but remove as soon as germination begins.

To mend a bare patch with turf, you must cut around the patch using straight lines to square the area off. Fork up the soil and add or remove soil as necessary to ensure that new turves sit flush with the surrounding grass. Fill in any cracks with a sandy top dressing or sifted soil. Water during droughts.

mending a lawn edge

Formal edges enhance your lawn and it's a nuisance when these get damaged. Mending them is easy.

1 Cut an oblong of grass, taking in the broken edge...

2 turn the cut turf...

3 ...so the broken part now faces inwards...

4 Add good soil or top dressing to fill the gap and then sow. Alternatively, cut the hole into an even-sided shape and plug it with turf cut from elsewhere.

caring for an established lawn

Anne: The extent of lawn care depends on the condition of underlying soil, the mix of grasses in the lawn and the character of the gardener. Keeping a fine lawn in tip-top condition, especially on a poor, well-drained soil, will be a time-consuming business requiring 100 per cent dedication. On the other hand, if you are a relaxed person with a hard-wearing lawn on good soil, you can get by with regular mowing, edging and the odd feed.

secrets for a healthy and beautiful lawn

Watch your lawn as carefully as the plants in your borders and assess its type. Think, too, about the type of soil underneath. Examine your own character, and decide whether you want a perfect sward or whether weeds will be tolerated. But even if you go for the latter approach, there is still work to do.

● Regular mowing is essential to maintain the quality and density of your grasses. It will keep weeds at bay and encourage tillering (spreading, sideways growth). Don't let grass grow too long, then shave it off, because this will seriously weaken the lawn. Aim to remove the tips on a weekly basis when in full growth during spring and summer.

● Trim edges regularly, or your lawn will look tatty and start to grow into borders.

● For turf on poor soil, or small, much-trampled lawns, autumn raking, aerating and top dressing will work wonders to relieve compaction and improve drainage and general condition.

● Feeding in spring and summer encourages dense, good-quality grass with good colour. A lawn will tell you it needs feeding by its appearance. There's no point wasting time and fertiliser on one that's already thick, green and lush. However, sparse, yellowing grass on poor soil will obviously be in need of a boost.

Mowing

There are many different mowers on the market, but they break down into only two basic types.

This beautiful, healthy green lawn meandering through informal borders is what we'd all like in our gardens.

Cylinder mowers have a series of moving blades fixed around a cylinder, passing over a fixed bottom blade to create a scissor-like cut. Efficiency is determined by the number of blades on the cylinder and how fast they go round. These mowers give the cleanest cuts and are usually chosen to maintain top-quality lawns. They are not so good on long, coarse or wiry grasses. Years ago, most people with small lawns used to have a hand cylinder mower and I still think these are great. You don't have to worry about electric cables or fuel, they are quiet and won't annoy the neighbours and you can keep fit while pulling and pushing the machine over your small lawn. For larger lawns, choose petrol-driven types.

Rotary mowers are the popular choice these days and are more versatile. A blade or blades rotate horizontally, supported either by wheels or, in the case of hover mowers, by riding on a cushion of air. Rotary mowers are better able to deal with longer, rougher grass areas, and are a godsend when you've let the lawn grow longer than it should. Hover mowers are especially good for wet grass and slopes, but are not designed for straight-line mowing. For really large grass areas, ride-on mowers are expensive, but will save hours of time.

For small areas, most gardeners choose electrical mowers. Always be aware of the cable and use a Residual Current Device, so the current is switched off automatically if there is a fault. For large areas, petrol-driven models will be more expensive to maintain, but give far greater freedom.

Grass collection

Leaving clippings on the lawn is messy, as they are often trodden into the house. Clumps of clippings are not good for the lawn, as they cut off light and air. On the other hand, stopping to empty a collection box is fiddly and time consuming. I would opt for a mower with a collection box. However, you might like to consider a mulch mower, which chops the clippings into tiny pieces and blasts them firmly down into the lawn, where they rot down to feed the grass and conserve moisture. A good compromise is to leave the first and last clippings of the season on the lawn because the grasses can benefit from the moisture, nutrients and shade conferred to the roots without the danger of clogging. Continuously leaving the clippings in situ brings with it the problems of thatch, that thick layer of dead grass and weeds that can clog a lawn, causing bad drainage, diseases and moss growth.

If you want stripes, you need a roller. These are usually associated with high-quality cylinder machines, but you can get them on rotaries as well.

When to mow
Mowing usually starts in early spring and carries through to mid-autumn, but be guided by the weather and the rate of growth rather than your calendar. Begin in spring by cutting grass that has grown to 4cm (1½in) back to 3cm (1¼in). As growth accelerates, reduce the height to 2.5cm (1in) for a durable lawn, and down to 2cm (¾in) or even 1cm (½in) for a fine lawn. When the grass is growing fast, mowing must take place at least once a week. Should mild wintry weather cause excessive growth, don't hesitate to cut the lawn to 3cm (1¼in) as long as the ground is not wet.

How to mow
Start by mowing the perimeter of the lawn, going round it twice. Mow around obstacles such as flower beds as well. Then mow in straight lines, up and down, overlapping slightly, to cut the lawn methodically. Make sure the lines are straight if you are using a mower with rollers to create stripes. It is fun and good for the lawn to change the direction of the cut from time to time – try cutting in the opposite direction, or diagonally. When cutting larger, informal areas with a ride-on mower, work inwards in ever-decreasing circles, mowing around trees and other obstacles as they arise.

Mower maintenance
Mowers need regular cleaning to prevent metal corrosion. Always disconnect the power before cleaning or attending to an electric mower and always remove the spark plug from the engines of petrol-driven mowers before cleaning and maintenance. Keep a small kit handy, containing rags, an oil can and a wire brush for cleaning down after use. Unless you are good with machinery, send the mower for a service once a year. Some companies give discounts if you book your machine in early, rather than leaving it until just before you need it in spring. There is always a spring rush and if you leave the service until the last minute, you might have an agonising wait while the lawn grows daily out of control.

Spring lawn care
A light raking with a spring tine will remove any leaves, twigs, stones and other debris left behind after winter. It will also remove some thatch and break up the soil so that roots can penetrate it. Where a spring application of weedkiller has left a lot of dead plant matter behind, it might be necessary to scarify in late spring (see opposite). In extreme cases, aerating and top dressing can also be carried out.

Feeding
Feeding starts in spring, but only after the grass has started growing. Never use a feed to push the grass into growth, because the roots will not be active enough to make use of the fertiliser. The normal approach is to apply a good, compound lawn fertiliser containing nitrogen to promote green, leafy growth, but also phosphates for healthy roots and potassium for general all-round good health.

Some gardeners who want to get rid of moss and weeds might be tempted to use a product that feeds the grass as well as killing weeds. These do work well, but weedkillers are usually at their most effective when applied after feeding. This is because the weeds have been stimulated to grow faster by the fertiliser, making the effects of the weedkiller more dramatic.

For many lawns, an annual feed in spring will be sufficient, but on poorer soils, a summer feed will help the grass stay healthy. There is no point feeding a lawn that has stopped growing because of prolonged drought – wait until the drought breaks and the grasses show signs of growing. Where lawns have taken a hammering during summer, take advantage of a long, mild, moist autumn to apply an autumn feed and put the lawn back on track before winter sets in. Always use a formula intended for autumn use, which is lower in nitrogen and usually supplies this element in slow-release form.

autumn lawn care

When the summer droughts are over and the lawn is moist, yet not waterlogged and freshened by autumn rain, now's the time to make up for the rigours of summer use.

1 Pampering your lawn starts with scarification. Using a spring-tine rake, begin by raking the lawn heavily to pull out dead weeds, moss and grasses clogging up the base of the turf. The picture shows speedwell, thatch, moss and dandelions, all raked out of a small patch of grass. On a large lawn, use a mechanical scarifier. The lawn will look pretty awful afterwards, but rake up the rubbish and take it away.

2 The next job is to open up the pores of the lawn to allow water to drain through and air to circulate among the roots. On small lawns suffering from minor compaction, this involves simply spiking the surface with a garden fork to a depth of at least 8cm (3in). If heavy soil seems really hard, use a hollow-tine fork.

3 Regular holes made deeply into the lawn help winter rain to drain away, especially when the surface layers are compacted by use.

4 Brushing a fine dressing of loam mixed with lime-free sand and organic matter into the surface of the lawn does it so much good. Suddenly, grasses can root out into a mixture more resembling potting compost than the compacted soil they are used to. This encourages valuable tillering (sideways growth) and makes the lawn thicker and tougher. Where lawns have been aerated, especially by hollow-tining, top dressing is the obvious next step, filling the holes with this loose, sandy, well-drained mixture. When calculating quantities of top dressing needed, aim to apply 1.3–1.8kg per square metre (3–4lb per square yard) and spread in small heaps over the surface.

5 Next, brush the dressing in using a besom (birch broom) or the back of a rake. Small hollows will be filled in during the process, but grasses must not be completely buried.

applying lawn feeds

● Having bought your product, keep an ear to the weather forecast. The ideal scenario is dry weather, but when the soil is moist and showers are likely after the event.

● Apply the feed a couple of days after mowing, so you can see where you've been and the fertiliser trail is not hidden under long grass.

● Do not apply during rain.

● If the expected rain does not fall after a couple of days, water the fertiliser in using a sprinkler.

How to feed

On small lawns, spreading fertiliser by hand is a feasible method. Read the packet thoroughly, measure out the required amount, divide into two lots and apply half over the lawn travelling in one direction, then the other half travelling in the other.

Wheeled distributors are a great help on large lawns. First make sure the equipment is clean and dry, so fertiliser doesn't clog up the holes. Use the distributor in a similar way to a lawn mower. Deliver one or two strips to either end of the lawn, or around the edge of a curved shape. Then make straight lines up and down, taking care not to overlap applications. You can see most fertilisers clearly – some even have a dye added.

Soluble fertilisers are quick-acting and at least you don't have to worry about whether it rains afterwards to wash the fertiliser in. The soil should still be moist, rather than dry, when they are applied, but do not apply to waterlogged soils. Tiny lawns can be treated using a watering can with a rose (sprinkler) on the end. For larger lawns, applicators are fixed to the end of a hosepipe; these dilute the concentrated fertiliser into the water as it flows past.

Watering

Lawn grasses are incredibly resilient and my best advice is not to water. When drought strikes and grass begins to look parched, the urge to fetch out the sprinkler is strong. But if you start watering, you are going to make your lawn more dependent, rather than less, and you'll be locked into a cycle of having to water until there's a hosepipe ban.

Keeping small lawns green by watering is a manageable prospect. Some gardeners need a good lawn to offset displays of bedding plants when they are entering competitions and they will opt to water their lawns.

If you decide to water, do so in the evening to cut down on evaporation and scorch. Position the sprinkler where it waters lawn and not path and make sure you apply enough water – otherwise you might as well not bother. A simple way of checking is to set a few jam jars under the water spray and aim to collect a minimum of 1cm (½in) of water up to 2.5cm (1in) – enough to replace a week's worth of loss during a drought.

If you don't water, you have to wait until the weather breaks and autumn rains replenish the lawn and encourage re-growth. The autumn lawn care programme of scarifying, aerating and top dressing will help restore its health (see page 155).

Weed control

The issue of weed control is an emotive one, as some gardeners are offended by even one weed in their perfect sward and others positively welcome them. I easily settle for a flat, more or less green surface where both moss and weeds are tolerated and sometimes even celebrated, unless they cause bare patches. If you like lawn weeds, they become wildflowers and I really like a rich green sward studded with daisies, clover, selfheal and speedwell, whose growth mingles well with the grasses. I do take exception to dandelions and plantains because their flat rosettes of large leaves stand out, even after mowing. Clover is actually good for a lawn, as it fixes nitrogen into the soil for grasses to use.

What is important is that your lawn looks healthy, and what you can get away with in terms of studied neglect depends largely on soil type. When we gardened on poor, sandy soil, where water and nutrients disappeared quickly, we were less tolerant of weeds. To prevent our rather sparse grasses from being out-performed, we were forced to control weeds and

taking care of edges

Worn edges let a lawn down and unkempt edges grow into borders, causing a big weed problem. Trimming edges and knocking the soil back away from them should be done on a regular basis, ideally after every mowing and at worst after every other mowing.

1 Trim edges using specially designed edging shears.

2 Always pick up the clippings, as they may contain portions of perennial weeds capable of rooting into the gully between the turf and the border.

3 Using the back of a hoe, flick the soil away from the edge back on to the border. Maintaining a gully between the two stops weeds and grass encroaching into the border. Weeding the rest of the border then becomes a joy, as your hard work will be beautifully set off by the crisp edge.

feed the lawn regularly. Failure to do this would have meant thin grass and bare patches.

By contrast, our current garden in Devon is blessed with a much heavier, richer alluvial (river valley) type soil and grasses thrive, creating a rich sward. We live in an area renowned for its dairy farming because the soil and pastureland is so rich. Here, we can neglect our lawn, confident that grasses will compete well with weeds. There is so much goodness in the

soil, we are almost scared to feed the lawn and would only step in to do so if it looked pale or patchy.

Size is also an issue when considering weed control. You can get away with a sprinkling of weeds (or wildflowers) in a large rural lawn, but a small urban equivalent might be deemed scruffy. Large lawns suffer less from compaction too, whereas smaller, well-worn areas are more likely to break up and turn patchy where weeds are allowed in.

Moss is usually an indicator of poor drainage and acid soil. I rather like springy, mossy lawns, but only when they stay more or less green and the grass still has enough vigour to grow well alongside the mosses. To get rid of moss and make sure it doesn't come back, improve drainage (see pages 128–31) and check the pH of the lawn (see page 123). Adding lime will raise the pH (that is, make it less acidic and more alkaline) and help to drive out the moss. Lawn sand gets rid of moss (see page 159). Other moss killers are available and if used in conjunction with weedkillers do a double job.

I find a sprinkling of daisies attractive and many lawns remain green and healthy despite them. Whether and what weeds you tolerate in lawns is all down to the condition of the sward and personal choice.

recutting edges

In addition to the routine maintenance described above, you may need to re-cut edges every year or so to improve straights and curves.

1 For straight edges, use a measuring stick to check the width of the border and make sure it runs parallel with the wall or fence behind. Mark long stretches with a line...

2 ...and lay a wooden board along the line to guide you when you cut. For curves, I draw on the lawn with the blade of my half moon until I am happy with the effect, then cut.

3 Fork up the unwanted turf, which should come away cleanly from the cut edge.

4 Remove the turf...

5 ...and carefully fork over the exposed soil, then flick it back away from the edge.

6 For a curved edge, draw the curve on the grass with one edge of a half moon blade to make sure you like the shape.

7 Cut along the edge...

8 ...remove the unwanted turf and weeds...

9 ...and flick back the soil as for a straight edge.

Hand weeding

You can go a long way to keeping a small lawn weed free by winkling out offenders regularly before they take hold. The easiest weeds to dig out are the tap-rooted kinds, such as dandelions, and a screwdriver worked around the root is the best tool for the job. Creeping weeds are more difficult to remove by hand, because their roots become mingled with those of the grasses.

removing unwanted grasses

● **Some grasses are considered weeds. If a lawn is suddenly spoilt by a tuft of coarse-leaved grass, take a half moon iron or a sharp knife and cut across the top of it in different directions before mowing. It will eventually give up.**

Weedkillers

Lawn sand

This mixture of ammonium sulphate, iron sulphate and sand will get rid of quite a lot of weeds and moss. It works in a simple way, by clinging to the larger, rougher leaves of broad-leaved weeds, but sliding down the grass blades. The clinging powder scorches the weeds, killing the tops but not the roots. This weakens the weeds and gives the grass an advantage. The ammonium sulphate washing into the lawn afterwards feeds the grasses and greens them up. Make sure the lawn is moist when treated and don't mow or tread the grass until after rain has fallen. Should no rain come, water after two days. Don't use lawn sand on new lawns (within a year if seeded, or six months from turf).

Selective weedkillers

Selective, translocated, or so-called 'hormone' weedkillers work because plants are divided into two different types – monocotyledonous and dicotyledonous. Grasses are monocots and the weeds lurking among them in your lawn are dicots. The chemicals in selective weedkillers affect the way dicots grow and develop, causing uncontrollable growth in a way they cannot sustain and they die. But because monocots (including grasses) grow differently, they are unaffected. Selective weedkillers kill the roots too. Selective weedkillers

are a common solution to weeds, especially in larger lawns. Products that feed the grass, but kill the weeds and moss in one application are popular. One application every spring would keep an average lawn healthy and weeds to a manageable level.

Look closely at your lawn and take the time to identify the weeds you want to get rid of before buying – clovers, medics and pearlwort are the hardest to get rid of. Then decide whether the weeds are covering the whole lawn or just part of it. There's no need to treat the entire surface if only a few patches are affected.

How to apply weedkillers

For killing small individual weeds, spot treatments are available. Weedkiller comes in ready-to-apply forms, which can either be smeared or sprayed onto the culprits.
To treat patches of weeds on the lawn, diluting a liquid weedkiller into a watering can or a sprayer will do the trick. Label the can or sprayer with the word 'weedkiller' in large writing and never use it for watering or to apply pesticides, as residues capable of damaging your plants might linger even after rinsing. Powder or granular weedkillers can be used to target certain areas. However, avoid ones containing fertiliser, or you'll end up with a patchwork effect. To treat the whole lawn, either choose a liquid weedkiller or a granular or powder type. All should be applied evenly either by hand (always wear gloves) or by distributor.

The most effective time to treat your lawn is during late spring and early summer. Choose a still day when the ground is moist, but the grass is dry and recently mown. There should be no wind, as both powders and liquids are liable to drift and could kill nearby plants. If you really want to be rid of all the weeds, one application may not be enough, but another six weeks later should do the trick.

When using weedkillers, read instructions thoroughly before use and follow safety precautions to the letter. Store leftover products carefully, locking them away from children in a safe, dry and cool place.

warning

● After using weedkillers (whether lawn sand or selective), do not put clippings from the next four cuts on the compost heap. Even after that, make sure the heap sits for at least six months before using the compost on the garden.

problems

Worms

Worm casts on lawns drive some gardeners mad, but I won't hear a bad word said against nature's helpers. They are busy conditioning and aerating the soil under your lawn roots. Stop moaning and brush the casts away on a dry morning.

Leatherjackets

One is normally blissfully unaware of leatherjackets (legless grubs of the crane fly) until hungry birds pecking and scratching at the soil arrive to get at them. Although leatherjackets feed on grass roots, they don't normally cause much harm – but the birds sometimes do. You can control leatherjackets by applying biological controls in the form of nematodes (minute, worm-like creatures), in this case called *Steinernema feltiae*. Water them into your lawn when the soil is warm in spring.

Ants

A lot of anthills are a nuisance, but ants do provide food for green woodpeckers. I would simply brush them away, but use ant killer if they really annoy you.

Bitches

Bitch urine leaves unsightly scorched patches. The only answer is to provide a resident bitch with her own toilet area. If an accident does occur, a quick flushing using a bucket of water or hosepipe will prevent scorch. Male dog urine doesn't scorch, but seems to feed the lawn, resulting in bright green patches.

Diseases and other manifestations

Circles of toadstools ('fairy rings') cause an inner ring of lush grass, a middle zone of yellowing grass and then an outer lush ring inhabited by the toadstools. Watering iron sulphate into the soil at 15g per 4.5 litres (½oz per gallon) is said to work, but the only sure cure is to dig the soil out 30cm (12in) deep under the problem area and 30cm (12in) either side of the rings. The soil must be replaced with clean soil and either re-turfed or sown. I prefer to let the ring enlarge until it burns itself out or falls off the edge of the lawn.

Regular bare patches on narrow grassy pathways probably mean that the area is getting too much use for the type of grass; you need to redesign it and put in a permanent, hard-wearing pathway.

If your lawn sprouts suspicious yellowing patches, with white or pale pink moulds (Fusarium patch or pink snow mould) or reddish needle-like growths (red thread), grey-black lichens or green slimy algae, then you need to think carefully about the efficiency of your lawn maintenance. Provide sufficient feed, without overfeeding, and good drainage to combat compaction and these kinds of problems can be averted. Treat fungal symptoms with the relevant fungicide and improve lawn care.

planting & managing a meadow

The easy method

The simplest method to enjoy a meadow is to stop cutting parts of the lawn. Leave some areas of grass long and others cut, including pathways to provide access to the meadow areas. The sculptural, three-dimensional effect this creates is beautiful and in a large garden, seriously reduces the time spent mowing and the mountains of clippings it produces.

An area of long, swaying grasses with a straight pathway through the middle creates an almost instant vista. A rectangular area can be divided into four squares with straight pathways around them. You can cut diagonally though an area with a straight or curving path, or take a completely informal approach and create curving pathways through an area of long grass.

What grows in your instant meadow will depend on what was present in the grassy sward originally. A previously well-kept lawn will probably only yield some very pretty grasses with long stems and interesting flower spikes. To our surprise, when we allowed our meadow to develop, it sprouted many wildflowers dating back from its days as grazing land. They were adapted to surviving as flat rosettes of leaves and had only risen up to flower on the wilder margins of the garden. Soon, cuckoo flower or lady's smock (*Cardamine pratensis*), buttercups and the corky-fruited water-dropwort (*Oenanthe pimpinelloides*), so much a feature of meadows in East Devon (where we live) and West Dorset, rose up. They were followed by clovers, achillea, cranesbills, chickweeds, knapweeds and meadowsweet.

Keep the path through a meadow area neatly mown and anyone who sees it will be lured along it.

A rich meadow containing purple knapweeds, pink ragged robin, white ox-eye daisies or moon pennies and yellow buttercups is usually a mixture of nature and nurture.

Maintaining your easy meadow

To save a meadow from becoming too coarse, cut it at least once a year, in mid- or late summer. Few ordinary mowers are versatile enough to cope with long grass, so you will need a different type of machine. For small areas, such as where long grass has been allowed to grow up under an apple tree at the bottom of the garden or surrounding naturalised daffodils, snake's head fritillaries and other bulbs, you can use hand tools. A sharp scythe, or a sharp pair of long-armed shears should do the trick. For larger areas, a mechanised scythe or brushwood cutter are the best tools. Take the cuttings away to prevent them rotting down and feeding the soil, making it over-fertile and favourable to grass rather than wildflowers, and to avoid patchy areas of re-growth in autumn.

As well as grasses and wildflowers, meadows will also attract wildlife into your garden. Small voles and grass snakes thrive near the roots, while some butterflies and moths lay their eggs or pupate on the grass stems. Increased insect life attracts more birds. So if you do have a large area, consider leaving a small portion uncut just to tide the wildlife over and give them a refuge. As you get to know your meadow better, you can favour various plants and animals by cutting areas more than once a season to suit them.

Introducing new plants to your meadow

You have the option of leaving your meadow as it stands, or adding wildflowers compatible with the soil and area. For instance, on my moist, fertile soil I might introduce ragged robin, daffodils (*Narcissus pseudonarcissus* 'Lobularis' is the closest you can buy to the wild native daffodil) and perhaps a few ox-eye daisies. The latter are lovely, but are really pioneer meadow plants and tend to die out after a few years of growth and cutting. I think they are worth re-introducing. I would love to see the parasitic yellow rattle growing. This annual usefully weakens grass growth and is best introduced from seed, sown in autumn so that it can experience a cold period prior to germinating. On lighter soil, you could add vervain, wild thyme or bird's foot trefoil. Always buy seed from reputable companies, making sure it is from native stock and as local to your area as possible. Raise in small pots or plugs and plant them into the meadow this way.

Another option is to add exotic species from other countries to your meadow. Check on their preferred growing conditions before buying – I could naturalise bulbs of moisture-loving, blue-flowered, North-American quamash (*Camassia esculenta*), prairie perennial (*Echinacea purpurea*) and, to shadier spots, the dusky cranesbill (*Geranium phaeum*).

The more difficult method

There is a school of thought claiming that really good meadows can only be created by seriously reducing fertility first, so that the grass doesn't grow too quickly and compete with the wildflowers. Gardeners on poor sandy or chalky soils won't have to lift a finger, but those of us with rich, fertile soil would have to scrape off most of the topsoil, revealing less fertile subsoil into which an appropriate meadow mix of grasses and wildflowers could be sown. If you try this approach, always leave behind a thin layer of topsoil, especially if your subsoil is thick and sticky, otherwise it will be really hard to make a tilth into which the seed can be sown.

You would undoubtedly gain a more colourful meadow this way and I think the idea works well where a garden is not influenced by a surrounding landscape of distinct character. However, if I were to treat my own meadow like this I think it would look odd compared to the fields and rolling verdant landscape all around.

Choose a seed mix to suit your soil and climate and avoid coarse, fast-growing grasses. Generally, one would opt for 80 per cent slow-growing grasses and 20 per cent wildflowers. Either sow during autumn (the best time) or in mid-spring, when the soil has warmed up but should still remain moist for a month or two more. Generally, 15–20kg per hectare (13–18lb per acre) is about right, or for smaller areas 5–7g per square metre (⅙–¼oz per square yard). During germination and growth, watch your developing meadow carefully and encourage the wildflowers by removing any coarse weeds. When the tallest grasses and plants reach beyond 9cm (3½in), mow to 4cm (1½in) and repeat this process until autumn, unless annuals are flowering. Dividing areas up and cutting them at different times of the year is a good idea, because an early summer mowing will favour the early-flowering plants by saving them from being swamped by grasses. But late-flowering perennials, such as scabious and knapweed, need more time to bloom and are best cut in late summer.

Meadow grass in an old orchard adds to the romantic feel.

Chapter 6

hedges & hedge care

Anne: When it comes to property, most of us have the urge to enclose the small plot of land we own. We can build walls or erect fences, but planting a hedge is often the cheapest, most serviceable and attractive boundary marker. These living screens are useful within a garden too. Large or small, there is often the need to divide a space into different sections, and hedges rising beyond eye level make effective barriers. Plants used for hedging must be amenable to clipping and happy to live in close proximity to each other for long periods. There is plenty of choice, but first decide what you want out of a hedge, then consider the range of plants capable of delivering the goods.

shelter

Windswept gardens need help in order for young plants to establish, ably supplied in the form of tough hedging plants. Hedges filter wind, slowing it down and softening its effect. You might think that walls and fences do the same, but solid barriers make the wind bounce up and over the top, only to have it crashing down into the garden further inside. Fences made of woven materials are good, because they have the same ability to filter as hedges (see pages 21–22). In exceptionally windy gardens, the hedge itself might need a windbreak of woven natural or man-made material for the first two or three years, in order for the young plants to settle (see page 168). Remove the windbreak once the plants have put roots down and developed a strong base. Cold winds, and those carrying salt or sand, blast budding shoots on the windward side, explaining why trees appear to lean away from the sea in coastal gardens; they are not only pushed over by the wind, but it also prevents them from making new growth on one side. If yours is a windy site, look for plants with small leaves that won't tear, or evergreens with shiny leaf surfaces, which protect the leaf from drying. Some hedge plants are tougher than others, while serving the same function.

Hornbeam, for example, is tougher than beech. If you want a conifer hedge, *Thuja plicata* withstands cold winds better than most.

Left: Mixed hedges of clipped holly.
Opposite: A *Rosa rugosa* hedge takes up a lot of space, but rewards you with both flowers and berries.

Wild windbreaks

A wild, mixed-species, natural hedge is great for reducing wind speed. In rural areas, such hedges sit naturally between your garden and the countryside, and in urban areas they bring in a little bit of countryside where appropriate. They are also extremely wildlife friendly, not least in providing roosting and nesting sites for birds as well as food. The bulk of a hedge is usually a mixture of hawthorn, blackthorn, field maple, holly, beech and hornbeam, but you can add the odd oak, ash or elder into the mix. Once established, add wild roses and honeysuckle (the native woodbine *Lonicera periclymenum*).

Seaside screens

Coastal conditions are particularly exacting, as hedging plants must withstand sea spray. Use stalwarts such as tough, hardy evergreen *Euonymus japonicus* and gummy, aromatic, red-flowered *Escallonia rubra* var. *macrantha* in the teeth of the gales. Other good choices include tamarisk (*Tamarix gallica*), whose feathery foliage is joined by plumes of pink flowers in summer. Sea buckthorn (*Hippophae rhamnoides*) is wonderful and looks so appropriate by the sea; narrow, grey-green leaves will be lighted up by orange berries, as long as a male bush is planted alongside several females for pollination. New Zealand daisy bushes including *Olearia albida* and *O. traversii*, whose leaves boast silvery undersides, are other good choices by the sea. Let the fascinating Chinese box thorn, sometimes known as Duke of Argyll's tea tree (*Lycium barbarum*), weave its lax stems of grey-green leaves and pinkish flowers followed by orange berries into seaside hedges.

Yew hedges at Powis Castle – formal screening on a grand scale.

formal screens and boundaries

Wild, woolly hedges are all very well, but as backdrops to plants and where gardens are more formal, neat, classy hedges are more appropriate. Yew (*Taxus baccata*) is the most obvious example and grows surprisingly fast and well where soil is good. The most famous conifer hedging plant of all is x *Cupressocyparis leylandii*, usually referred to simply as 'Leylandii'. Much-maligned, this fast-grower makes a successful, dense hedge as long as somebody takes charge of its training, stopping and clipping (see pages 170–72). Beech (*Fagus sylvatica*) creates a classic hedge, especially where height is needed, and never quite loses its leaves in autumn. These hang on, making a russet boundary throughout winter, but can be annoying when they do finally drop in spring. New growth is a fabulous light green and house sparrows are fond of roosting in the branches. Laurel hedges make a grand statement, but privet and *Lonicera nitida* are rather suburban looking and out of vogue.

interesting hedges

All kinds of shrubs make interesting, middle-sized hedges, some of them floriferous or strung with berries. Forsythia (*F. x intermedia* 'Lynwood') in full bloom makes a burst of yellow, but I'm not sure if a couple of weeks of glory is enough payback for looking less than beautiful during the rest of the year. One could say the same of flowering currant. The evergreen barberry *Berberis* x *stenophylla* has been a popular choice, and makes an especially thorny, burglar-proof screen. But though the effect is informal, with arching stems of golden-yellow flowers in spring, followed by purple berries, and looks good all year, it appears to be out of fashion. Firethorn hedges (*Pyracantha* spp.) are more popular and serve a similar function, providing thorny stems, flowers and fruit. *Garrya elliptica* is not a fast-growing shrub, but eventually makes a good hedge, strung with pale tassels of flower early in the year. If you've the space and want an unusual flowering hedge, go for the hedgehog rose (*Rosa rugosa*). Rare in being virtually disease free because tiny hairs on the leaf surface hamper the ingress of disease spores, a row of these shrub roses makes an exuberant though wide hedge (height 1.5m/5ft and width 1.2m/4ft). Expect large, fragrant, single flowers in pink or white, followed by rosehips.

short hedges or edges

Although I've mostly dealt with hedges reaching eye level and beyond, there is a place in gardens for rows of plants knitting together to make low, dense hedges along paths or lawns. Evergreen box is a good example, though recently plants have been assailed by box blight. Hedges of lavender, hyssop (*Hyssopus officinalis*), rosemary (the variety *Rosmarinus* 'Miss Jessopp's Upright' is a good choice) and shrubby germander (*Teucrium fruticans*) are attractive. Good choices for rose hedges include the small Dwarf Polyantha type, pink-flowered 'The Fairy' or Floribunda (cluster-flowered) roses, in particular the cream-hued, fragrant 'Gruss an Aachen'. All kinds of lavender make lovely hedges. You can plant all one type, such as *Lavandula angustifolia* 'Twickel Purple', grow slightly variable plants cheaply from seed, or do as I've just done and plant *Lavandula angustifolia* 'Miss Katherine' alternately with French type *L. stoechas* 'Fathead'.

planting hedges

Matt: The traditional and still the best time to plant hedging plants is from leaf fall to just before bud burst – that is, mid-autumn to early spring, provided that the ground is not waterlogged or frozen. Mid-autumn is ideal, particularly on light soils, but timing all depends on location, soil type, and whether the previous summer's weather has been wet or dry;. after a very dry summer, wait until rainfall has moistened the soil before planting. Early spring planting is recommended for exposed locations to avoid winter chill. Dig clay in autumn, so that frost action breaks down the clods, and allow the soil to settle before planting. Light, sandy soils can be dug at any time of year.

The planting season is also governed by the fact that hedging is usually sold 'bare rooted' and is not lifted until after leaf fall. Containerised hedging can be planted at any time of the year, but establishes better in the traditional planting season; it is also expensive. Specialist hedging suppliers advertise in the back of gardening magazines, so shop around for the best deals; ordering early ensures the widest choice of good-quality plants.

If the hedge is going to run at right angles from an existing house or fence, use a 3-4-5 triangle to ensure the angle is correct (see page 68). Accuracy is particularly important when planting boundary hedges. It is worth discussing the subject of cultivars and hedge lines with your neighbours beforehand to ensure that they are happy with your proposals. Communication is the key!

Matt's planting tips for hedges

● Avoid standing on the cultivated area. If the ground is moist, stand on scaffolding boards to reduce compaction.

● Always tease out the roots of containerised plants before planting. Shovel the soil back into the hole and gently firm (but not compact) it with your heel.

● Tease bare-rooted plants gently from the bundle; tugging them apart can damage the roots. Cut back damaged roots to healthy growth, spread the roots out carefully, ease the soil between them and firm.

● After planting, water and mulch with a layer of well-rotted organic matter 7.5–10cm (3–4in) deep. Alternatively, plant through landscape fabric, tucking the edges into the soil to keep it in place.

Protecting a young hedge

Staking is not necessary for hedging plants. Erect a temporary windbreak on windy sites; it should be at least 30cm (1ft) taller than the tallest plant and 60cm (2ft) away. It should remain in place for at least a year or until the plants become established. Windbreak netting and stakes can be bought from the garden centre.

planting a hedge

1 First, mark out where you are going to dig your trench. It should be 30–60cm (12–24in) wide (roughly the same width as a mature hedge).

2 Skim off the turf and stack it to one side of the trench, on a sheet of hessian or polythene. Use a sharp spade (keep a file in your pocket to re-sharpen it if necessary, or use an old spade with a thin blade) or hire a turf cutter for large areas.

3 As hedging plants grow close together, and will be doing so for decades, thorough ground preparation is essential. Dig out the area to one spade's depth, removing large stones, debris and weeds, and stack the soil on the other side of the trench. Fork over the base, incorporating organic matter; add organic matter to the soil piled by the trench too. Bury the stacked, chopped up turves upside down in the bottom of the trench.

4 Before planting, fork over the area, breaking down the soil into smaller clods and rake it roughly level. Run a garden line down the centre of the cultivated area; two if you are planting a 'double' hedge; make sure the lines are parallel. Water the plants thoroughly before planting, preferably by plunging them in a bucket or water butt for half an hour, or by watering containers using a watering can or hose.

7 Plant at the correct depth, returning the soil back into the trench. For bare-rooted specimens, the correct depth is at the junction between the bark and the root system where the tissue changes colour (this is the same level as they were planted at the nursery). For containerised plants, plant at the same depth as they were in the pot; lay a cane across the planting hole to ensure that the depth is correct. Remember; the soil will settle, so if in doubt add a bit extra.

5 Trim off any damaged roots with a pair of sharp secateurs.

8 Information on spacing should be supplied with the planting instructions from the nursery. Planting distances vary from 30–60cm (12–24in). Single rows are narrower and more elegant; double planting may be ruled out by cost but makes a dense barrier that is more wildlife friendly.

6 Space the plants out along the edge of the trench. Check the spacing against a tape measure.

9 The plants for double-row hedges more than 90cm (36in) wide are often staggered between two rows spaced 45cm (18in) apart, with plants 90cm (36in) apart and the second row planted opposite the gaps in the first. In areas prone to waterlogging, plant hedges on a ridge.

looking after your hedge

Matt: Water plants thoroughly after planting and for the next two years, preferably before dry periods to reduce stress. Creating a ridge of soil around the base of each plant ensures that the water soaks down to the roots rather than disappearing as run off. On dry sites, install a temporary irrigation system that can be removed once the hedge is established.

Top-dress around the roots annually with general-purpose fertiliser or sulphate of ammonia at 30–40g per metre (1–1½oz per yard) from mid- to late spring, and top up the mulch as required. Alternatively, keep the surrounding area weed free; avoid hoeing too deeply as this could damage the roots.

At the end of each season, remove and replace any dead plants.

safety

● Take care when handling hedge-trimming equipment, particularly power tools; they can be lethal.

● Wear goggles, gloves, ear defenders and safety boots; don't wear loose clothing.

● Ensure stepladders are secure and on level ground. Hire a portable scaffolding tower for taller hedges; they are more stable than ladders. If you're using a couple of planks between two ladders, don't step back or overstretch!

● Buy electric or petrol trimmers with adequate safety mechanisms. Switch off machinery and think before moving away from the working location.

● Use a Residual Current Device (RCD) for electric trimmers. This automatically cuts out if there are electrical problems or thre is damage to the cable. Ensure the cable is draped over your shoulder, rather than hanging free. Ideally, there should be someone else with you at all times in case of injury.

● Only use hedge trimmers when you're feeling fine. The machine should be well oiled, not you!

● Do not allow small children into the working area.

● If you want to catch the attention of someone using a hedge trimmer, wait until they have stopped working and the machine is switched off. Take care – fingers cannot be replaced.

● Avoid using hand tools above your head, it gets very tiring. Hand shears made of light alloy with extendable handles make trimming easier.

Trimming

Whether you are using secateurs, hedge trimmers or hand shears, keep your equipment well maintained and sharp; it makes the job easier. Ideally, a hedge should be no higher than 1.8m (6ft) tall for ease of maintenance.

Pruning

Hedges are usually divided into three groups for pruning purposes. The frequency of trimming depends on the style of hedge and its rate of growth. Make a note of birds' nests and 'do not disturb'.

When trimming hedges, ensure that the ladder is stable.

Lay hessian or polythene sheeting at the base of the hedge before starting work – it makes it easier to gather the prunings. Formal hedges are those that are neatly trimmed to shape; informal hedge plants are allowed to develop their natural shape.

Group 1

Cut upright plants, like hawthorn, privet, blackthorn and 'Myrobalana' plum back to 15cm (6in) when planting and lightly trim the laterals the following summer. In late winter or early spring of year two, cut back all stems by fifty per cent. Continue trimming the side shoots through the summer to create and maintain a shape with tapered sides. It may be three or four times a year – in late spring, mid-summer and late summer to early autumn, depending on the rate of growth. You can save time by trimming just once in late summer but the hedges will look untidy until then.

Cut back the stems of evergreens like box, escallonia and *Lonicera nitida* by one third at planting time. Repeat the process in late winter or early spring the following year. In later years, trim back the top growth and side shoots every four to six weeks from late spring to early autumn to retain the desired shape. For accurate shaping, use a template shaped from plywood (see page 176).

If group 1 hedging plants are planted late in the season, leave pruning until the second year.

Group 2

This includes deciduous shrubs that are naturally bushy at the base, like hazel, beech and hornbeam. After planting, cut back all shoots by one third to an outward-facing bud. Repeat in late winter to early spring the following year to keep the hedge compact and to thicken up the base. Prune established hedges in late summer, trimming to the desired shape.

Privet responds well to clipping.

An archway through a beech hedge changes colour and form with the seasons.

Group 3

This includes conifers and most evergreens, including the Lawson cypress, holly, laurel, yew and cotoneaster. After planting with individual supporting canes, leave the leading shoot unpruned and tidy up the straggly side shoots. In summer, trim the side shoots again and tie in the leading shoot to the cane. In future years, clip to the desired shape up to three times during summer. Stop trimming in late summer so the shoots have time to ripen before the onset of frost. Stop the main shoot once it reaches the required height.

flowering and fruiting hedges

Informal hedging plants that flower on the current season's growth, such as hardy fuchsia, dogwood or *Buddleja davidii* can be pruned back to the base as you would individual shrubs in spring. This is also the ideal time to clear out debris or weeds, and apply feed and mulch.

For pyracantha and chaenomeles, which flower on one-year-old shoots, reduce the current season's growth by 50 per cent in mid- to late summer and trim lightly again in mid-autumn if a second flush of growth occurs. Alternatively, for an informal hedge, thin out congested growth after flowering. This will remove some of the berries on fruiting plants such as pyracantha, but helps to retain the shape.

Flowering hedges such as camellia are better left alone, except for trimming untidy shoots after flowering. Camellias are best treated as semi-formal or informal hedges.

Cotoneaster hedging – formal yet with flowers and fruit.

John's tip for laurel hedges

● **Large-leafed shrubs such as laurel are difficult to cut without ending up with lots of the foliage being cut in half. Short lengths may be cut with secateurs – slow work, but at least the finished hedge will be tidy.**

shaping

Hedges should be wider at the base than the top to prevent shading, which discourages growth, and to stop snow from accumulating on the top. The sides should be slightly tapering and flat or rounded at the top. When trimming, check regularly to ensure the shape is correct.

1 If you find it difficult to cut a hedge to the desired shape, put two canes into the ground, in line with one another, attach two lines between them, one marking the top and another near the base, to act as guidelines.

2 Carefully clip the hedge using the lines as a marker. Take care not to cut the lines!

3 Trim the top of the hedge, checking that the top edge is horizontal.

pleached hedges

Matt: Pleached hedging or 'hedges on stilts' have been a feature of formal gardens since Roman times. In *Much Ado About Nothing*, William Shakespeare writes about 'Walking in a thick pleached alley in mine orchard'. The most suitable trees for pleaching are ones with strong, flexible branches such as apple, pear, beech, hornbeam, plane, lime or hawthorn. These were traditionally planted in a line and, as they grew and intertwined, the branches grafted together naturally, or were encouraged to do so by gardeners who took a sliver of bark from touching branches so they grew together.

Before planting, build a framework of wood, metal or post and wire to which the trees are trained. This framework should include an end post beyond the final trees so the 'hedge' is flat at each end. The spacing between the trees depends on how fast they grow; it can be up to 2.5m (8ft).

Pruning pleached hedges

After planting, cut off any lower branches growing below the frame. Tie in any side branches to the left or right, using soft twine. Also tie in as many lateral shoots as possible. Allow the main stem to grow vertically.

Towards the end of the following summer, as the growth matures, shorten long laterals back to a side shoot. Once the leading shoot reaches the top of the frame, it can be bent horizontally and tied in. Any shoots that cannot easily be bent and tied to a supporting wire should be removed. In future years, weave the branches together where they meet and tie in any well-placed new shoots; cut back shoots growing in the wrong direction to an outward-facing bud.

A simplified form is to plant a line of trees 1.2–1.5m (4–5ft) apart, remove branches from the lower part of the trunk, cut out the leading shoot and prune out the upper stems, keeping only the lateral growth. The branches will eventually intertwine to form a dense, twiggy 'hedge'.

Pleached limes create an elegant avenue.

At Amport House in Hampshire, Gertrude Jekyll created a magnificent feature using lime trees. Rather than growing the branches horizontally, they were trained to hang like swags and are delightfully elegant.

topiary

Matt: Topiary, the art of creating shapes from evergreens, traditionally uses small-leaved plants such as yew, box and privet that respond well to trimming. Individual specimens can be grown successfully in pots, but on a larger scale in the garden they need an open sunny site, sheltered from strong winds to encourage even growth, with access space for maintenance and viewing. Topiary should be trimmed regularly and slow-release fertiliser and mulch should be applied in spring to encourage healthy growth.

Most topiary is based around a wire framework. Flexible young shoots are tied into the frame to create bushy growth and side shoots are regularly cut back to two or three buds, encouraging branching. While the shape is forming, check the ties regularly to ensure they are not cutting into the stems. Vertical growth is the quickest, followed by side shoots; downward-pointing stems, which should be tied into the framework regularly throughout the season, growing slowest. Some stems are known as 'frames', and stay in place throughout the life of the topiary, while others are 'formers', which can be removed once the shape is established.

Shapes can be bought or you can create your own from chicken or fencing wire and canes – the only limit is your imagination! There are magnificent examples of formal topiary at Levens Hall in Cumbria and at Tulcán Cemetery in northern Ecuador, which includes elephants and astronauts. Planes, trains and even sofas grace many of Britain's smaller gardens, often developed from existing hedges. While curves can be cut freehand, geometric shapes are more difficult and you will need spirit levels, plum lines and a straight edge, as well as a lot of patience and time, to keep them tidy.

Growth rate determines how often you have to clip the plant – yew only needs one cut each growing season, while faster-growing *Lonicera nitida* may need three cuts. If topiary needs repairing, cut back the damaged stems and tie in new replacement shoots. Start trimming in early summer; if in doubt, don't trim. Pause regularly to review your progress.

Levens Hall, a fine topiary garden – let it be your inspiration!

Cloud pruning

Cloud pruning takes two forms: traditional Japanese pruning of trees to create bare stems with dense 'clouds' at the tips, which highlights the shape of the plant, and hedges trimmed into dynamic billowing forms. There are some wonderful examples of cloud pruning in country houses throughout Britain. If you're looking for inspiration, visit Walmer Castle in Kent. Box, yew, thuja and cupressus can all be pruned in this freeform style to create rounded shapes.

Cloud topiary – living sculpture.

step-by-step topiary

1 Cones and pyramids in pots are a good place to start. The simplest method is to make a cane pyramid, stand it in the pot...

2 ...and tie any long shoots to the cane with twine to form the outer edges.

3 Prune the plants to the 'pyramid' template to maintain the shape.

creating ivy 'topiary'

If you haven't the time or patience for topiary, another easy method is to create a frame from chicken wire and train ivy over it. Again, start with simple shapes like cones or spheres.

1 Put a 5cm (2in) drainage layer in the base of the pot.

2 Fill the pot with a 50:50 mixture of John Innes No. 2 and multi-purpose compost.

3 Insert the wire frame into the compost to keep it steady, leaving room to plant several small ivies round the sides. Pack the frame with moss from the lawn.

4 Once the frame is full of moss, remove it and plant your ivy cuttings around the side of the pot.

5 Replace the frame and train the ivy cuttings up through the wires. Spray the moss with water to keep it damp and water the compost regularly. Keep away from bright sunshine until the ivy is established.

rejuvenating hedges

Matt: When a hedge outgrows its allotted space, is neglected, weedy or bare at the base, drastic action is necessary. Tough hedges such as holly, hawthorn, beech, pyracantha and yew (the only conifer that will re-shoot from old wood) can all be cut back hard to rejuvenate and reshape them. This is done in late winter, so re-growth starts almost immediately, healing cuts and improving the appearance. Feed the hedge well the growing season before, so that it is healthy, vigorous and ready to re-grow.

Because cutting back hard places such demands on a plant, pruning should be carried out in stages: usually, the top and one side in year one, the opposite side in year two. If the hedge doesn't respond well after the initial prune, leave it for another growing season before cutting back the opposite side. In total, you should be able to prune away up to 50 per cent of the hedge.

Before you start, make sure all cutting tools are sharp and in good condition. You will need a bow saw, loppers, secateurs, a pruning saw, gloves and goggles. Use the bow saw for thick branches, loppers for those a little smaller and secateurs for twiggy growth.

Start from the base and work upwards. If possible, place a shredder nearby and enlist the help of an assistant gardener to tidy the material as you work.

Trim the top of the hedge last. Don't be alarmed by the effect – simply marvel at how hedges can recover from such butchery! After pruning, feed with slow-release general fertiliser, mulch with well-rotted organic matter and water well before the onset of drought.

Cutting windows in a hedge creates an element of surprise.

leyland cypress hedges

Think hard before planting a Leyland cypress hedge (x *Cupressocyparis leylandii*). If it is maintained responsibly and trimmed regularly, it makes a superb, fast-growing hedge, but if it is left to its own devices it rapidly becomes a problem, not a pleasure. 'Leylandii' impoverish soil, create shadow and sometimes generate anger; make sure you prune your hedge well from the start to avoid problems later on. If it is allowed to become too large, you will be faced with an expensive bill for topping and trimming. In the first year, trim back side shoots to create the required shape. You should do this twice – once at the start of the growing season in mid-spring and again in mid-summer (or when the leading shoot reaches the required height). Cut back the leading shoots to about 15cm (6in); the new growth will fill in the space. If they become too tall, younger plants can be cut back by one third in mid-spring, but take care when reducing width as these plants do not re-grow from older wood.

Hedge laying is a work of art.

hedge laying

Old hedges deteriorate over time, but it is possible to rejuvenate them by laying. This involves thinning out old stems and debris and laying down the younger stems to form a living barrier that eventually re-grows to become a hedge. Traditional hedgerows containing hawthorn, blackthorn, hazel and field maple are the most suitable for laying. Well-laid hedges can last for more than 50 years before they deteriorate. Laying is a wonderfully creative art and part of our rural heritage. Why not give it a try? Many agricultural colleges, the British Trust for Conservation Volunteers and the National Hedge Laying Society run training courses; the latter also has lists of hedge-laying contractors.

Chapter 7
planting

choosing healthy plants

Bob: It makes sense to start with the best and to choose good quality plants that are healthy and true to type, as any problems may not show for years. Many pests and diseases would never appear in your garden in the first place if it wasn't for you bringing them in on plants or in their compost.

Above: The best plants come from seeds sown in situ, like this chestnut.
Opposite: A 'Rambling Rector' rose growing round a pear tree.

Therefore, where you buy is important and, although it may cost a little more to buy from specialist nurseries, on the whole they offer a bigger range of cleaner and better quality plants than the cheaper 'bargains' in the lay-by or on the market stall (where you may still find some very good plants, but probably only the most commonly in demand and not choice sorts).

Seedling plants are nearly always cheaper and more vigorous than those propagated from slips, cuttings or buds. Many may be free of disease, but there will always be some that are affected or, worse still, that prove too vigorous. Propagating your own plants from slips, cuttings or buds is certainly an inexpensive way to increase your stock of some plants, but it can bring its own set of problems, especially with blackcurrants and raspberries. Never, ever propagate from a plant that looks weak, unhealthy or not true to type. The worst problem-bearing plants are usually the free ones from other gardeners who should know better!

What to look for
Having decided which plant you are after, ascertain the best quality option available. For example, you might choose a rhubarb or strawberry plant that is certified virus free, ensuring excellent performance, at least initially, compared with non-certified stock. Plants grown in sterile compost under cover may be free of many soil-borne pests and diseases, compared to soil-grown ones. Be especially vigilant not to import brassicas, stocks or wallflowers grown in the soil, as they may bring in clubroot disease. Only buy these if they are grown in sterilised compost!

Bob's tips for buying healthy plants

There are various ways in which you can improve the odds that the plant you are getting is healthy and vigorous. First of all, does it basically *look* healthy and is there sufficient young growth? Are there plenty of strong young buds or leaves and shoots? If not, keep looking.

Then there are specific dangers to watch out for.

1 Check for any signs of damage or disease. A plant with split stems is likely to be vulnerable to infection. Also look out for aphids on the tips, scale insects on the stems and the pale, flecking and spotting of red spider mite. If the latter has reached the cobwebbing stage, abandon any thought you may have had of buying the plant.

2 Dead and dying patches on the leaves in any quantity are bad signs, as are holes – especially pea-sized notches on the edges, which indicate the presence of vine weevils.

3 If your plant is in the pot, knock it out to see if the roots are healthy and fill the compost, or are old, dying or wrapped around a hundred times (not a good set of signs).

4 Are there any suspicious-looking grubs, worms or root aphids? And are there masses of weeds, mosses and liverworts on top of the compost – these indicate the plant has been sitting around a while.

5 Don't be seduced by plants that are covered in flowers, however pretty they may be. Much better to buy something in bud or with just one or two flowers, so that you can enjoy the display when the rest open in a day or so.

Severe drought or waterlogging are also such serious signs that you should shop elsewhere.

When to buy

The best time to buy depends on the plant. For the very best results, regardless of time and effort, sow from seed – preferably in situ, or in a seed bed or in small pots (see pages 230–35). Next best is to root a cutting or slip, again preferably in situ or in a seed or nursery bed (see pages 235–41). If none of these are possible and you are forced to buy in your plants, bear in mind that any plant raised elsewhere and checked in transit will never do as well as one grown in situ or close nearby and which is moved without pause or hindrance into a similar soil and situation.

If you are after a flowering plant, it may be a good idea to buy it when one or two flowers have opened, so that you can be sure of its exact shade or form. Bedding plants and many house plants are forced into premature flower by growers to make them more appealing and many resent being moved. To encourage them to establish quicker and put on an eventually better show, remove flower buds and flowers from most sorts of bedding before planting out.

For most plants, it is generally better to peruse catalogues and buy at leisure, ordering well in advance from specialist mail-order suppliers who will send you the plants at suitable planting times. It's true that most plants can be potted on or planted out at almost any time of the year with some care, but greater success will come more easily if plants are obtained when they are dormant or just starting into growth.

The best time to buy the majority of deciduous trees and shrubs, both ornamental and fruiting, is for delivery in early autumn and they should be planted as soon as possible. Most evergreens should be bought in and planted during spring like tender plants. Planting times for bulbs vary, with one sort or another needing planting almost any month of the year, although some, such as snowdrops, are better bought 'in the green' in pots rather than as dried up bulbs. Most herbaceous plants benefit from being planted in autumn, but if they are to be split at the same time then early spring is often surer.

Tulips for spring need planting early the previous autumn, but then you can look forward to a display like this.

Bare roots or pot-grown?

You may have the choice of bare-rooted stock for many trees, shrubs and bulbs. The advantage here is that it allows you to inspect the roots thoroughly for quality and infestations before buying. In general, if they are planted promptly, bare-rooted purchases make better specimens than many pot-grown ones. However, in either case, a smaller, younger and still vigorous individual will always do better than a larger and more expensive one, which will usually be slower to become established. If in doubt, choose the smaller – not the bigger – example. For more on container-grown plants, see page 190.

I personally think it foolish to buy almost any tree that will grow to above head height as anything other than bare rooted. With large trees, it is important that the roots are strong and splayed out from the start if they are to support the tree throughout its life – they will be no good if they are wound around in circles inside the pot (so always remember to unwind them before planting!).

planning your planting

Anne: Gardeners plan their planting from a variety of starting points depending on the state of their garden.

Starting from scratch

Those who've started from scratch will have plotted the outline of their garden, laid lawn and dug their borders over before beginning to plant. Some will have designed their plots down to the last bulb, labouring long and hard over the gardening encyclopaedia and catalogues to specify every single plant. With a vision in their minds and excitement in their hearts, they will have visualised year-round colour, spring borders, late borders, colour co-ordinated climaxes and dramatic combinations. They then embark on the long, hard and often expensive road of tracking all these plants down.

By contrast, other gardeners think they have finished the creative work when they lay the last brick or roll out and pat down the final turf. They don't have a plan for their planting, but make lots of trips to the garden centre, filling their trolleys with small plants and acquiring clumps of this and that from their friends. Three years later, when they should have the bones of a good garden taking shape, you can still see their walls and fences and there's hardly any colour in winter.

A good middle course is this: take an overview of the finished outlines of the garden and think about how you would like to divide the plot up into parts you can see and parts you can't. Blocks of planting designed to reach head height or more are really important and the sooner they go in the better. Either plan it on paper, initially sketching in the areas where you want height, or, if visualising plants on paper is difficult, take a series of tree stakes and canes into the garden and push them into the ground to get a feel for this backbone of plants. Think about the impact of trees on your neighbours and make notes of their eventual height. Some trees, like birches, cast only light shade, whereas others virtually block out all the

A colourful early summer mixture of nepeta, foxgloves and alliums.

New planting can be planned to incorporate existing features such as mature trees.

light. Even the tiniest garden might have room for a tree at the bottom, especially when the ends of several gardens butt up together. I always think an apple tree is great for this situation, especially one that is underplanted with wild or semi-wild plants as a contrast to more formal planting around the house.

So plot the trees first. Good small types include the Allegheny serviceberry (*Amelanchier laevis*), which will eventually reach a height and spread of 8m (25ft). This North American bears pretty white blossom in spring, joined by bronze new leaves. Blue-black fruits follow, and then autumn colour. *Malus* 'Golden Hornet' might eventually reach 10m (33ft) and is an ornamental crab apple bearing delightful spring blossom and a profusion of persistent golden fruits in autumn. They soften and become palatable to birds in the new year, providing a valuable food source. One of the smaller magnolias such as *M.* x *loebneri* 'Merrill', able to tolerate alkaline soils and reaching up to 8m (25ft), might be lovely. A multi-stemmed specimen of the Tibetan cherry (*Prunus serrula*) should remain under 8m (25ft) and its reddish, peeling bark is of interest all year round. Site where winter light will catch the bark.

The larger shrubs come next, such as viburnums, the smoke bush (*Cotinus* spp.), the spindleberry (*Euonymus alatus*) and the sacred bamboo (*Nandina* spp.). Look up their height and spread, and give them the room they need for development. Measure their space, set them out and plant them. Don't be afraid to group a tree and a couple of large shrubs together to create a bank of planting. Initially, these small plants, destined to grow large, will look silly with wide open spaces around them. But the idea is to fill these gaps with smaller, shorter-lived shrubs, climbers, herbaceous perennials, bulbs and bedding plants. These smaller types can gradually be removed as the larger, backbone trees and shrubs mature and meet.

tight budget?

● If you have only a small budget for plants, put in the trees and shrubs first so they can start growing. Fill the spaces around them by sowing cheap packets of annual and biennial seeds until you can afford more permanent plants.

Introducing new planting schemes to existing gardens

When I used to garden for other people, I was often called in to redesign perhaps one tired border and give it a new lease of life. Good, established trees and shrubs would be left in place, but most other plants removed and the soil dug and conditioned. I would draw a rough scale plan of the border on graph paper, so that one square on the paper represented a square metre on the ground. Standing in front of the border, I would sketch in what was needed, setting trees and shrubs the correct distance apart, noting where the smaller shrubs would go and when there would be three of one type together to make a group, or two or three evenly spaced along the border. Then I'd put in the blocks of herbaceous plants, almost always planting in groups of three, five or more, rather than ones and twos. Crosses denoted individuals, allowing about 45cm (18in) between each plant. Gaps could be left for bedding plants, set about 23cm (9in) apart, and bulbs could be added in season.

I would hardly ever specify individual plants, as seeking them out would have cost my clients a lot of money. We would discuss the general effect they wanted, take into account a few preferences, then they left the exact choice of plants to me. I would then visit three nurseries in one day and, using my plan as a guide, select virtually all the plants I needed in one hit. I would choose the healthiest looking plants and look for bargains, all the time building pictures in my mind of how they would look and gradually filling in my plan.

planning a planting scheme

● Check what space each plant needs by looking it up in an encyclopaedia.

● Plant smaller shrubs and herbaceous plants in generous groups or drifts.

● Be prepared to take out smaller shrubs and herbaceous perennials as the larger shrubs and trees grow and knit together.

● Evergreen shrubs are great for year-round interest, but too many can create a heavy, rather gloomy atmosphere. Aim for perhaps one third evergreens to two thirds deciduous. This way, the winter garden will look markedly different to the summer garden.

● Some plants need partners. For a good set, fruit trees such as apples need a pollinator, so plant another apple tree nearby, but of a different variety that flowers at the same time. Hollies are usually all male or all female, so for the females to set berries, a male cultivar must be growing in the vicinity. But if you have room for only one holly, *Ilex aquifolium* 'J. C. van Tol' is hermaphrodite and will fertilise itself.

Choosing plants of varying heights and shapes is one way of adding interest to a border.

By all means specify a few plants for a new border, but tracking down unusual plants you've seen in magazines or books can cost a lot of time, money and postage. Be flexible about the exact plants, but stick to a plan showing how many you need of each rough type and make sure there is interest all year – in this way, you can enjoy shopping on impulse but in a controlled way. Now, when I replant, I might order a few special plants, but buy the rest from nurseries, garden centres and plant shows. I almost always save money by raising some from seed.

Planning for seasonal impact

Mixed borders of trees, shrubs and herbaceous perennials designed to look good all year round sound good in principle, but in practice they might not deliver the impact you were hoping for. There's a lot to say for designating certain borders to seasons. A winter garden should be visible from the house, so you can look out at winter flowers, colourful stems and classy evergreens without having to don boots and set off on a hike to find them. Many winter-flowering shrubs have fragrant blooms (*Viburnum* x *bodnantense* 'Dawn' and witch hazels, for instance), so put them somewhere sheltered where the scents can linger.

Instead of having two borders, one on either side of a lawn, trying to be everything to all people throughout the year, plant one predominantly with spring-flowering plants and the other mainly for late summer. This way you can concentrate your forget-me-nots, spring bulbs, pretty primroses, aquilegias and early summer treats in the spring border, with one or two surprises for later, such as a glowing smoke bush (*Cotinus* 'Grace'). Keep the other clear, ready for stunning displays of hot colours –from cannas and Mexican sunflowers to rudbeckias and dahlias.

Interplanting

Rather than laying your plants out in blocks – perhaps putting three Russian sage (*Perovskia* spp.) together for impact, a whole mass of *Arum italicum* for their pretty marbled leaves in winter, or a bold display of grasses – consider mixing plants up in layers, so that as one finishes its performance, another rises

Libertia peregrinans growing through the purple thyme *Thymus* 'Bertram Anderson'.

up to take its place. This tactic is particularly valuable in small gardens. Spring bulbs pushing their way through herbaceous perennials, whose growth then swamps the dying bulb leaves, is an ideal example.

Evergreen, gold-leaved *Libertia peregrinans* is ideal for slotting between other plants because its leaves are very slender and it propagates itself into an easily divisible clump. Dibble small sections in among summer-flowering plants and you'll hardly notice them, but when those plants look nothing in winter, the libertia will shine out.

Colours

Like many gardeners, I don't think I worry about colour as much as I should when planning my garden. When plants do look great together, it's usually an accident. Occasionally there are some spectacular clashes. One can be more analytical about colour by using a specially designed wheel. Colours that blend are next door to each other on the wheel and those that contrast are opposite, so you can see how to be subtle or dramatic. If you take blue, for instance, the colours next door such as white and purple are harmonious, but on the opposite side of the wheel are exciting shades like orange, yellow or red to make your blues really shine.

Plant compatibility

In the wild, plants grow in certain environments because they have adapted to the climate and soils available. They may suit bogs and wetlands, for example, or dry, parched areas, dappled woodland, mountainous regions or grassy meadows. For our gardens, we have adopted plants from all over the world and countless different habitats, and yet we expect them all to settle in one plot and look good together.

Amazingly, most do on both counts. But because some plants come from vastly different environments in the wild, they can look a little odd placed cheek by jowl.

how to plant

John: Making a hole and burying the roots gets the job done – badly. There is every reason to believe that the unfortunate plant will survive, but that is not the objective. I want you to give each plant the very best conditions to cater for its every whim. Find out what makes your plant happy. Would it prefer the soil to be wet, moist, dry, alkaline (limy) or acid? Would it rather be in sun, shade or something in between?

Some deciduous plants, such as roses and hedging, may be purchased with bare roots in late autumn and winter and Bob has dealt with the advantages and disadvantages of each (see page 185). Occasionally you may be offered ball and burlapped plants, where the rootball has been wrapped in hessian or polypropylene netting and securely tied at the neck of the plant. The wrapping should be removed before the plant is set into its planting pit.

Most trees and shrubs are sold in pots as container-grown (good) or as containerised plants (bad). Container-grown plants will have been grown in the container in which they are sold, so will have a healthy rootball holding the compost together. Containerised plants, on the other hand, will have been grown bare rooted and transferred to a container during the winter. It is not until late summer that the roots spread out through the compost, so if the plant is sold before then, the compost falls off when you take it out of the container and the plant suffers a check.

Right: A sure sign of a containerised plant – the roots haven't had time to spread through the compost, which has fallen off the moment the plant is removed from the pot.
Opposite: One of John's favourite trees, *Betula utilis* var. *jacquemontii*, planted as a specimen.

planting a shrub

Anne has explained how to choose the right spot for the plant, so let's welcome it to our garden and settle it into its new home.

A well-planted shrub will be a joy for many years. This is one of John's favourites, *Mahonia media* x 'Charity', whose soft young reddish leaves become green and spiky as the plant matures.

1 The planting pit should be larger than is needed to hold the spaced-out roots of the shrub – on average, at least twice the size of the pot or roots.

2 As you dig out the pit, separate the topsoil, piling it beside the hole for filling back around the roots. Discard the harder, clay subsoil and any stones larger than 2.5cm (1in) in diameter. Try the shrub in the hole to check that it is deep and wide enough to accommodate the roots.

3 Loosen the soil in the base and around the sides of the planting hole with a digging fork to allow roots to penetrate and water to drain.

4 Soak container-grown shrubs or the rootball the day before planting. Tease out and loosen any roots that are tangled into a tight ball. Damaged or broken portions of root should be removed using a sharp knife or secateurs and the cut ends dusted with flowers of sulphur. With bare-rooted plants, including trees, spread the main roots in all directions.

5 Place a layer of old, well-rotted farmyard manure in the base of the hole to help hold moisture. Mix a handful of bonemeal fertiliser through the topsoil.

6 Plant the shrub at the same depth as it was in the pot with its collar at soil level.

7 Return the soil, layer by layer, working it around the roots while taking care not to damage smaller, fibrous roots. Lumpy soil may tend to leave air pockets causing the death of any roots that grow into them.

8 Give the soil a final firming with your foot and tread the surface around the tree down into a 'dish' shape so that water does not run off before it has had time to penetrate the soil.

9 Water the shrub to settle the soil around the roots.

10 A 5cm (2in) surface mulch of composted bark applied to damp soil will help retain moisture around the roots and deter weeds from germinating.

planting and staking a tree

Most trees above 1.2–1.5m (4–5ft) should be supported with a stake to prevent windrock. A short stake tied at a height of 60cm (24in) will allow the tree to move in the wind while the root is held steady. This movement will thicken the tree trunk, so that after a short time it will be able to stand without support.

After the plant has settled in the soil, secure it to the stake with a tie and pad. The pad acts as a buffer between the stake and the branch, protecting the bark from rubbing. Buckle ties are easy to use, but remember to pull the end of the strap back through the clip to prevent it slipping. Straps that are fed through slits on either side of the pad need to be nailed to the stake. Wire will cut into the bark, so avoid using it, even as a temporary tie. Check ties regularly to ensure they are not too tight. Depending on the speed with which the trunk expands, ties may need to be slackened in spring and again in autumn. For more information on staking, see opposite.

1 Make the planting hole larger than the root area of the tree to allow room for the roots to spread out. Keep the topsoil in a separate pile to the subsoil – you will know when you hit subsoil as it is harder and of poorer quality. Fork up the base of the hole to improve drainage and to allow the roots to penetrate the subsoil.

2 When the hole is ready, unwrap the roots of the tree (don't do it earlier or they will dry out) and place the tree in the hole.

3 If a stake is going to be needed (see above), work out the best position so that it won't interfere with the roots. Positioning the tree in front of the stake will hide the stake from view. Remove the tree before you drive in the stake to avoid damaging the roots.

4 Spread a layer of well-rotted farmyard manure in the base of the hole – this will help get the tree off to a good start and retain moisture when it needs it. Cover with 15cm (6in) of topsoil.

5 Put the tree back in the hole and spread out the roots. Prune any broken roots back to healthy tissue, taking care not to damage the small fibrous roots. Dust the cut ends with flowers of sulphur to prevent disease entering the wounds. Plant the tree at the same depth as it was in the container – there will be an obvious soil mark on the bark to guide you.

6 Mix a couple of handfuls (90–180g/3–6oz) of bonemeal and some well-rotted farmyard manure into the topsoil.

7 Backfill around the roots, shaking the tree to settle the soil. Firm the soil with your foot to exclude air pockets, and 'dish' the surface so that it collects water in the area immediately above the root zone. Water well after planting to settle the soil around the roots. For the first season, keep the soil in the vicinity of the roots well watered and spray the foliage to prevent the tree from drying out and wilting.

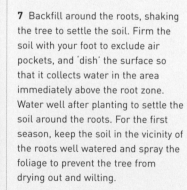

8 Use a strap and pad to hold the tree firmly to a timber stake.

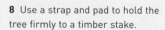

A mature hawthorn in all its autumn glory.

Planting large specimens and semi-mature trees

Large specimens and semi-mature trees are usually supplied in large rigid plastic containers or with their rootballs wrapped in hessian and held securely with wire netting. A machine will be required to dig the planting pit and position the tree in place. Such specimens will require long-term support and a normal tree stake will be of no use. The most secure systems consists of four metal posts concreted into the base of the pit before the tree is lowered into position. Two planks are then laid across the top of the rootball, parallel with one another, with one on either side of the trunk. These are held in place and tensioned with two wires tied across the top of the planks and secured to the metal posts.

I have always preferred round wooden stakes that are pointed at one end. Square-cut posts always seem to twist as they are being driven into hard, stony soil. Tanalised stakes that have been impregnated with a preservative are more expensive than untanalised ones, but worth it because they last longer. Where a stake is required, always drive it in vertically and firmly before you place the plant in the hole. To avoid splitting the stake when using a sledge hammer, make sure that you hit the top of the post with the flat of the hammer. There is a marvellous purpose-made tool called a stake thumper. It is a heavy steel tube sealed at the top with a handle on either side. It is placed over the top of the stake, raised up and allowed to fall. The weight drives the stake into the ground.

transplanting a tree – a one-year plan

Even large trees may be lifted successfully but, where time allows, it is best to prepare them the year before.

1 Measure a circle 1.2–2m (4–6½ft) in diameter around the tree to be transplanted.

2 Excavate a 30cm (12in) wide and 30–40cm (12–16in) deep trench along this circle ...

3 ...and cut through any roots.

4 Fill the trench with a mixture of soil and homemade compost to encourage new fibrous roots to grow into the area. The tree may be lifted the next year after the root area has been given a final, thorough watering. Prepare the new planting hole before lifting the tree.

planting bulbs

A trick to protect your bulbs from vermin and make it easier to dig them up at the end of the flowering season is to plant them underground in a pot. You can buy special pots for this purpose with holes in the side that allow water to seep into the soil and prevent the bulbs becoming waterlogged.

1 Fill the pot with garden soil rather than potting compost, and plant the bulbs according to the instructions that came with them – as a general rule, the larger the bulb the deeper it should be planted.

2 Bury the pot in the bed or border so that the top is flush with the surface of the soil.

3 Cover with fine wire mesh to prevent the local small mammals getting at the bulbs. Remove the mesh when the shoots from the bulb start to appear. When flowering is over, dig up the pot and store the bulbs in the garden shed or other dark, dry place ready to start again the following year.

aftercare

Watering

Matt: Water plants thoroughly after planting and until well established, preferably before the onset of dry periods to reduce stress, and in the evening so water soaks into the ground. Creating a 'dish' or ridge of soil around the base of trees and shrubs ensures the water soaks down to the roots, rather than disappearing as run off. Alternatively, you can bury a vertical piece of pipe that leads down to the rootball at planting time, so water can be poured directly down to the roots; or cut the base from a plastic bottle, bury it vertically and use it as a funnel. It's possible to buy specially designed systems with a plastic cap over the end to prevent water loss. Water newly planted perennials carefully to avoid washing soil away from the roots. On drier sites, it's worth putting a temporary irrigation system in place that can be removed once plants are established.

If you are moving plants, particularly conifers and evergreens, reduce stressful water loss from the leaves by spraying with anti-transpiring spray, sold as anti-needle-drop spray for Christmas trees. Lightly misting the plant with water or putting in irrigation systems can also reduce transpiration.

Weeding and mulching

Keep the surrounding area weed free because these will compete with your plants for moisture and nutrients. Mulch with a layer of well-rotted organic matter at least 7.5cm (3in) deep, less if planted through landscape fabric. Scrape away the mulch and top dress annually around the roots with general-purpose fertiliser or sulphate of ammonia at 30–40g per metre (1–1½oz per yard) from mid- to late spring to encourage root growth and re-apply mulch as required. If mulching or laying landscape fabric is not practical or desirable, it is better to hand weed or hoe, but avoid hoeing too deeply as this can damage the roots.

Protection

Protect plants in exposed areas with a screen of windbreak netting in front of the plants, facing the prevailing wind. This can be attached to tree stakes and should be one third taller than the height of the plant; leave it in place until the plant is established. The same technique can be used to shade plants from scorching sunshine.

Pruning and checking for pests or disease

Prune trees and shrubs according to their needs to ensure they develop a good shape (see pages 208–19). It is easier to do this when they are small and growing vigorously when pruning cuts will heal rapidly. Remove dead, diseased, dying, crossing, weak and rubbing branches and any that are spoiling the overall shape. Tie climbers into training wires and support perennials with frames, or birch or hazel twigs (see pages 222–25). Check regularly for pests or disease, which weaken young plants, and treat any problems immediately (see pages 262–77).

With sufficient shelter you should be able to grow exotics such as *Musa basjoo* (the banana-like leaves in the centre of the picture) and *Eucalyptus gunnii* (the grey-green foliage bottom right) that would hate an open, exposed site.

Chapter 8

pruning & training

why prune?

John: There are plants in your garden that require regular pruning throughout their life. There are others, maybe planted alongside them, that will never need to see a pair of secateurs. What you shouldn't do is prune for the sake of it just because you have the tools to do it. So why prune? There are four main reasons: to promote or restrict new growth, to create an attractive shape, to encourage flowers, fruits or berries and to remove diseased or unwanted growth. Pruning will have an effect on a plant's shape, size, health, life expectancy and its ability to flower and fruit and, as with our children and animals, early training (of both you and your plants!) is beneficial.

Timely pruning has created this riot of clematis – *C.* 'Perle d'Azur, *C.* x *jouiniana* 'Praecox', *C.* 'Polish Spirit' and *C.* 'Arabella', in shades from deepest purple to almost white – over a trellis screen and archway.

To promote or restrict growth

Probably the most important reason for pruning is to promote new growth, whether it is in a young shrub that you have grown from seed or a mature fruit tree that has suffered years of neglect. When we remove the growing tip from a tree or shrub, it produces new side shoots from growth buds along the stem. If we prune these regularly, they will build up into a dense framework of strong, healthy shoots or branches.

Pruning is important not just from an aesthetic point of view. A garden hedge that has been pruned regularly once or twice a year will not only look good, it will also provide privacy, shelter and security with its dense framework of branches.

It is not just our garden plants that need regular pruning. Regular cutting of grass will thicken the surface (sward) of a new lawn. If left uncut for a long period after germination, however, the grass will remain thin and straggly. Bear in mind that a lawn is made up of thousands of individual plants of grass, so each time the grass is cut the plants are being pruned.

I have said that pruning promotes growth. However, pruning twice a season can restrict growth in vigorous plants, such as ivy and the ubiquitous Leyland cypress. These plants need to be taught who's boss or they will run riot, swamping less vigorous neighbours. Trained fruit trees that are grown against a wall or along wires are pruned in summer and again

Opposite: *Fremontodendron californicum* can be trained into a variety of shapes against a sunny, sheltered wall and if it likes its conditions should reward you with flowers for at least six months of the year.

in early winter to restrict surplus growth and build up fruiting wood. Wisteria should be treated in the same way, resulting in more flowers and less unmanageable growths.

It is not just the stems of plants that are pruned to restrict or promote growth. Pruning a plant's roots is an effective way of reducing leafy growth and preventing it from causing structural damage to foundations, walls and piped services. Root pruning is practised in the Japanese art of bonsai. Artificially dwarfed trees can live for hundreds of years, perfect replicas of mature trees but only 30–45cm (12–18in) high. The key to their success and longevity is regular root and stem pruning. There are people who claim that this form of cultivation is cruel, because they believe that plants can feel (but there are also people who believe in Santa Claus and leprechauns).

For shape

Some plants, by their nature, are untidy and need shaping to control their awkward branches. Mahonia, for example, has a habit of producing the occasional tall stem, bare of foliage, with a perfect cluster of flowers at the top. This is best

A peach tree (*Prunus persica*) trained against a barn wall.

removed, preferably after the fragrant flowers are over, by cutting the stem level with the remainder of the shrub. Magnolias, hamamelis, pieris, rhododendrons and camellias are all likely at some stage to send out an awkwardly shaped branch, which you should cut off using a sharp blade.

Other plants are in continual need of pruning to retain their shape. Fruit trees that are grown into espalier, cordon or fan shapes are a case in point, and these need to be trained at least twice a season to control their growth (see page 210). The early stages of topiary involve frequent cutting to give a compact shape (see pages 175–77). With care and continued pruning to bulk out the plant, peacocks or even elephants may be fashioned from small-leaved plants such as privet – but one wrong cut and your peacock becomes a one-legged hen, your elephant a well-fed sheep!

When talking about pruning, gardeners sometimes roll off technical terms, such as pleaching, pollarding and coppicing. Lovely-sounding words, but boiled down to everyday language, they merely describe where you make the pruning cuts to achieve a desired shape. In brief, pleaching means to weave or intertwine branches. When the heads of a line of lime, beech, hornbeam or plane trees are properly pleached the result is what appears to be a solid hedge on stilts.

Pollarding is cutting the branches forming the head of the tree, usually each spring, leaving stumps 2m (6ft) above ground level, eventually producing a mass of brightly coloured stems – ideal for trees with coloured bark on their young growths. While I admit that a tree such as a willow can look spectacular when pollarded, I can't help feeling that it looks like an odd sort of lavatory brush! I prefer coppicing, which is the same as pollarding but at ground level. Again, willow makes a wonderful specimen, but the deciduous dogwoods (*Cornus* spp.) with their brilliant red, orange, yellow or near-black young growths act like a bright light in the winter garden.

To encourage flowers, fruits or berries

One of the fundamental reasons for pruning is to encourage more flowers, fruits or berries. In the border, pruning is used to

Gooseberries like this 'Whinham's Industry' are easier to pick if you keep the prickly bush under control.

encourage a long flowering season in annuals. Nipping out the growing tip of sweet peas, stocks and antirrhinums, for example, encourages them to branch, resulting in a bushy plant with more flowers. Chrysanthemums and geraniums are also treated in this way.

To produce fruits, a plant must first produce flowers. With some plants, such as apple trees, flowers appear on stems that are two years old. With others, such as vines, flowers and grapes are produced on the new shoots that appear each summer after winter pruning. Before you prune a fruiting plant, therefore, it is important to establish when is the best time to prune it and which growths you need to remove, or you may end up with no fruits or flowers that year (for more advice on when to prune, see pages 203–08).

Fruit trees grown against a sunny wall are usually pruned into shape to allow all the fruits to benefit from the sun's rays. Apples, pears, plums, peaches, cherries and figs are traditionally pruned into cordon, fan, pyramid or espalier shapes for this reason. Bush fruits, such as redcurrants and blackcurrants, are pruned to keep the centre of the plant open for sunlight and ease of picking. Gooseberry bushes are pruned for the same reason and also to avoid the spines when picking the fruits.

In the vegetable garden, pruning is carried out to improve the quality and size of the crop. By removing the side shoots from tomatoes, cucumbers and melons, the bushiness of the plant is restricted, reducing the number of fruits but increasing the size and often the flavour. Reducing the amount of leaf growth also ensures better air circulation, thus reducing the risk of botrytis and other fungal diseases.

When you harvest asparagus, you are in fact pruning the plants. If left to grow, the flavoursome shoots would turn into ferny shoots. If you remove them in mid-summer, however, they grow back as leafy growth, which dies down in autumn, strengthening the plant for the following year. The longer you continue to prune or harvest asparagus after mid-summer, the fewer spears there will be the following season,

Thinning an exceptionally large crop of fruits by hand could be called a form of pruning. I fully support the idea that a

John's top tips to prevent disease

The downside to pruning is the risk of disease entering the plant through the wound. The most common diseases to enter in this way include dieback, various killer cankers, silver-leaf and fire blight. Disease spores spread quickly, landing on fresh cuts and soon penetrating the branch. Sap from infected trees is transferred to healthy plants on the blades of cutters. So, to keep your plants healthy:

● always clean equipment after use (see page 220 for tips on cleaning)

● cut trees with diseases such as apple canker last.

● seal large wounds that will be slow to callus over with a proprietary paint to prevent spores entering

● prune when spores are dormant (which will be winter for apple canker but summer for silver-leaf disease)

● burn infected prunings immediately.

small number of large, juicy plums, for example, is better than a large number of inferior ones. Often the plant is of the same opinion and, if it feels that it can't sustain a large crop, it will cast off some of the fruits as they begin to swell. In the Northern hemisphere this is referred to as 'June drop', although it may occur earlier or later in the year according to the variety and conditions. If this 'drop' doesn't occur naturally, it is advisable to remove large crops of fruit by hand lest their weight prove too much for the branch, which, unless supported from below, may break or tear, letting in disease.

To control pests or disease

If your plant is suffering from a disease, it's best to find out what it is before attempting to remove it (see pages 270–77). Some diseases can be pruned out, providing the main trunk isn't affected; other diseases will eventually kill the plant anyway and could, in the meantime, spread to neighbouring plants.

Severe attacks of blackfly tend to concentrate on the young growing tips of a wide range of plants, from broad beans to cherry. The best way to control blackfly is to cut off affected areas and burn them. To prevent disease spreading to other plants, always collect up and burn diseased material and remember to clean your tools before using them on healthy plants.

Other reasons for pruning

Variegated plants

When a branch of a variegated plant reverts to its 'true' or original species and its leaves lose their variegation, any green shoots should be pruned out to leave only the variegated leaves. Otherwise, they will grow more quickly and smother the weaker, variegated leaves.

Dealing with suckers

Suckers that appear below the graft on fruit trees, roses and rhododendrons must be cut off because they will be more vigorous than the grafted variety. Remove them when they are small and without leaving any stem, as that could re-sprout with two or more new suckers.

On a variegated plant, prune out any leaves that have reverted to plain green.

Climbers

The rules of when and how to prune are especially important for climbers, such as clematis, climbing roses and wisteria. With correct pruning and training, plants such as these will plaster themselves with flowers, while little or no pruning will result in masses of long, thin, non-flowering growths and a few miserable flowers high up on the plant. Virginia creepers, clematis, ivy and *Hydrangea petiolaris*, if they are grown against a building, need to have their extension growths removed before they find their way through the soffit into the roof space and under roof tiles.

safety

● It is frequently necessary in urban areas or close to buildings or roads to reduce the overall height and spread of mature trees to make them safe. Regular inspections will determine if diseased branches need to be removed.

● In the case of mature trees, especially where safety and the use of a chain saw is involved, pruning is best left to a qualified tree surgeon. Always check on a firm's experience, whether the workers are qualified and that their public and employers' liability insurance is sufficient to cover a worst-case scenario.

when to prune

John: Pruning is an on-going operation. There is always some plant in need of pruning in the garden and I seldom walk through mine without a pair of secateurs in my pocket ready for use. But when is the best time to prune? This depends on whether a plant flowers on growth made during the previous year or growth made earlier the same year.

After flowering

Plants that flower on growth made during the previous year usually need to be pruned after flowering. This gives the plant time to form new wood during the growing season ready for flowering the following year. Early-flowering deciduous plants, such as forsythia, fall into this category, and need to be pruned immediately after they have finished flowering by removing all of the flowering wood. Failure to do this would result in a tall plant with flowers high up.

The bride's blossom or mock orange, properly labelled philadelphus, flowers in summer with exquisite fragrance. It also needs to be pruned after flowering by shortening back the flowering shoots, leaving the new young shoots to flower

Forysthia is most familiar as a cheering early spring shrub, but can be pruned to make an eye-catching hedge.

John's top 40 (or so) plants for pruning

Here's a quick guide to the best times to prune the plants you are most likely to want to prune.

Betula	winter
Buddleja	early spring
Buxus	spring and summer
Camellia	after flowering
Ceanothus (evergreens)	after flowering
Ceanothus (deciduous)	spring
Chaenomeles	after flowering
Choisya	summer
Clematis	late winter, or after flowering for winter- and spring-flowering varieties (see page 215)
Crataegus	autumn/winter
Euphorbia	early spring
Fagus	spring
Ficus	late winter
Forsythia	late spring
Hedera	winter
Hamamelis	early winter if necessary to maintain a good shape or to restrict growth
Ilex	for Christmas!
Lavandula	early spring
Lonicera (shrubs)	after flowering
Lonicera (climbers)	winter
Magnolia (evergreens)	late spring
Magnolia (deciduous)	winter
Mahonia	after flowering
Malus	winter
Passiflora	early spring
Philadelphus	after flowering
Pieris	late spring if necessary to maintain a good shape or to restrict growth
Prunus (evergreens)	after flowering
Prunus (shrubs)	mid-summer
Prunus (trees)	mid-summer
Pyracantha (shrubs)	winter
Pyracantha (hedges)	after flowering
Pyrus	winter
Rhododendron	after flowering
Roses	winter/early spring
Syringa	after flowering
Taxus	spring
Viburnum (evergreens)	winter
Viburnum (deciduous)	after flowering
Vitis	late autumn and winter
Wisteria	late summer and winter (see page 216)

the following year. Climbing roses are another example, where the new stems that are formed after flowering take the space occupied by the older flowering shoots.

After last frosts

We have learnt that pruning encourages growth, but only if carried out at the right time of year. Some plants produce growth buds early in the season and these can be damaged by late frosts in spring, especially if you have removed their protection. For example, the growth buds of hydrangea form under the previous year's flower heads. If you have pruned the flower head, exposing the buds to frost, and a bead of water becomes lodged behind a new bud, when the ice expands, it pushes the young bud away from the stem, causing it to fall off and die. So it is always better to prune hydrangea after the frosts have passed. Early pruning of bush roses (before you are confident that spring has arrived) is risky in cold northern gardens.

Shrubs that flower in summer on growth produced that year require pruning in spring to encourage flowering wood and compact plants. Bush roses and buddleja are pruned after all risk of frost has passed. Regular feeding helps the plant to produce lots of strong stems that flower within six weeks. Most hedges need pruning regularly to keep them neat and tidy. However, evergreen shrub or conifer hedges are not as resilient as they appear. They might look solid from the outside, but when you look beyond the fresh green outer 'skin', you will discover that the inner shoots are completely devoid of foliage. During a prolonged spell of cold weather, the frost can penetrate to the inside of the plant, causing damage or even killing parts of the hedge. To prevent frost damage, avoid pruning them too late in the year and wait until after the last frost before clipping in spring. Conifer trees are also susceptible to frost damage if they are drastically reduced in height in late autumn.

At planting time for shape

Early training of trees and shrubs will prevent badly shaped plants with crossing or weak, narrow and angled branches. Most climbing shrubs, such as wisteria, clematis and honeysuckle, benefit from being pruned at planting time to encourage strong shoots from the base. Fruit trees intended for growing against walls or trellis should also be shaped from an early age to ensure that their branches grow correctly to form espalier, fan, pyramid or cordon shapes (see page 210).

Spring pruning for bark colour

With many trees and shrubs noted for their colourful bark, it is the young stems that make the best display. As branches become older, the bark loses its colour. Prune dogwoods, especially the *Cornus alba* varieties (red) and *Cornus sericea* 'Flaviramea' (yellow), every spring. To encourage strong, well-coloured branches from the base, make sure you cut the branches close to the ground before they come into leaf. If you are coppicing and pollarding willows for bark colour, do this at the same time (see page 200).

When plants are dormant

Most fruit trees are pruned in winter (when they are dormant and before the sap rises) but there are always exceptions. The spores of fungal diseases such as silver leaf and bacterial canker, which affect plum and cherry trees, are less active at the height of summer and therefore less likely to enter pruning wounds, so that is the best time to prune these trees.

Some deciduous plants tend to 'bleed' if they are pruned as the sap is rising in the spring. Vines, both ornamental and those grown for fruit, should be pruned in winter when the plant is dormant. Any birch trees that need shaping should be pruned before spring. If pruning is left until the leaves start to emerge, the sap will drip for weeks. (The Norwegians distil this sap to make an alcoholic drink.)

Regular pruning of vigorous plants

While I don't advocate constant clipping and snipping of plants, formal hedges should be pruned on a regular basis. The number of cuts will depend on the species of plant and the speed of growth. Usually two cuts a year will be necessary to keep a hedge tidy, but some owners are rightly proud of

their manicured hedges and clip them every fortnight. No matter how often you prune, always check your hedge for nesting birds and, if you are lucky enough to have such residents, don't cut until they have finished breeding.

For some plants, 'regular' pruning means nothing more than once a year. With evergreen flowering shrubs such as escallonia, which make wonderful flowering hedges and produce blooms on new growth made during the spring, the timing of the annual trim is crucial. Most varieties will flower all summer and well into the autumn. In mild areas, they may be pruned in spring, but where there is a likelihood of late spring frosts I prefer to sacrifice some of the late flowers and prune in early autumn.

Pruning out old growth gives the young shoots of this *Cornus sanguinea* 'Midwinter Fire' the chance to glow.

Escallonia bifida: prune in early autumn even if it is still flowering.

Double pruning

Where you have limited space, pruning in summer and again in winter can be an effective way of restricting growth while building up flowering or fruiting wood. Double pruning is practised on trained fruit trees to encourage many more fruits to be produced in any given area of branches. The best time to carry out the initial pruning is in mid-summer; the second pruning takes place in winter when the plant is dormant. The following spring, the plant should have built up a strong framework of mature, short-branched stems (spurs) with many fat, rounded fruiting buds. See page 210 for step-by-step instructions.

Wisteria also benefit from pruning twice a year – see page 216 for detailed instructions.

After fruiting

Pruning soft fruits such as raspberries, blackberries and loganberries may be summed up as: remove the old, retain the new. These plants produce their fruits on year-old shoots. Immediately after fruiting, cut these out as close to ground level as possible and tie in the new stems to replace them.

For summer-fruiting varieties, prune after they have finished fruiting. Start by cutting all the canes (stems) that carried fruits to ground level. This leaves only the new growth. Tie in the strongest growing, unfruited canes to their supporting wires at intervals of 7–10cm (3–4 in). In early spring, reduce any tall canes to 15cm (6in) above the top supporting horizontal wire.

For autumn-fruiting raspberries, cut all the canes to ground level in late winter or early spring. As new shoots appear in late spring, tie them in to the supporting wires without thinning. Burn the prunings to prevent the spread of fungal diseases such as cane spot. Cut new plants down to 25 cm (10 in) after planting.

I prefer to prune cane fruits such as blackcurrants after they have fruited. Cut out the oldest stems to encourage strong, new growths that will fruit the following summer; at the same time get rid of any diseased leaves. For ease of picking from thorny gooseberry bushes it is important to keep the centre of the plant open and free of growths. Do the main pruning in winter with another light prune of vigorous plants in summer.

To prevent seed formation

When you look at the size of a lupin seed head, it is easy to imagine the amount of energy it took to form. Producing seed diverts a plant's energy away from making new growth and this can prevent certain plants from repeat flowering. With lupins, flower spikes should be removed directly after flowering to enable them to flower a second time, albeit with smaller spikes of flower. Annual sweet peas need constant deadheading to encourage repeat flowering. You also need to remove the dead flowers of roses, otherwise seed hips will form, which delay the onset of a second flush of flowers. Removal of the large flower heads of rhododendrons allows next year's flower buds to form during late summer. If not removed, the buds produced on either side of the seed head will be more likely to be growth rather than flower buds.

There is another very good reason for pruning to prevent seed formation. Some excellent perennials, shrubs and trees scatter their seed so profusely that their progeny can invade our gardens like weeds. *Leycesteria formosa* can be a real headache,

pruning blackcurrants

1 Remove old branches with dark bark as close to the ground as possible.

2 Remove thin and crossing branches using secateurs or by hand.

pruning raspberries

1 Once raspberry canes have fruited prune them close to the ground, to prevent the stumps becoming diseased and to encourage strong shoots from the base.

2 DON'T leave stems as long as this. The dead stems are hollow, so rain can penetrate and rot the plant.

with its sea-green, hollow stems and trailing flower stems resembling gypsy earrings. Birds love their deep purple berries, attractively camouflaged by paler mauve bracts, and they are responsible for the spread of this quick-growing shrub.

The perennial *Alchemilla mollis*, better known as lady's mantle, causes a similar problem. I wouldn't be without it, but you can have too much of a good thing. Its seedlings can appear all over the garden and fast become a nuisance. But there is a simple solution – as the frothy, greenish-yellow flowers start to fade, remove them using hedge clippers or secateurs, along with all the tired foliage. Not only will you prevent unwanted offspring, but new, soft, grey-green leaves will appear again to brighten the border.

how to prune

John: We have covered the various reasons why a plant is pruned and the importance of timing. Now we get to the crux of pruning – the hands-on work. Here are a few general tips on how to make your plants the best in your neighbourhood.

As I said at the beginning of this section, early training of trees and shrubs is essential. For a start, it is so much easier to prune a pencil-thin stem than, if you leave it a few years, a branch as large and round as a dinner plate, overhanging other plants.

The shaping of a young plant is governed by a little knowledge and a lot of common sense. Buds are important and each one represents a branch. Break or damage a bud and there will be one branch less. Who knows, it might have been the one suitable branch to hang a garden swing from in 20 years' time.

The best tip you will ever use to your advantage is that a shoot and eventually a branch will grow in the direction that a growth bud is pointing. So, if your rose bush is a bit one-sided, pruning shoots on the weak side to a bud pointing outwards will encourage growth in that direction. Where a new shoot is heading in the wrong direction, it needs to be cut back to a suitable bud (heading in the right direction) or removed altogether. By the end of the growing season, you will have a balanced plant.

The strongest shoots are produced at the base of a plant. Further up the stem they tend to be weaker and thinner. For this reason, many new plants are pruned low down after planting. Raspberry canes, for example, are cut back to within 25cm (10in) of the base straight after planting. Climbing and rambler roses are treated in the same way. Bush roses will also throw out strong shoots if pruned to within two or three buds of the base and this will encourage them to flower that summer.

If necessary, prune rhododendrons like this *R. loderi* 'King George' to maintain a good shape. Old plants may be rejuvenated by severe pruning (see pages 211–12).

understanding pruning

Before discussing how to prune, it is helpful to understand the gardening names for those parts of a plant associated with pruning, as well as the terms used to describe the operation. While I seldom see the need to be totally technical when discussing plants, it is easier to converse if gardening terms are understood. It is far simpler to say 'shorten by half the laterals leaving the spurs to fruit', for example, than 'shorten by half the small branches growing out of the sides of the main branches leaving the short stems of older wood which carry the fruit buds'. I haven't used all these terms in the text, but you may find them useful as you become more of a pruning addict.

Axil The V-shaped area between the stem of the plant and the leaf growing away from it. The bud produced in this area is called the axillary bud.

Branch A stem growing from the leader branch or trunk, complete with shoots and foliage.

Branch collar A swollen ridge of bark on the lower side of the branch, close to the main trunk.

Bud (apical) The bud at the tip of a shoot that allows the stem to grow. Also called a terminal bud.

Bud (growth) A swelling where a new shoot will form.

Bud (fruit) A rounded swelling that will produce flowers.

Callus A protective layer of corky, bark-like growth that grows over a wound to seal it.

Canopy The total spread of the head of a tree or shrub.

Central leader The young main stem that continues the line of the trunk or main branch.

Coppice An area of trees, such as hazel, willow or eucalyptus, that are cut back to within 30cm (12in) of ground level and allowed to regrow with many straight stems.

Crotch The angle between two large branches or between the main trunk and a large branch.

Crown (head) The branches of a tree.

Dieback A fungal disease that causes the end of a shoot to die. If not controlled, it can spread gradually down the stem towards the base. Dieback often enters a plant through a pruning cut.

Deadhead The removal of dead flowers before they set seed.

Disbud The removal of some growth buds to reduce overcrowding of branches, or the removal of flower buds to increase flower or fruit size.

Extension growth The growth a plant makes beyond the point to which it has been pruned back, resulting in added height.

Feathered tree A young tree with side shoots off the main stem.

Fork The angle between two branches.

Lateral (side shoot) A stem growing off a main branch.

Leg A short length of stem on a woody plant.

Limb A branch.

Maiden A year-old tree or shrub without side shoots. Often used to describe a fruit tree the year after grafting.

Nicking and notching The removal of a small amount of stem above or below a bud to inhibit or stimulate growth.

Open centre The area in the centre of a tree or shrub where there are no branches.

Pinching out The removal of the growing tip of a shoot using your fingertips.

Pleaching A method of shaping trees, such as limes, where the branches are trained in tiers horizontally along wires or canes to form a dense, formal head.

Pollarding The hard pruning of the branches of a tree, such as a willow, leaving stubs.

Rootstock A rooted plant that is grafted on to a tree or shrub.

Root sucker A shoot growing from the base of a woody plant.

Shoot A stem or young branch.

Split leader A branch that forms two main side shoots, each competing to become the leader.

Standard A tree or a shrub with a length of unbranched trunk capped with a multi-branched head.

Stem A shoot or young branch.

Spur A short, branched stem producing flowers.

Sucker Either a root sucker (see above) or, on grafted plants, any shoot that arises below the graft union.

Tip pruning Removal of the growing tip of a stem to encourage side shoots.

Trunk The main stem or bole of a tree.

Water shoot (water sprout) A vigorous, thin shoot growing from a main branch in the centre of the tree, often appearing after severe pruning.

Whip A young, bare-rooted tree consisting of an unbranched single stem. fruit tree the year after grafting.

Where two shoots are vying to be the leading shoot, always remove one of them. This will prevent a narrow angle forming between the two branches. If left, the fork in between will become a weak area and eventually the branches may split. Always select the weaker shoot for removal, or the one that is slightly angled.

making a pruning cut

Always make a downward sloping cut, starting above the bud. This will encourage water to run off the cut, away from the bud or branch. This is particularly important with large pruning cuts, which need to be encouraged to heal quickly. Small buds are also at risk, especially in cold weather, when they can become dislodged by frozen water droplets.

Pruning a shrub

The correct amount to be removed by pruning depends on the number of shoots produced and the length of the growths. A well-maintained, mature *Philadelphus*, for example, may have 15–20 main branches. Each summer, after flowering has finished, you will need to remove about one third of them to encourage new growth for flowering the following year.

To maintain a compact, bushy plant the cuts should be made close to the base of the shrub where the shoots are strongest. As a general rule, always select for removal the oldest branches (usually those where the bark is almost black or a darker shade of brown). Make a sloping cut using loppers or, where the branches are thick, a small, folding hand saw. A bow saw is too large and awkward for use among a mass of branches such as these. Remove the branch as close to ground level as possible, since stumps encourage disease and in time may clutter up the base of the shrub.

In contrast, a young *Philadelphus* – say two to three years old – should have all its branches cut by about one-third, to

shaping a young fruit tree

In its first year a young fruit tree forms a single stem up to 1.2m (4ft) high. Ideally, in the second year it should produce side shoots evenly round the main stem at a good angle from the trunk. If left to nature, a variety of long and short side shoots would grow, some with narrow or weak angles. Successful training, on the other hand, produces a balanced framework of strong, healthy branches.

Shorten the main stem to a suitable height. I prefer the lower branches to be well clear of the ground – branches tend to bend under a weight of fruit, making grass cutting more difficult if they come close to the ground. So I would cut the stem at 1m (3ft). Use a sharp knife to cut immediately above a healthy bud, sloping the cut downwards away from the bud to encourage water to run off. The six buds below this cut are important and from this area the framework of branches will develop that is maintained throughout the life of the tree. (If there are more than six buds, remove the rest.)

'Nick' the top bud closest to the cut by cutting out a small crescent-shaped 'V' from the stem immediately below the bud. This bud will be trained as a 'leader' to produce a second tier of branches, but its growth needs to be

restricted by reducing the flow of sap to it alone. If not restricted, it will take advantage of all the sap, at the expense of the other branches.

Remove the next bud (beneath the top bud) by pushing it off with your thumb, or it will grow into a narrow, angled branch. Leave the third and fourth buds untouched, as these will grow out at a desirable angle from the main stem.

'Notch' the stem immediately above the two lowest buds by scraping away a small, shallow, crescent-shaped piece of stem with a sharp knife. This diverts additional energy to the lower buds. The result is a balanced tree, well furnished with branches, none of which is weak or at narrow angles to the main stem.

If you are growing your fruit tree as a fan, only three branches (rather than five) need to be encouraged to grow. Follow the basic instructions above, but cut the stem closer to ground level and to the graft. Remove the top bud (which would form the leader) and take off the two buds underneath as well (or pinch them out as they start growing). Allow only the fourth bud and the two lowest buds to remain. Notch above and below the lower two buds to divert energy towards them.

produce a strong, non-spindly framework that will bear flowers at a reasonable height.

Cutting a large branch

This can be a tricky operation. Ideally, a team of two gardeners works best, with one person supporting the weight of the branch while the other person cuts. (This way, the branch shouldn't pull away from the cut and leave a gaping wound with torn bark on the underside.) Always use a sharp blade, never one where the edge is notched. A clean pruning cut will heal more quickly and reduce the risk of fungal spores entering the wound.

Renewal pruning

Renewal pruning is suited to shrubs with arching branches, such as *Philadelphus* 'Virginal', weigela, bush apple trees and some shrub roses. When a branch becomes too low, cut it back to an upward-pointing side shoot that, in time, will arch over. At this point prune it again in the same way.

Rejuvenating an old shrub

When a shrub becomes very old, its lower branches devoid of foliage, with all the new growth and flowers high up, it is time to reassess its value in the garden. There are three options: leave the plant alone, remove it by the root and replant it somewhere else or try to rejuvenate it.

Rejuvenation requires a lot of heavy pruning and some species adapt better to it than others. I have cut escallonia that were over 40 years old, leaving knee-high stumps about 15cm (6in) across. Within three years, the shrub had revived as a compact flowering plant. Rhododendron, griselinia, forsythia and philadelphus can also tolerate being cut well into the old wood, leaving just stumps. Within a few seasons, these plants will make a complete recovery with lots of new branches growing from low down on the plant. Other plants – including lilac (*Syringa* spp.), broom (*Cytisus* spp.), lavender and most of the conifers (other than yew) – are less likely to produce new growths from very old wood and are liable to die if pruned back too heavily. When rejuvenating a shrub in this way, pay particular attention to timing (see pages 203–08), as any new

cutting a large branch

1 Start by selecting a suitable place to cut. The best place is near to where there is a natural 'collar' or ridge of bark close to the main trunk. If possible, leave the ridge intact as healing is usually quicker in this area.

2 Make a small V-shaped cut part way through the branch on the underside. This should prevent the bark from tearing if the branch falls.

3 Cut the branch from the top side, supporting it from underneath. A saw cut part way through the branch on the underside and a top cut a few centimetres further out on the branch will prevent damage if by chance the branch does fall. To speed up callusing of large wounds over 10cm (4in) in diameter, smooth with sandpaper. To prevent disease, also trim any ragged saw marks on the surrounding bark using a sharp knife.

4 When a large quantity of old branches is removed high up on a tree or shrub, especially fruit trees such as apple or pear, thin, spindly shoots known as water shoots are likely to form on the remaining branches in the centre of the tree. These will never become good-quality fruiting material, so remove them close to the base of the branch or trunk without leaving a stub that may produce more shoots. Remove and burn any clippings, as water shoots are prone to canker disease, which may spread to other areas of the tree.

shoots will need plenty of time to firm up and become woody before the first hard frost. High-potash liquid fertiliser, applied in late summer, will harden the young growths.

When rejuvenating an old plant by heavy pruning, it is very important to make the large cuts at a downward angle (see page 210) to encourage water to run off. Otherwise disease will enter the plant. A proprietary wound sealant should prevent spores from entering the cut, but keep applying it as necessary (perhaps once every six months) over the next couple of seasons, as it may be years before the wound is fully callused over.

Shaping a plant

Some plants are in continuous need of pruning to retain their shape. The most obvious example of this is topiary, which is covered in Chapter 6, but even standard trees require a fair amount of pruning and training in their infancy. Standard trees with a 1.8m (6ft) clear stem, before the branches form the head, are pruned to that shape by removing all the side shoots as the plant grows. Support the stem with a bamboo cane to keep it straight. At the desired height, remove the growing tip and allow branches to form. The mini standard form, with a 1m (3ft) high stem, suits plants such as fuchsia, *Euonymus* 'Emerald Gaiety' and *Cotoneaster* 'Conspicuus'. Wall-trained fruit trees such as apples, pears, cherries and peaches need to be pruned twice a year during winter and summer to retain their espalier, fan or cordon shape. Apart from extension growth and that needed to build up fruiting wood, most other growth is removed or shortened. If left unpruned for more than a year the plant will become bushy and the skeleton shape will be lost.

Wall-trained shrubs such as pyracantha (grown for its flowers and berries), *Garrya elliptica* (long, male catkins) and fremontodendron (saucer-shaped flowers) benefit from regular pruning to keep them in check. To maintain a compact shape, trim back the side shoots of trained pyracanthas every two or three weeks once the fruits start to swell.

pruning requirements of favourite plants

Grape vine

John: There are two types of vine: ornamental and fruiting. Ornamental varieties include *Vitis* 'Brant', *V. coignetiae* and *V. davidii*, each with large leaves offering brilliant autumn colour. Pruning of ornamental vines takes place every year in late winter to encourage new growth. Plants grown in a confined space may also benefit from an extra trim in summer to cut back long growths. If your vine has been neglected, cut out the oldest stems close to the base of the plant to rejuvenate it.

Fruiting vines have a more defined system of pruning. If the operation is mismanaged, there will be no crop that year.

There are three main types of vine cultivated for their grapes: the European grape (*Vitis vinifera*), the American grape (*V. labrusca*) and hybrids between these two. The difference between the European and American types is that *V. vinifera* produces the bunches of grapes close to the base of the new growth, while varieties of *V. labrusca* and the hybrids tend to fruit further along the growth. Both types are usually grown on a straight main stem, with fruits appearing on side growths produced that year.

The most important period for pruning fruiting vines is during winter dormancy, when an enormous amount of the previous year's growth is removed. European vines are spur-pruned, which means that all of the previous year's growths are cut back to within two buds of the old cane. When the new shoots appear, one is removed, leaving a single stem to grow. (The reason why two buds are left to grow on as shoots is in case one is damaged.) Ideally, fruiting shoots are pencil thick with 15–30cm (6–12in) gaps between the leaves. American varieties of *V. labrusca* tend to form their fruiting buds further along the stem and they should be pruned back to about ten buds (cane pruned). When pruning, any thick canes may be left longer than the ten buds.

Vitis vinifera 'Purpurea' is grown more for its foliage than its grapes, and is not over-vigorous, so needs less pruning than many vines to keep it under control.

Europeans have grown grapes under glass for centuries. The best time to prune them is in mid-winter before the sap starts to rise. Pruning later in the season will cause the vine to 'bleed' copious amounts of sap from the wounds, draining its energy. To prune grapes grown under glass, follow the basic instructions on page 212, but once the cluster of flowers gives way to a tiny bunch of grapes, pinch out the growing tip of each shoot, leaving three leaves beyond the bunch. Shorten subsequent laterals to one leaf. Good air circulation is essential when growing grapes, especially in glasshouses. Where bunches of grapes are tightly packed, remove some of the leaves around them to increase air movement and reduce the risk of disease. For improved quality and size (albeit fewer bunches), restrict each stem to one bunch of grapes.

The white-flowered *Clematis montana* var. *wilsonii* belongs to Group A (see opposite) and needs to be pruned only if it is getting out of hand.

clematis

Total confusion seems to have grown up among amateur gardeners regarding the correct method for pruning clematis. It is slightly complicated, but only because clematis fall into three groups: A, B and C. If you know the species or variety you are growing, follow the instructions below. If you haven't a clue – either because you have taken over a mature garden or have simply lost the labels – then here is a rough guide that will save the day (and the clematis!). If your clematis flowers before early summer on the previous year's growths, leave it alone with no pruning. If your clematis flowers in mid- to late summer or autumn, on growths produced that year, prune it hard in late winter. Trust me, it will work.

Group B

Varieties that flower before early summer (or a few weeks later in colder parts of Britain and northern Europe), including those that are double flowered. This group includes *C.* 'Arctic Queen', *C.* 'Royalty', *C.* 'Vyvyan Pennell' and *C.* 'The President'.

1 Using secateurs or a sharp knife, prune out all the dead, damaged and weak stems in late winter before spring growth starts. Starting at the top of the plant, work your way down each stem until you find a healthy fat bud. Cut immediately above it. Note that if you prune the double-flowering varieties hard, the flowers that season will be the same colour but single. They will revert to double flowers for the second flush in autumn.

2 Four weeks after pruning, the plant is showing healthy growth.

Group A

Clematis alpina, C. armandii (evergreen), *C. chrysocoma, C. cirrhosa* (evergreen), *C. macropetala* and *C. montana*, which flower in winter and spring.

1 As a general rule, the clematis in this group do not require annual pruning. However, if they are bare at the base, or are wandering far and wide beyond their allotted space…

2 …prune them immediately after they have finished flowering. The new growths made during the summer will flower the following year. Old plants of *C. montana* and its cultivars may be cut back severely with little risk of losing the plant.

Group C

Late-flowering, large-flowering hybrids such as *C. orientalis, C. texensis* and *C. viticella*.

These clematis flower on growths made during the same year and should be hard pruned in late winter before growth commences.

1 Start at the base of the plant and follow each stem upwards until you come to a pair of healthy, fat buds.

2 Prune each stem immediately above these buds. Remove and burn all the growths. Where a plant has clambered over other shrubs or a big, old tree, this can be a slow operation, but persist and I promise your patience will be rewarded.

Wisteria floribunda lives up to its name and flowers profusely – provided you prune it properly!

wisteria

'How do I get my wisteria to flower? It is growing well, but has not produced any flowers.' If I had a tree for every time that question has been submitted to the *Gardeners' Question Time* panel I would have a forest!

If the plant is more than three years old then it should be flowering. The problem is either the result of overfeeding with a high-nitrogen fertiliser, which makes growth at the expense of flowers, or it has arisen because the wisteria has not been pruned or has been pruned incorrectly. These vigorous climbers have a habit of making masses of long, thin, non-flowering growths during summer which, if cut back in winter, will produce more of the same the following year.

To encourage a wisteria to flower, it must be rigorously spur-pruned twice a year: once in the summer, to remove all the shoots that are not required as extension growth, and again in winter to encourage side shoots. The short lengths of maturing stem that remain will produce flowering buds the following year.

1 Starting in summer, reduce all the side shoots to within five or six buds from the main branch.

2 In winter, reduce these stems further, leaving two to three buds at the base. This builds up flowering wood and it is this spur that will flower next year.

3 Some people like to prune and train their wisteria as espaliers or standards, but bear in mind that these are vigorous plants and be prepared to spend a considerable amount of time keeping the plant in shape.

roses

Up to a point roses are very forgiving. What they don't appreciate, however, is years of total neglect followed by drastic pruning into old wood that isn't really capable of producing new growth. Even with regular pruning, bush roses do become old and while a 30-year-old rose may still be flowering it will not be performing as well as a new plant. Be prepared to replace it.

Where there has been a serious attack of black spot disease, the stems of susceptible varieties will be marked. Where possible, removed affected stems during winter pruning before spores are allowed to spread in late spring. Dieback disease can be a problem with roses. It starts at the tip of the shoot and gradually moves down the stem and kills it. To control dieback, cut off diseased shoots at least 5cm (2in) below the area of stem affected.

Where older branches are being removed, cut them out as close to ground level as possible. Avoid leaving a stump. This also applies to climbing and rambler roses. If old stems that are past flowering are removed at ground level, this will encourage new basal shoots to form, which will clothe the base of the plant with foliage. This is a good way of hiding 'bare legs' and encouraging flowers to form low down on the plant. Too many stems will cause overcrowding and where crossing branches are rubbing, damage will occur unless they are thinned out.

Rosa 'New Dawn' is one of the great roses, with a particularly lovely scent.

1 Roses have alternate buds, rather than opposite pairs. This means that when you prune them, you need to make the cut above a suitable bud and sloping away from it. Always prune above a healthy bud pointing in the direction you would wish the shoot to grow. If there is no visible bud, prune 15–20cm (6–8in) above ground level. When the dormant buds break, you can prune as you wish.

2 Bush roses are usually pruned in spring. However, if your garden is windy, shortening the stems by one third of their height in early winter will reduce the risk of winds rocking the plant and loosening its roots.

3 It is important that all suckers from the rootstock are removed when they are small (the thinner, pale green shoot on this pot-grown rose is actually a sucker that has grown from the rootstock; if not removed it will eventually take over the plant). The best way to deal with suckers is to pull them off by hand. (If they are cut with secateurs, the stump that remains will regrow, producing even more suckers.) This is also necessary with standard roses, which have been grafted up the stem, and you should remove any suckers that appear on the stem below the graft.

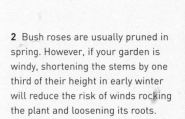

hydrangeas

The most familiar hydrangeas are the large, blowsy, mop-headed *Hydrangea macrophylla* that make a show from summer until the first frosts. Pruning is not essential for these, but the quality of the flowers will be improved if they are pruned annually.

I do not recommend deadheading of hydrangeas after flowering is finished (unless they are grown in a warm climate). The large flower heads offer some frost protection in early spring to the new buds that are high up on the stem. On top of that, in the dead of winter, their faded, papery appearance, enhanced by a light frost, can be appealing.

Pruning of mop-headed hydrangeas takes place in mid- to late spring. Cut out any thin, weak shoots as close to ground level as possible. At the same time, remove two or three of the oldest branches to encourage new basal shoots to form. Trim off the old flower heads, cutting immediately above a pair of healthy, fat buds.

There is seldom any need to prune or shape newly planted hydrangeas. Neglected plants, on the other hand, may be cut back hard, but not all in one go. Better to prune over two years or there will be no flowers during the year of cutting.

Hydrangea paniculata flowers during late summer and autumn on shoots produced that season. For large panicles of flowers, prune in late spring, removing all the previous season's growths to within 5cm (2in) of the older wood.

The deciduous climbing hydrangea *H. anomala* subsp. *petiolaris* produces its creamy-white summer flowers on the previous year's side shoots. These require little pruning, although it is a good idea to shorten any strong, outward-growing laterals after flowering has finished.

Hydrangea anomala subsp. *petiolaris* is one of Matt's favourite hardy climbers, with bronze bark that means it looks good even in winter.

buddleja

There are some plants that need to be taught manners and the butterfly bush falls into this category.

spring pruning buddleja

1 If left unpruned, buddleja will become an enormous plant within a few years, with the flowers almost out of sight at the tips of the branches and laterals.

2 Buddleja flowers in summer on the growths made that year. In spring, cut back all of the previous year's growths to within 5–10cm (2–4in) of the old wood.

3 The new stems will grow as much as 2m (6ft) in a few weeks, with large flowers at the tips of every branch. There is a lot of satisfaction to be gained from pruning this shrub and every butterfly in the area will show its appreciation by visiting your garden.

broom

Unfortunately, the spring-flowering broom (*Cytisus scoparius*) is a short-lived shrub. However, an annual pruning immediately after flowering has finished and before the black seed pods appear may extend its life. If left unpruned, it will produce masses of seed that will weaken the plant.

Pruning couldn't be simpler. Using hedge clippers, trim off all the long, thin growths that have flowered. Note that established plants do not respond to hard pruning and will show their displeasure by sulking or dying. Main branches become woody quickly and if you try pruning into old wood there will be little chance of re-growth.

dogwood

With these wonderfully showy plants, it is not the flowers or berries that are of interest but the brightly coloured bark. Colours include red (*Cornus alba*), yellow (*C. sericea* 'Flaviramea'), orange-yellow and red (*C. sanguinea* 'Winter Beauty') and purple-black (*C. alba* 'Kesselringii'). After the leaves drop in autumn, these beauties come into their own with the stems glistening in pale winter sunlight. Pruning is done in late spring, when the stems are cut to within 6–8cm (2½–3½in) of the ground. These are replaced during the growing period with new coloured shoots.

Where there is a large clump of dogwood, stems may be cut to various lengths to give an impression of tiers of colour. The following year, long growths are cut low down and short ones are pruned at a higher level.

pruning tools

John: Anne has covered the main gardening tools on pages 100–103, but here are some extra ones that are essential for pruning. These should be stored separately and kept solely for pruning plants. I have seen secateurs with blades that looked as though they had been chewed by a vine weevil on steroids! The excuse – they were the handiest thing for cutting wire. Blunt pruning tools result in wasted effort and an inferior cut that is more prone to disease.

I store my tools in a cupboard in the garage (the cars are never in the garage and I don't have a potting shed). This is what they consist of:

● folding knife
● by-pass secateurs (I don't like the anvil type with one blade – the blade presses the stem of the plant against flat metal, which can damage soft tissue in plants such as pelargoniums)
● petrol-driven or electric hedge trimmers
● long-handled loppers
● extension loppers (for pruning tall plants), with a rope-operated blade and pruning saw
● folding pruning saw
● bow saw
● hatchet (for severing tree roots)
● long-handled slasher
● chain saw (petrol)

If you have only one apple tree and a few compact shrubs, then a shoe box will probably hold all the pruning equipment you need, namely secateurs, a knife and a pruning saw. I also keep several sharpening stones, an oil can and fine files for sharpening the chain saw. I do have a small shredder to mulch up the prunings, but it is so noisy I seldom use it. A winter bonfire is much more satisfactory and disposes of diseased wood, leaving an ash rich in potash that is ideal for fruit trees. A couple of pairs of tough gloves, thick enough to stop all but the most vicious thorns, completes the inventory.

Safety

Electrically powered equipment, such as hedge trimmers, can be dangerous and should be used responsibly, as there is always the risk of cutting through the power cable. To ensure the power cuts out if the cable is severed, fit a circuit breaker. Make sure you inspect plugs, sockets and cables regularly for damage.

caring for pruning tools

I am constantly losing tools by setting them down and forgetting to pick them up again. By the time I notice their absence and find them, they are starting to rust. One solution is to store each piece of equipment in the same space so that any gap is easily noticed. Here are a few tips on how to look after your tools:

● Keep your cutting blades sharp. A blade that you treat with respect will repay you with many years of service. A whetstone and file are essential for sharpening blades. A file is used to remove notches and flattened areas of the cutting edge, not to sharpen fine blades such as secateurs and loppers. I haven't the patience or the expertise to sharpen the teeth of a hand saw, and anyway bow saw blades are cheap to replace.

● Anvil-type secateurs have only one blade and it is sharpened on both sides. By-pass pruners have two blades, which should be sharpened only on the outside away from the other blade. Unbolt the two halves of the cutters and sharpen each blade separately. Before using the whetstone, coat the upper surface with a light oil or water. As you sharpen the blade, keep applying oil or water to the whetstone. Keeping the existing angle on the blade edge, push it along the surface of the stone as though you were removing a thin sliver of cheese. Avoid forming a curved edge on the blade.

● Don't check your tools for sharpness by running the ball of your thumb along the blade. If it is sharp, you will have to clean up the blood! Instead, test it on a piece of branch.

● When buying, most of the cost of the tool should go towards the quality of the steel rather than a fancy handle, fastening clip or leather holster. English, French or Spanish steel is generally good, but rely on a good manufacturing 'name' rather than gimmicks.

● Clean tools to remove dirt after every operation and always before storing at the end of the day – a wipe with an oily cloth will usually suffice. Diseases, especially viral and bacterial problems, are easily spread from plant to plant by contaminated sap on secateurs, knives and saw blades. Paraffin oil will remove all but the most hardened sap stains. Every few weeks, apply a few drops of light oil to moving parts, such as springs, pulleys and bolts.

● Rub wooden handles with an oily cloth a few times a year to prevent them splintering.

Keeping pruning tools clean helps to prevent the spread of disease, and keeping them sharp makes any pruning job easier.

supports

Bob: Pruning is only part of the job, though; in order to get our plants to the 'right' shape with flowering or fruiting growths where we desire them, we must also train them. This means removing the unwanted, then either coaxing, bending or forcing the wanted into place. The sooner this is done the easier it is, as younger, thinner growths are more pliant and become tougher the older they get. This requires an eye for the way things look best – and a delicacy of touch combined with firm ruthlessness. It also requires ties, preferably broad, rigid supports or a frame to tie to, strong enough to withstand the wind as well as the weight of the growth and all its leaves, flowers and fruits. And even if we don't actively wish to train we may still need to support many plants.

Why support?

We support plants for many reasons, although in nature they must find their own supports or do without. We support trees in their formative years to keep them upright until their new roots have established and can take over the job for themselves. Some trees are grafted onto such weak roots that we have to support the tops all their lives. Extra support is necessary where we expect the branches to be trained in odd directions and then carry heavy crops, and where the limbs of trees are being trained into unnatural shapes such as espaliers, fans or cordons. Other softer growing plants, such as tomatoes, brambles and lax bedding plants, are supported mainly to keep their flowers or fruits off the ground and to separate the growths from one another so that each receives ample light and air. We may even support individual fruits, such as melons, to help increase their size.

Stakes and posts

The simplest support is a stake or post driven into the ground beside a young tree and tied in place. It has been shown that a short stake at knee height is quite sufficient to keep a tree stable and prevent rocking and root disturbance. Taller stakes are usually no better because they prevent the trunk developing fully (although they may be desirable for grafted trees with weak roots or those prone to breaking at the graft).

To prevent root damage, it is best to put the stake in the ground before the tree. I usually dig the hole first and hammer in the post. Then I put the tree's roots in place around the support, carefully filling with soil and firming it down and finally tying the tree to the support (see page 194). Driving in the support after planting risks spearing the roots; tying the two together before filling the hole may prevent the soil from packing down properly, leaving the tree (and its roots) suspended. Ideally, place the support some distance from the trunk and insert a piece of packing between the two, held by the tie, to ensure the tie does not pull the tree off vertical.

Rather than a single stake or post parallel to the trunk, some gardeners prefer one driven in at an angle to the ground and tied where it crosses the trunk. Others prefer two posts with a crossbar tied to the trunk – this is certainly the sturdiest for windy conditions or for trees with heavy heads or crops. It is also the safest to erect after the tree is in the ground, because the posts can be spaced some way from the trunk and therefore away from most of the roots.

On a smaller scale, the stake and tie method is also suited to soft fruit bushes, tall shrubs, tomatoes, aubergines and sweet peppers, standard roses, dahlias and show chrysanthemums. Often much less care is taken over staking these smaller plants, when in fact they need more support. They also swell fast and need frequent tie adjustment.

Choosing posts and ties

Stakes and posts are usually made from untreated timber. Treated wood is not only unnecessary, since in most cases the support is temporary, but it can harm the plant's roots. To prevent fungal infections, it is a good idea to remove stakes and posts as soon as they become superfluous. For permanent or long-term use, it makes sense to use metal, plastic or even concrete supports. For easy replacement, do not fix wooden posts directly into the ground, but insert them in pieces of plastic gutter pipe fixed in the ground. Once the original support rots, it can be easily pulled out and a new one slipped in. For smaller plants, bamboo canes and broom sticks are the usual supports. Many gardeners tend to buy long canes of the largest size in bulk, which they break up into plenty of smaller, shorter ones over the years. Avoid using metal supports on delicate or valued plants as it chills and burns in frosts and heat. Instead, fix the plants to canes and tie these to the metal support.

Ties need to hold the plant closely to the support to prevent rubbing, but not so tight as to strangle it. Broader softer materials, therefore, are better than wire or string. Proper strip ties are available, but many gardeners prefer to use old tights and nylon stockings or rubber inner tubes, cut into strips, from bicycles. Whichever ties you choose, make sure you check them every few months and adjust them regularly, especially after strong winds. Commercial ties have a rubber or plastic block to act as a spacer and shock absorber, but you might find that a chunk of dense plastic foam packaging does the job just as well.

Smaller softer plants, such as tomatoes and roses, are often tied with wire to canes or supporting wires. To prevent wire cutting into shoots, either pad the stem of the plant with a strip of cloth or wrap the tying wire in plastic beforehand. It is far kinder to tie soft plant growths with woollen twine, thin strips of cloth, raffia or natural string than to use wire or plastic string that cuts in more and never rots if neglected.

Canes or wires?

There is a long-running debate as to whether tying plants directly to supporting wires is better than fixing them to canes and tying the canes to the supporting wires. As I've already said, wire can rub and cut into plants, especially if roughened by rust, and in cold weather metal certainly gets very cold compared to cane. Therefore it is probably better, and neater, to fix bamboo canes to supporting wires for long-term use, such as on fan-trained trees and trained ornamentals, or for tender specimens. I wouldn't bother with canes on grape vines or brambles, where the shoots are replaced every other year anyway – tying to the wires should be satisfactory and seems to work well enough.

Frame supports for espaliers or cordons

While most trees and shrubs just need to be staked to keep them upright, others need a more rigid frame to keep all the limbs in their correct place, as well as to support the crop. The surface area of a row of cordon-trained apples is enough to propel a large ship, so sturdy supports are essential. Trained fruitd such as these are usually supported on very strong wires (possibly with canes as well) tensioned between braced posts. These need to be very substantial, especially in windy areas. Steel or concrete constructions are sensible and long lasting; softwood ones are far too short term.

Wall supports for climbers

Walls and fences can make good places to grow plants, as they benefit from the microclimate. However, unless they are self-clingers such as Virginia creeper or ivy, they need support. This might be fixed either to the wall or fence or to posts in front of it. The frame does not need to be quite as strong as a freestanding arrangement, because of the shelter of the wall, but it still needs to be sturdy.

Raspberry canes spaced and supported by wire.

Arrangements of lath, cane or cane-and-wire supports are ideal here. In most cases, we do not want the plants to be actually touching the wall or fence but held a finger's length or so away from it where they are exposed to more air and less direct heating. Special screw-in fixings called vine eyes are available for supporting wires on walls or fences, although they are often too short and the plants end up too close to the wall or fence. A better solution is to fix vertical wooden battens on the wall or fence and to fit wires or crossbars onto these.

Supports for brambles, grapes, roses and similar

Whereas trained fruit trees need very substantial supports to hold the weight of their fruit, brambles, grape vines and weak climbers, including many ornamentals and swag-trained or lax roses, require less rigid supports because their supple stems need little forcing into shape. They are usually trained directly onto wires fixed up to about shoulder height between braced end posts. Raspberries, being the weakest of the bramble family, are either wound around a single strained wire or held between a pair of horizontal wires a foot or so apart.

Rosa 'Cecile Brunner' on wires against a wall.

Trellises for climbers

Whereas fruiting plants are usually trained – and therefore
need an open regular framework of canes or wires –
ornamental climbers such as honeysuckle and jasmine are
mostly left to grow as they wish within their allocated space.
Most often they are given a piece of wooden or plastic trellis
to grow through, usually fixed on top of an existing fence or
wall. Trellis makes an excellent support for the climber,
provided it is fixed securely to a substantial framework, and is
itself sturdy enough to withstand buffeting by the wind. It is
foolish to fix trellis to an old or insecure fence, but if that is
all you have it is probably best to erect separate posts and
rails to carry the trellis.

Supports for container plants

Most gardeners use canes, stiff wires or plastic rods as
supports for container plants, but the big danger here is the
risk of ramming the support through the roots. Single
supports also work loose and wobble. Therefore it is much
more secure and sensible to use three lighter canes in a tripod
arrangement. For small, delicate or young plants, such as
sweet peas, especially ones grown under cover, a twiggy stem
cut from a bush offers more support than a neat, clean cane. I
grow my own bamboo canes and use them for this purpose
without removing the feathering.

Supports for herbaceous plants

The stems of herbaceous plants are especially prone to
flopping, but it is difficult to support them individually
because they come in clumps. Many gardeners insert canes
around the perimeter and tie the canes together with string
when the clump is part grown. When the stems mature they
hide the supports. Others prefer to use special, usually green
coloured, plastic hoops and rings instead. Old wire baskets do
a similar job but are considered rather naff.

This *Clematis armandii* may soon need more space – gorgeous scent, though.

Supports for tomatoes, peas, runner beans and melons

Tomato plants are usually tied individually to canes with garden string. However, where a short row with several plants is grown to produce a heavy crop, they are better supported from a wooden crossbar on a couple of posts. This can also support a temporary plastic cover when the plants are small or during rainy weather. Where tomato plants are tied with string, it's kinder to wind the string around the stem in a spiral fashion and fasten it to a leaf stem, rather than fastening to the main stem.

Peas are traditionally grown up twiggy stems, cut from hazel or other bushes. However, today they are more usually grown on nets suspended from stakes. As most climbers prefer a rigid support to a flexible one, plastic nets for peas should be fitted very tautly. I prefer galvanised chicken netting as it is more rigid, lasts forever and any unremovable haulm can be burnt off at the end of the season.

Runner beans grow very tall unless topped. They too prefer rigid supports rather than strings, especially lax ones. A wigwam of rigid canes is much better than one made of strings. A traditional top, consisting of an old bicycle wheel, spaces the canes or strings further out most conveniently.

Melons (and other cucurbits) grow much bigger if they are supported while they swell rather than if they are left hanging. Pieces of fine net or cloth, tied to supports, can be used as pouches for ripening fruits. If the fruits rest on the soil, or on metal, glass or plastic they may rot, so place a flat piece of untreated wood underneath them.

Left: Sweet peas on a wicker wigwam – pretty, but not a very practical design! Sweet peas must be picked or deadheaded regularly, as any setting seed will stop the plant flowering and the wigwam will make this task more difficult. However, if you are prepared to put in the effort, the results are eye-catching.
Right: Runner beans and *Rosa* 'Madame Alfred Carrière' both benefit from support in the kitchen garden.

Chapter 9

propagation

John: When it comes to job satisfaction in the garden, propagation has to be the most rewarding work. I never fail to be impressed however often I manage to produce plants. Whether it is by sowing seeds that are smaller than dust or rooting a leafless stem, the marvel of the resulting plant remains constant.

Turning begonia leaves, stems of shrubs such as hebe or whole branches of willow into plants with roots is not difficult even for the amateur gardener. It is a rewarding job and after your first few successes you, like me, will be hooked, spending the rest of your gardening life propagating plants by every conceivable means.

There is no need to become big-headed and boastful – nature has been doing a good job for millions of years, whether by wind, water, animals and birds spreading seeds far and wide or plants spreading naturally by root, sucker and stolon.

The easily propagated plants can be found growing in margarine tubs and yoghurt pots at church fêtes and school sales. They root naturally, are lifted complete with roots and are potted up for sale. They include rampant spreaders such as dead-nettle (*Lamium*) and periwinkle (*Vinca*).

Towards the end of this chapter (see pages 251–54), Bob has given guidance as to which forms of propagation are best for which plants, but here first of all are the details of the different methods.

sowing

The principles of seed sowing remain the same whether it's a row of carrots, a display of summer annuals, a garden lawn, an oak tree or a 50 acre field of wheat. The secret of success is in the detail.

In the wild, seeds ripen on the plant, fall to the ground and, if the conditions are favourable, some will germinate. The 'wings' on the seeds of sycamore allow them to spiral down, carried by the wind, to well beyond the spread of the tree. The seeds of fleshy berries eaten by birds pass through undigested and can be deposited miles away from where they were growing.

In the wild, not every seed will survive. Many will 'fall by the wayside', and even those that do germinate may be eaten or damaged and never grow to be mature plants.

We can, however, with common sense and artificial conditions, improve the odds and increase the percentage of seeds that become seedlings.

The essential requirements for germination are heat, air and water. Moist compost allows water to enter the seed and mobilise the enzymes, but only when the air and compost are warm. Since oxygen is essential, avoid waterlogged conditions where the pockets of air are replaced by water.

Although *Verbena bonariensis* is a perennial, if the seed is sown in early spring, it may flower in the first year.

Sowing outdoors

Sowing seed in the open ground, where there is no form of overhead protection, leaves the gardener (and the seed!) at the mercy of the elements. Successful germination will often depend on the gardener's patience and knowledge of when the conditions are right for sowing.

The weather will dictate the best time to sow. A delay of a few days to allow the soil to warm up will result in quicker germination and sturdy seedlings. In colder northern latitudes you may have to sow several weeks later than in warmer areas. Remember, patience.

Cold, wet, sticky soil is a recipe for disaster. Proper soil cultivation (see pages 140–41) should reduce the soil to a fine tilth without large lumps or stones. To test whether your soil is ready for cultivation, squeeze a handful of soil into a ball with both hands, as if you were making a snowball, and drop it onto the ground. If it breaks up and crumbles, the ground is ready to work and rake. If the ball stays solid or breaks into two pieces, it is not yet ready.

To bring forward sowing dates, cover and protect areas of soil with glass or clear plastic cloches or a cold frame. This should encourage the soil to dry out and warm up ready for planting.

Weeds are a nuisance for small seedling plants. Every time you cultivate the soil, you bring more weed seeds to the surface. As they germinate, they compete for light, water and food, smothering the small seedlings around them. There are two ways to reduce the problem of weeds and give your seedlings a head start. After the final raking, leave the seed bed for a week to allow any annual weed seeds to germinate. Then, burn off the weeds with a contact weedkiller such as paraquat or a flame gun and sow the seeds with a minimum of soil disturbance. Another method of dealing with weeds, and this one is slightly more risky, is to sow the seed immediately after raking and, just before it germinates, apply a contact weedkiller. When using chemicals, make sure you are properly protected with waterproof clothes, gloves and a face mask (see page 112).

Ox-eye daisies (*Leucanthemum vulgare*) will self-seed year after year and are ideal for wild meadow gardens.

sowing outside

1 Before sowing rows of seeds, use string and pegs to mark out the line of each row.

2 Use the back of a rake to excavate a shallow furrow (known as a drill) in your prepared soil. As a rule of thumb, fine seed should be sown close to the surface, larger seed should be sown more deeply, so the depth of the drill can be varied accordingly. A broad bean seed, which is about the size of a thumbnail, can be planted 3–5cm (1½–2in) deep, whereas fine seed can almost lie on the surface, covered with only a thin layer of fine soil.

3 A clever tip is to pour boiling water along the open drill a few hours before sowing. Not only will this kill any weed seeds in the ground, but it should also warm up the soil and encourage your sown seeds to swell.

4 Sow seed thinly and evenly along the row, following the instructions on the seed packet. Carrots and other root crops, which are not going to be transplanted, should be sown at their finished spacing. With most other plants you will be thinning them out in due course so you can be more generous with the seed.

5 Rake the soil back into the drill to cover the seeds. Water with a fine rose on the watering can so as not to wash the seeds away.

tip for helping germination along

● Many seeds are protected with a hard shell, which makes water absorption (and therefore germination) difficult. To speed up germination of hard seeds such as sweet peas, prepare the seed beforehand by chipping or pre-soaking.

● Chipping involves scraping a portion of the hard, outer coating of the seed with sandpaper, a nail file or a sharp knife to allow water to penetrate. Make sure you choose an area of the seed coat away from the 'eye' (the scar visible on the outer coat of larger seeds).

● Alternatively, soak the seed in aired water – that is, water that has been left to reach room temperature – for up to two hours. Once it starts to swell, sow immediately in compost. Do not allow the seed to dry out before sowing.

● Pre-chilling is another way to speed up germination – especially of the seeds of some trees. Seeds naturally fall from their parent plant on to warm soil in autumn, then lie dormant during cold winter weather prior to germination in spring. To simulate these conditions, sow the seed onto moistened seed compost and place the container in a clear polythene bag. Seal and store for three to four days at a temperature of 15–18°C (60–65°F). Then place the bag in the refrigerator for the period recommended on the seed packet – it varies from species to species, but 5–10 days is a rough guide. At the end of this period, the seeds should be convinced that they have just emerged from a cold winter and be ready to go into action.

Sowing under cover

There are clear advantages to sowing seeds in a greenhouse: you (and the seeds) are not at the mercy of the elements, temperatures can be controlled and the compost kept uniformly moist by watering, and weeding is kept to a minimum as bagged compost is weed free. Compost for sowing seeds is available as peat-based or peat-free formulas. Both sorts should be moisture retentive and free draining. On no account use a potting compost high in fertiliser for sowing seeds. Seedlings have little need for nutrients until they are potted up or planted out and too many nutrients will force them into soft growth with little root.

Of course, growing seeds under glass is not without its problems. Pests, such as slugs and snails, can cause havoc in the greenhouse, munching their way through soft stems, and these need to be baited or trapped on a daily basis. Seedling diseases, such as damping off, need to be kept in check as they can destroy a pot or tray of seedlings within days of germination.

sowing under cover

1 With fine seed, choose a peat-based or peat-free compost suitable for seeds. Fill the container or seed tray to the top with compost and firm the surface lightly with a wooden block. Water the compost by standing the container in a tray of water. If possible, do this the day before sowing.

The compost should be moist, not wet, when you sow. Open the packet of seeds and pour some into the palm of your hand. If the seeds are very fine, add half a teaspoonful of dry, silver sand to the packet, shake to mix the seeds and sow in the usual way.

2 Sprinkle the seeds evenly over the surface of the compost. Firm lightly with a wooden block, dusting off any that stick to the wood. For fine seeds, don't cover with compost. Water the compost by standing the container in a tray of tepid water. Don't water from above as this will disturb the seeds. Cover with a sheet of glass or clear polythene to retain moisture.

Germination times vary. Cress, for example, will germinate on a warm windowsill within 3–5 days of sowing. Other seeds, including many species of tree, may not germinate for as long as 6 months, or they will appear erratically in ones and twos over a period of 12–18 months. Once again, your best friend is patience.

3 With larger seeds such as marrow or cucumber, sow one or two to a pot to give the seedlings plenty of room.

When planting seeds, always read the packet carefully for planting depths and optimum conditions. Depth of sowing, in particular, is critical to success, with smaller seeds requiring only the thinnest covering of compost or soil. Sowing depth need not be so precise with larger seeds, such as peas and beans, which have plenty of food reserves within them until they reach the surface and light. Also pay attention to where is the best place to germinate trays of seed. Some seeds like to be kept in total darkness until germination. Most, however, need light – but it should be subdued, to avoid leaf scorch.

Saving and storing seed

Many seed producers package their seeds in airtight, waterproof packets. However, not all the seeds need to be sown at the same time. Packets of lettuce, for example, may be resealed and sown in batches every fortnight throughout the growing season. Storage periods for packaged seeds vary from plant to plant, with viability rates dropping dramatically after the second or third year. Celery, marrow and cabbage seed will remain viable for four to five years after opening, whereas the seed of parsnip, onion and sweetcorn is not worth keeping after one year.

Bought seed is, of course, convenient. However, many gardeners like to harvest their own seed as well. If you plan to do this (and it can save you a lot of money), make sure you follow these basic rules. Always harvest seed when it is ripe – you can tell because the seed pod will be brown or black and so will the seed. Timing is critical here, since some plants disperse their seed as soon as it is ripe. Don't leave it until the seed case starts to rot on the plant. If possible, harvest the seed on a dry, sunny day.

Use paper bags to hold the seed after collection. Label the bag straightaway with the full name of the plant, placing another label with the same information inside the bag. As soon as possible, dry the seed indoors on a sheet of paper and separate any pods, debris, bits of casing or broken seed. Store the seed in an airtight container. The black, plastic containers that camera film comes in are ideal for storing small seed. Once again, label inside and out. See also page 251.

cuttings

I have been propagating plants from cuttings since I was fifteen. As a boy, chrysanthemums and cacti were my passion. In the intervening years, I have never lost that original sense of amazement and pleasure every time I manage to root pieces of plant. Many plants are easy to root from stem cuttings, but there is more than one method, depending on whether you are propagating from softwood or hardwood cuttings.

Whichever method you follow, avoid propagating from cuttings that are diseased or infested with pests. Your mission is to increase your stock of a particular plant, not to spread pests and diseases that may destroy other plants.

Softwood cuttings

Propagating from softwood cuttings is the technique commonly used for many shrubs and some climbers. These cuttings root easily, especially if they are cultivated in a propagating frame with some bottom heat and high humidity (see pages 256–57). The best time to separate them from the parent shrub is in late spring or early summer, before the shoots become woody and firm: 'softwood' means precisely that, using the current year's growth.

Many gardeners use a hormone rooting powder or gel to encourage cuttings to root more quickly, especially hard-to-root plants such as camellias and rhododendrons. To prevent a potential spread of disease from one batch of plants to another, avoid dipping cuttings directly into the full container of hormone powder. Instead, use small amounts of hormone at a time, decanting it into a clean dish.

The cutting will need a good root system before it is ready to be potted on. Try not to disturb the roots while they are forming. Wait for small white roots to appear at the base of the container and leave the cutting in the container for at least another seven to ten days to enable them to develop further. Once the root system is established, the cuttings can be separated and potted as individual plants.

softwood cuttings

1 The best time to remove cuttings is in the morning, before the leaves start to transpire. Choose a soft, new growth, such as a young side shoot, and remove it from the parent plant either with a sharp knife or by pulling away the entire shoot with the fingertips. Make sure the 'heel' from the main stem is intact. Place the cutting in a sealed, clear polythene bag and store in a cool, shaded room until ready to plant (preferably not more than a couple of hours). Cuttings quickly lose moisture and they will wilt if they are not kept in a moist atmosphere.

2 Prepare the cutting using a sharp knife or a razor blade by trimming it immediately below a leaf joint or node – this is the area with the highest concentration of plant hormones. With most plants, you will end up with a cutting 5–10cm (2–4in) long. Cut or pull off the lower leaves, taking care not to damage the stem or to leave a stump of leaf stalk. Failure to do this will cause the leaves to rot when you insert the cutting into the compost, killing the cutting before it has time to root. Nip out the growing tip of the cutting if there is a flower bud forming.

3 If you are using hormone rooting powder, dip the cutting in it and shake off any excess.

4 Choose a free-draining compost without nutrients. A homemade mixture of equal parts of peat and coarse horticultural grit will be every bit as successful as a proprietary mixture. Fill a seed tray or shallow flowerpot with compost to within 2cm (1in) of the rim. The compost should be moist, not wet. To check whether it is sufficiently moist, remove a handful from the bag and squeeze it in your hand. If it retains its shape, it is fine. If water drips out as you squeeze, it is too wet.

Use a dibber (I use a pencil) to make a hole first, ensuring it isn't too deep for the cutting. The base of the cutting should rest on the base of the hole without an air pocket and the lowest leaves should be clear of the compost. Insert the cuttings in the compost, spacing them 5cm (2in) apart.

5 Firm the compost by hand and water from overhead using a fine rose. Cover with the propagator lid or a clear polythene bag secured with string or a rubber band.

John's tip for taking heather cuttings
You may wish to try this method if you want to root a considerable number of heathers. It works a treat for me.

Fill a seed tray to within 2cm (1in) of the rim with moist rooting compost. Remove enough short (5cm/2in) lengths of heather, taking them from current growths. Nip out the growing tip of each cutting with your fingernails. There is no need to trim off any leaves. Lay the cuttings horizontally on the surface of the compost and dampen with water through a fine rose.

Cut a sheet of clear, horticultural glass slightly smaller than the dimensions of the top of the seed tray. Place it directly on top of the cuttings, pressing down gently to make sure the cuttings are in contact with the compost. Cover the glass with a sheet of newspaper. After a few days, remove the paper and place the tray of cuttings in subdued light, away from strong sunlight. Within a few weeks you will see, through the sheet of glass, small, thread-like, white roots appearing on the surface of the compost. You can now remove the glass and pot up the individual rooted cuttings in pots of fine compost – this time they are inserted vertically – and water them in. Maintain high humidity by covering them with clear polythene for the first few days. And all at no cost.

Semi-ripe cuttings

Semi-ripe cuttings are sometimes referred to as semi-hardwood. Either description is accurate, since the material that is taken for propagation is current-season growth that has started to firm up and become woody at the base. Semi-ripe cuttings are normally taken from shrubs, and the work can be done any time from the middle of summer through until early autumn.

The instructions for taking semi-ripe cuttings are similar to those for softwood cuttings (see opposite).

Hardwood cuttings

As with softwood cuttings, the name is self-explanatory: in this instance the cuttings, though still from the current year's growth of shrubs and some trees, are taken later in the season – in late autumn or winter, when the stems have hardened up.

The recipe for propagating hardwood cuttings is as follows: a dash of common sense, a pinch of know-how and a dollop of patience. Expense doesn't come into it at all. For more details, see page 238.

semi-ripe cuttings

1 Choose a soft, pliable, new growth, such as a young side shoot, making the cutting 7.5–15cm (3–6in) – slightly longer than a softwood cutting . Once again, try to keep the 'heel' intact as this encourages the firm wood to root more quickly. To reduce transpiration from plants with large leaves such as hydrangeas and laurels, cut each leaf in half with a sharp knife. Remove the growing tip from each cutting with your fingertips (this will encourage it to form side shoots as soon as it is rooted and starting to grow).

2 Dip in hormone powder or gel.

3 Use a dibber or a pencil to make a hole first, deep enough so that the base of the cutting rests on the base of the hole, with the lowest leaves clear of the compost.

4 Insert into the rooting compost as for softwood cuttings and cover with clear polythene or a propagator lid. Water as necessary, but avoid overwatering to the level that the compost remains wet and heavy. Check regularly for signs of disease and remove any dead or dying leaves. Rooting times vary, with some plants taking four to five weeks and others needing as long as six months, only showing progress the following spring. Young cuttings should be over-wintered in a cool greenhouse or garden frame. Avoid strong, direct sunlight.

hardwood cuttings

1 Select a fully ripened, firm stem of current year's growth. The length of the cutting will depend on the amount of growth made during the year, but it should be between 20–30cm (8–12in). Where there has been sufficient growth, it will be possible to make two or more hardwood cuttings from each branch. Prepare the cutting by trimming the base straight across immediately below a node or leaf joint. The top sloping cut should be made above a bud and angled downwards away from it. Try to get into the habit of making the top cut as a sloping cut and the bottom cut as a straight cut, as this should help you to identify the top end from the bottom and prevent you from planting the cutting upside down. Cut or pick off the lower thorns of plants such as roses and gooseberries to make them easier to handle. With evergreens, remove the lower leaves.

2 You can either root your hardwood cuttings in a container in the cold frame or plant them directly into the ground, usually in a nursery bed (see page 256). There is no need for hormone rooting powder with hardwood cuttings. I have always rooted hardy plants outside in the open ground in a sheltered part of the garden. Dig a trench 15cm (6in) deep with one side vertical. If your soil is heavy, line the base of the trench with a 2.5cm (1in) layer of coarse grit or sand to assist drainage.

3 Place the cuttings vertically, 15cm (6in) apart...

4 ...in a line along the side of the trench with the bases in contact with the grit.

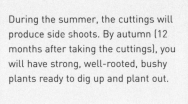

5 Backfill the trench...

6 ...and tread the topsoil around the cuttings, taking care not to damage the parts of the cuttings that are above the ground. Use a fork or a rake to loosen the surface of the soil, then apply a deep mulch of bark or compost to deter weeds.

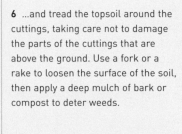

7 These cuttings can now be left to develop.

During the summer, the cuttings will produce side shoots. By autumn (12 months after taking the cuttings), you will have strong, well-rooted, bushy plants ready to dig up and plant out.

Leaf cuttings

Propagating by leaf is an efficient way of increasing your stock of house plants. *Begonia rex*, mother-in-law's tongue (*Sansevieria* spp.) and Cape primrose (*Streptocarpus* spp.) are all easy to root and are capable of producing many young plants from a single leaf. They may be rooted at any time of year, but in late spring they will root more quickly.

For mother-in-law's tongue, cut the leaf lengthways into sections 5–8cm (2–3in) long. Dust the lower cut edge of each section with hormone rooting powder or gel and insert upright in a tray of moist cutting compost. Position the tray away from strong sunlight. The cuttings from the base of the leaf will root more quickly than those close to the leaf tip. After a period of up to three months plantlets will form at the base of each section of leaf where the vein is in contact with the compost.

leaf cuttings

1 Select a healthy, unblemished leaf (here, *Begonia rex*) and remove it from the plant.

2 Remove the stalk from the leaf, then cut through the main veins on the underside of the leaf using a sharp knife.

3 Fill a seed tray with cutting compost. Water lightly with a fine rose and place the leaf on the moist compost, underside down. To make sure the cut veins are in contact with the compost, peg the leaf down flat using u-shaped pieces of fine wire, or weigh it down with stones. Keep the tray away from direct sunlight.

4 Plantlets will form at the cut veins, but be patient, as in some cases this can take months (this picture shows the begonias at six weeks).

5 When the plantlets are well rooted (here after about three months), they may be lifted and potted up.

Cape primrose leaves may also be cut lengthways. With a sharp knife, cut along either side of the main, central vein to give two leaf portions. Discard the central vein. Dust the cut edge of each leaf portion with hormone rooting powder or gel. Insert the cut edge into a tray of cutting compost. Keep the compost moist, but avoid damping the foliage of the streptocarpus as the fine hairs on the leaf's surface tend to rot easily. Eventually, little plantlets will form all along the base of the leaf. Again, be patient, because this can take anything from 8–20 weeks depending on the time of year.

Leaves of African violets (*Saintpaulia* spp.) are propagated without removing the leaf's stalk. Healthy, fully grown leaves may be rooted at any time of year. Cut the leaf off the parent plant with as long a stem as possible. Fill a container with rooting compost, having added one part grit to every five parts of compost to ensure good drainage. Make a hole in the compost with a dibber or pencil just off centre. Trim the end of the stalk, making a clean, straight cut. Take care not to bruise the soft stalk.

I don't use rooting powder for African violets, simply because I have found that they don't need it. Insert the leaf stalk upright, keeping the leaf slightly above the surface of the compost and facing into the pot to leave space for the new plants. Within six weeks, new plants will have formed on the surface. These may be separated and potted on.

rooting a cutting in a jar of water

● Most people have, at sometime in their life, rooted a cutting in a jar or glass of tap water. Many plants including pelargoniums root within weeks. Once the roots have formed, pot the young plant into compost, taking care not to damage the soft roots. Keep the compost wet until the roots spread out and the plant starts to grow.

Leaf bud cuttings

This type of cutting comprises a full leaf attached to part of the plant stem with a growth bud in the axil of the leaf where the stem and leaf stalk join. This method is most likely to succeed with camellias. The cuttings are taken in summer from current year's growth that has started to firm up.

Cut the stem immediately above a leaf with a healthy bud, angling the cut down and away from the bud. Make a horizontal cut 2.5cm (1in) below the leaf. Split the stem cutting lengthways, leaving it the same length but half the thickness, to make a larger wound from which roots will sprout. Dip the stem in rooting powder or gel and insert it in moist cutting compost. Position the leaf at, or just above, the surface. Place the pot in a heated propagating case and spray regularly with a fine mist of aired (i.e. room-temperature) rainwater. Where there is no propagating case, cover the pot with a clear polythene bag and place in a warm, shaded position. In the case of camellias, the cutting should be well rooted within three months. Take care when potting it up, as the roots will be brittle at this stage. Camellias hate lime, so use an ericaceous compost for potting.

The same method is successful with mahonia, especially if the cuttings are taken in early autumn. Cut the large, spiny leaf in half to reduce transpiration, but don't split the stem.

Root cuttings

A simple and very effective way to increase your stock of some plants is to propagate from root cuttings. The best time to propagate a plant from root cuttings is when the plant is dormant, ideally between late autumn and late winter. When digging up clump-forming herbaceous perennials, such as phlox and acanthus, it is practical to wash off the soil before removing the roots for propagation. This is also a good time to divide the clumps (see opposite). When propagating large trees, such as *Paulownia tomentosa*, it is often impractical to remove the parent plant to take root cuttings. Instead, you will have to dig down into the soil to find the young roots. In the case of the shrub *Chaenomeles*, take portions of young root from close to the centre of the rootball.

root cuttings

1 Dig up the parent plant and wash off the soil to expose the roots. Remove as many young, healthy roots as you need, as long as you don't kill the parent plant! Use a sharp knife to make a clean cut. Ideally, choose roots that are pencil thick; thinner, thread-like roots can be propagated but in a different way (see below). Store the roots in a labelled polythene bag until you are ready to use them, which should ideally be no more than a couple of hours. Replant the parent plant as soon as possible, firm it in and water to settle the soil around its roots.

To prepare the roots, remove any thin side roots and put to one side. Cut the remaining roots into sections 7.5–10cm (3–4in) long. You will need to know which end of the root cutting is the top and which is the bottom, so cut the top end (closest to the crown of the plant) straight across and the bottom end at an angle. Thin roots should be cut into shorter lengths, 5–7.5cm (2–3in) long. Dust the cut ends of each root cutting with flowers of sulphur or a fungicidal powder to reduce the risk of fungal disease.

2 Fill a pot with a mixture of free-draining rooting compost and grit. With the aid of a dibber or pencil, insert the cuttings vertically, 5cm (2in) apart. The top (straight cut) end should be level with the surface of the compost. Plant any small, thin lengths of root separately in a seed tray of cutting compost. Lay the fine roots horizontally 5cm (2in) apart on the surface of the compost, lightly cover with compost and water from a fine rose.

Place the root cuttings in a cold frame or in a sheltered position outdoors over the winter months. In spring, the cuttings will have produced more roots and the adventitious buds will have produced shoots and leaves. By summer, the plants will be well rooted and ready for potting into a compost containing nutrients.

division

Clump-forming plants, such as herbaceous perennials, and some alpines that produce more than one stem at ground level, may be divided to produce several plants complete with roots, crown and growth buds. This method is not suitable for increasing your stock of single stem plants – the Oriental poppy (*Papaver orientale*), for example, cannot be divided but should be propagated by root cuttings (see left).

There are two times when division is most practical – early spring (when growth is just about to start) and late autumn (when the plant's foliage is dying down for the winter). With plants that come into growth early in spring, such as hostas and agapanthus, I prefer to divide in autumn when there is less risk of damaging the new shoots. Clump-forming perennials with fine roots, on the other hand, such as asters, polyanthus and gentians, are easy to tease apart and don't suffer from being lifted out of the ground in early spring. Choose a day when the soil is moist. For more details, see page 241.

Border irises that produce rhizomes (thick, fleshy roots) may be divided in summer after they have finished flowering. As the plants become old, the leaves and flowers form a circle away from the centre of the plant. The rhizomes are easy to see because they tend to grow close to the surface where they are exposed to sunlight. Dig up the plant, exposing the roots. Using a sharp knife, cut away the old woody part of the root and discard it. This leaves the young portion closest to the leaves. Trim the fan of leaves to 15cm (6in) and replant or pot up, keeping the rhizomes at soil level.

Some house plants lend themselves to division. We have already discussed propagating mother-in-law's tongue by leaf cuttings (see page 239). However, these plants can also be propagated by division, especially as they mature and naturally form a clump in the pot, with numerous leaves growing directly out of the compost on fleshy roots. When you come to repot the parent plant, it is a good time to tease out some of the rooted offsets and cut them from the main plant. They can then be planted up separately in pots.

dividing clump-forming herbaceous perennials

1 Dig up the clump and, where possible, tease it apart by hand.

2 For congested clumps, you may have to resort to using two garden forks to separate the roots. I have never been very successful using this method, but try it yourself. Push two digging forks into the centre of the clump, back to back, and lever the roots apart without causing the plant too much damage.

3 If necessary, use a sharp spade or hatchet to cut the clump into several pieces, taking care not to damage the growth buds.

Left: *Uvularia grandiflora pallida*, **a beautiful spring flower for moist woodland areas, can be propagated by division in early spring.**

4 The youngest, healthiest roots are the ones towards the edge of the clump, so try not to damage these. The centre of the clump, which is the oldest part of the plant, will have become woody with old roots and this should be discarded.

5 Plant the divided clumps at the same depth as before, directly in the soil or in containers of potting compost. Water thoroughly to settle the soil around the roots.

layering

There are many methods of layering, all of which are achievable for the home gardener. The most common is simple layering, which nature has been doing forever.

Simple layering

There are many plants that, with a little encouragement, can be rooted by simple layering. The big advantage is that the resulting rooted layer is usually a significant size. It is particularly useful for propagating difficult-to-root plants, such as rhododendron, witch hazel (*Hamamelis* spp.) and daphne.

Simple layering may be undertaken at any time of the year, but rooting is usually speeded up if the layer is made when the plant is actively growing – typically, during spring or summer.

The age of the shrub or tree isn't important, as long as you select a young branch that is no more than two seasons old. Older wood may not root at all, or it could take a long time to form roots.

Mound layering or stool layering

Mound layering (also known as stool layering) is an easy, albeit slow, way to propagate woody plants such as weigela, philadelphus, gooseberry and blackcurrant. This method is most reliable with youngish plants, as older ones may not produce new shoots at ground level.

In winter, cut the shrub down to 45cm (18in). The following year, allow all the shoots to grow until winter and then prune them to 2.5cm (1in) above ground level. In spring, lots of shoots will commence growing. When the shoots reach 15cm (6in) high, cover them over with a mound of well-cultivated soil to which sand or grit has been added. Leave only the tips of the shoots exposed. As the shoots grow during the spring and summer, mound up more soil around them (in a similar way to earthing up potatoes) until the mound reaches a height of 25–30cm (10–12in). In autumn, when you remove the soil, you will see that each shoot has produced roots. These can now be cut off from the parent plant, leaving a 2.5cm (1in)

stump behind. The rooted layers may be planted in containers or planted out in the garden to grow on for a season. If necessary, repeat the mounding practice the following spring, when additional shoots will have formed.

Drop layering or plunge layering

This is the opposite of mound layering. It involves digging up the parent plant, but there is less chance of the soil drying out during a dry summer. Drop layering is most suited to heaths (*Erica* spp.), heathers (*Calluna* spp.) and *Gaultheria mucronata*.

Dig up the parent plant in spring or early autumn. Enlarge the planting hole to accommodate the entire plant (shoots and all) and replant it, leaving only the tips of the shoots above ground level. Spread the buried shoots out to separate them and carefully fill in between them with cutting compost. Water to settle the compost around the stems. Six to seven months after replanting, dig up the entire plant. You will notice that the stems have formed roots and these may now be cut off and potted up or planted out. Pinching out the growing tip of each stem at planting time will encourage the plant to produce side shoots and become bushy.

Serpentine layering

This is a form of simple layering especially suited to climbers such as clematis, honeysuckle, jasmine, fallopia and wisteria. As with simple layering, propagation may be carried out at any time of the year but rooting will be quicker during spring and early summer.

Select a stem of current season's growth that is capable of being laid along the ground. At the point where the stem touches the ground, prepare the soil by digging in a bucket or two of sand and peat formula to encourage rooting. If space is limited, the stem may be curved around the parent plant (away from the root zone) to form a circle. Instead of laying the stem flat (as you would for simple layering), loop the stem in and out of the ground until it resembles the Loch Ness monster. Make sure you allow at least four to five leaves between the sections that are to be buried. Remove the leaves from any sections that will be underground, then

simple layering

1 Select a branch that is at ground level, or one that can be bent to touch the soil. At the point where the branch will meet the ground, dig over the soil to loosen it, then add sand and peat to form a free-draining medium that will encourage rooting. Scoop a depression in the soil, where the stem will be positioned.

2 Strip off any leaves within 15cm (6in) on either side of where the stem will touch the soil to encourage all the plant's energy to produce roots.

3 Wound the stem at the point where it will come into contact with the soil. Follow that with a long, sloping cut part way through the stem and wedge the cut open with a piece of matchstick or, if you prefer, twist the stem to crack it at the right position.

4 Peg the stem firmly in place, using a U-shaped piece of wire or a flexible stem to hold it down, making sure the wound is in direct contact with the prepared soil.

5 Peg the shoots upright, so that they grow straight upwards and will be easier to lift later. If necessary, tie the portion of stem beyond the area for rooting to a cane or stake to prevent the wind blowing it. This should also train the plant to grow upright and not at an angle.

6 Cover the stem with more compost and water to settle the soil. Place a large stone or concrete block on top of the stem to prevent movement and disturbance.

Rooting may take as long as 18 months, but most plants should be well rooted within a year. Keep the ground watered. The following autumn, ease the branch out of the ground with a garden fork. If it is well rooted, cut the stem on the side closest to the parent plant. Think carefully about where you are cutting; it would be an awful mistake to make the cutting between the growing tip and the new roots! Try to lift the newly rooted layer with as much soil as possible to reduce the shock to the roots, then pot it up in a container or plant it out.

Hamamelis x intermedia layers well, but these branches are too upright for layering – you need a branch that can be bent to touch the ground.

wound the stem (as for simple layering, see page 245) below a node where the leaf was removed. Securely peg your Loch Ness monster down at intervals using U-shaped wires pushed into the ground. Cover the stems to be buried with cutting compost and ensure the soil remains moist.

After about twelve months, the layers should be well rooted and ready to dig up. Dig up the entire stem, exposing the rooted sections. Cut the stem immediately behind the rooted section, leaving each plant with a looped area of growth that was above ground level. Pot up in containers, or plant out in a sheltered area of the garden to grow on for a year before planting in permanent positions.

Air layering

So far, all the forms of propagation by layering I have described involve bringing the plant into contact with the soil. However, there are many occasions where this isn't possible. Stiff, upright branches of witch hazel (*Hamamelis* spp.), rhododendron and house plants such as rubber tree (*Ficus* spp.) and croton (*Codiaeum* spp.) physically cannot be bent down to ground level. So with air layering, the gardener brings the rooting compost to the plant, not the other way round. This is best done any time from mid-spring to mid-summer.

air layering

1 Select a firm, healthy one-year-old stem. Midway between two leaf joints (nodes), make a sloping cut part way through the stem.

2 Wedge the cut open with a piece of matchstick to prevent it healing over.

3 Dust the wound with hormone rooting powder or gel.

4 Pack damp sphagnum moss around the wounded area.

5 Wrap a bandage of clear polythene tightly around the moss. Seal it around the stem, top and bottom, with tape or raffia to prevent moisture loss.

6 Cover the clear polythene with an outer layer of black polythene and seal it again. Unfortunately, house plants will look a bit odd – but use it as a talking point!

7 Remove the black covering once a month to check on progress. If the moss appears to be drying out, loosen the top tie, pour in some water and reseal. Eventually, white roots will appear. In the case of house plants, this may take 8–10 weeks; for trees and shrubs, rooting can take as long as 12–18 months.

When the stem is well-rooted, carefully unwrap the plastic and remove any loose moss. Cut the stem immediately below the rooted area and pot up the new plant. Trim the stem of the parent plant back to a leaf, bud or side shoot to encourage it to branch out.

Strawberry runners

Strawberries are propagated by layering plantlets (see below). The established strawberry produces new plants on long stems called runners, which are so prolific that they can be a nuisance where they are not required for propagation.

Only propagate runners from healthy strawberry plants.

strawberry runners

1 In early summer select the number of new plants you require, choosing the biggest of the plantlets and only one per runner. Cut off any that are growing beyond the first plantlet. Sink a 7–10cm (3–4 in) pot flush with the soil alongside the parent plant and fill it with a loam-based compost.

2 Peg the plantlet, using bent wire to hold it in place, on top of the compost.

Water the compost during dry periods.

Within weeks the plant will have rooted into the compost and the runner may be severed from the parent plant. In autumn the pot-grown plant will be ready for planting out. The plantlets will root directly into the garden soil but will take longer than in the pot. Cultivate the soil between the plants to encourage rooting.

grafting

Please don't be deterred from grafting plants by the amount of detailed, skilled knifework involved. Practice makes perfect.

The first graft I attempted was a brilliant success, resulting in an old apple tree being given a new lease of life with better-quality dessert fruit. Since then I have had failures, but I still get enormous satisfaction every time a graft 'takes'.

In layman's terms, grafting involves placing the cut surfaces of two plants together and encouraging them to bond and grow as one plant. The rootstock is the plant retaining its roots; the different plant being grafted onto it is called the scion.

One of the main reasons for grafting is to combine the best attributes of two plants on one plant. The rootstock may be strong growing, with a good root system. The new species or variety being grafted onto it (the scion) may be a top performer for flower, fruit, shape or other attributes (but it may have a weak root system). Combine the two by grafting them together, and you end up with a top performer with a strong rooting system. This technique is ideal for creating dwarf fruit trees, where vigorous growth is not wanted (in which case, the tree might be grafted with a suitable rootstock that will make less growth). Grafting is also an excellent method for propagating lilac, which is difficult to propagate by root cuttings.

There are many and varied forms of grafting, but the most successful for a range of plants are whip-and-tongue and saddle grafting. The ideal time for both methods is in early spring, just before trees and shrubs commence their annual growth.

Rootstocks may be purchased from specialist nurseries or, in many cases, you can grow your own from seed. It is usually necessary to graft plants that are related to the rootstock. Rowan (*Sorbus* spp.) is compatible with apple and hawthorn, because they all belong to one family (Rosaceae). Any species of rose can be used as the rootstock on which to graft a bush, shrub or climbing rose variety.

Saddle grafting

I prefer to graft when the rootstock is planted, especially if there are a few to do, as it's easier on my back. Alternatively, the job may be done at a table and the completed graft planted afterwards. I recommend saddle grafting for rhododendrons, hamamelis, maple and rowan tree.

saddle grafting

1 For your scion material, select a stem or branch of growth made the previous summer. Using a sharp knife or secateurs, cut it to form an inverted 'V' or wedge shape.

2 For the rootstock, choose a stem equal or similar in diameter to that of the scion. Cut the rootstock close to the ground with a corresponding 'V', that will lock into the scion material.

3 Check that the two ends of stem fit neatly together without any gaps between the wood. The scion may now be cut down to 2–3 buds. When the two are joined together, the two cuts should fit perfectly together without any gaps and the cambium and bark layers should be touching.

4 The graft union may now be sealed to stop disease entering the wounds and prevent shifting or drying out. I am old fashioned and still swear by raffia for tying. More modern materials include plastic tape. Paint the wrapping with pruning paint to form an airtight seal. A dab of the same on the cut tip of the scion finishes the job.

Whip-and-tongue grafting

The technique for whip-and-tongue grafting is the same as for saddle grafting, except for the shape and size of the cut. This method is most commonly used for plants such as fruit trees, rhododendrons, witch hazel and acers.

Make the first cut on the rootstock 10–15cm (4–6in) from the ground, cutting upwards with a sloping cut, 3.5–5cm (1½–2in) long. One third of the way down the sloping cut from the top, make a 1cm (½in) vertical cut to form the 'tongue'. Make a sloping cut on the scion stem at the same angle as the cut on the rootstock stem, finishing the cut just below a growth bud. Now make a vertical cut one third of the way up from the bottom of the sloping cut, again 1cm (½in) deep. Bring the two prepared pieces of stem together, locking the two tongues as one. Secure and seal as for the saddle technique.

Bud grafting

This technique is normally referred to as budding. It is a popular and reliable method for grafting bush roses. Budding takes place in summer, usually on roses that are growing in the ground or in containers. The difference between budding and grafting is in the material used. Whereas both whip-and-tongue and saddle grafting use two stems of the desired variety, with bud grafting a single growth bud is grafted onto a rootstock. An ordinary sharp knife can be used for making the cuts, but a budding knife is best. This has a flattened end to the handle for opening the rootstock (see page 250).

bud grafting

1 Select a well-ripened stem of the current year's growth, making sure that there are dormant buds at the leaf axils. Remove the stem and take off all the leaves. Prepare the bud before opening the rootstock. Cut a single bud from the selected stem with the minimum of wood. Remove the sliver of wood from under the bark using the point of the knife and discard. This leaves the bud and the cambium layer attached to the bark. Keep the bud moist while you prepare the rootstock – the simplest method is to hold it between your lips. It will be difficult to talk and don't chew on it!

2 Now prepare the rootstock to receive the bud. Make a horizontal cut 2.5 –5cm (1–2in) above ground level and discard the top growth. Clean the stem of the rootstock with a rag.

3 Once the neck of the rootstock is clear you are ready to bud.

4 Make a T-shaped cut deep enough to expose the cambium layer below the bark. The stroke of the T should be less than 1cm (½in) long; the upward cut 2.5cm (1in) long.

5 Use the flattened end of the knife handle to open the two flaps of bark on the rootstock. Slip the prepared bud, pointing upwards, under the flaps of bark, making sure that the two cambium layers are together. Trim any surplus bud bark level with the stroke of the T.

6 Secure the union with raffia above and below, avoiding the bud. Some gardeners prefer to use budding strips made of thin rubber. These may be stretched over the bud union and held with an open staple.

Once the bud starts to grow, you can remove the raffia (if you use a rubber strip, it will perish). In early spring, cut the rootstock above the new bud growth leaving it to flourish and flower that summer.

which method, which plant?

Bob: John has given details of how to carry out the techniques, so here are a few guidelines on which method is likely to prove most useful for which plant – and a few pitfalls to look out for.

Sowing

Most flowering plants (in the botanical sense, so including vegetables) can be grown from seed – it's what the enthusiasts do – and many non-flowering plants can be grown from seed-like materials, such as ferns from spores and mushrooms from spawn. However, in many cases the seed does not give you exactly the same plant as the parent. It will depend on how the particular variety was originally come by. Varieties that arose from a chance seedling being spotted as different and multiplied often give at least a percentage of similar offspring. All the differently coloured Shirley poppies, for example, were obtained from the plain wild form by selecting and growing on those plants that were slightly different and slowly 'improving' their differences. The seed from these plants produces, mostly, forms much like the parents. But other plant varieties come about as mutations, such as bud sports on fruit trees: one bit of a plant starts to behave differently and, by detaching it and growing it on separately (maybe on its own roots or grafted onto a rootstock), we manage to preserve and multiply it. These bud mutations must nearly always be propagated this way – vegetatively, as it is called – as a mutation does not usually affect any seed produced. In other words, if you propagate your sport by grafting, you will produce another sport, whereas if you use its seed you will commonly only produce the original form.

Seed producers use various techniques to ensure you end up with pretty much what you see on the packet when you sow their flower or vegetable seeds. This is not always the case when you collect and harvest your own seed. If you sow your own 'Cox's' apple pips or 'Iceberg' rosehips, for instance, you will probably not get a 'Cox' or 'Iceberg' among the offspring but an assortment of apples and roses, varying wildly and many resembling the original wilder forms.

So seed may come true, or as expected, if carefully produced, and this is most likely when it is grown from commercial packets. Failing that, you will have to buy at least your first plant if it is to be exactly the right cultivar – that is when it is normally propagated vegetatively. So if you want a 'Victoria' plum, a 'King Edward' potato, a 'Belle Etoile' philadelphus or a 'Sarah Bernhardt' paeony you can't grow them from seed, though you may be able to grow something very, very similar or very, very dissimilar – but that's half the fun of it.

Keep in mind that propagating from seed may not in practice be easier, quicker or even cheaper than buying a plant – especially if you want only one or two. But where you want many plants then sowing is usually incredibly cheap. If you do a good job, most seed will grow and if carefully managed just one packet could be enough to fill a large plot. Also, seed-grown plants tend to be the most vigorous and productive. Those sown in situ and left undisturbed often make the very finest specimens, especially if they are well thinned and weeded from early on.

As a general rule, we most commonly sow annual flowers, biennial flowers, some varieties of herbaceous perennial flowers and most vegetables.

Self-saved seed

Bought packets of seed should do what they say and show on the packet. Self-saved seed might be free, but as I've already said it does not always come true, and is often not even viable (but that shouldn't put you off at least having a go). It is extremely satisfying to raise plants from seed you have collected yourself, and it is also quite easy even for the novice to create a particular variety in only a few years by careful selection. Conversely, inadvertent selection can reduce your variety to something quite undistinguished in equal time. For example, seed saved from a mixture of sweet peas will produce just the wild purple/violet form in only four or five years. Avoid saving seed (unless you really know what you're doing) of wallflowers, stocks, cabbages and other brassicas, marrows, squashes, cucumbers and other cucurbits, lettuces, carrots, sweetcorn and most other vegetables, as well

John & Bob's 75 (or so) plants for propagation

Although it can be fun to try the sophisticated techniques of propagation, most gardeners will rely mainly on sowing seed, taking cuttings or division to increase their stocks. Here's an at-a-glance guide to the easiest way to propagate some of the plants you are most likely to want to propagate.

	seed	softwood	semi-ripe	hardwood	root cutting	leaf cutting	division
Alcea	●						
Begonia	●					●	
Brassica	●						
Buddleia		●	●	●			
Buxus		●	●				
Calendula	●						
Camellia			●				
Campanula	●	●					
Capsicum	●						
Ceanothus			●		●		
Choisya		●	●		●		
Chrysanthemum		●	●				●
Citrus		●	●				●
Clematis		●					●
Cornus		●	●	●			
Cotoneaster	●	●	●	●			
Crataegus	●						
Cyclamen	●						
Dahlia	●						
Daphne	●		●				
Dianthus	●		●				
Digitalis	●						
Erica	●		●				
Euphorbia	●	●					●
Fagus	●						
Ficus				●			
Forsythia	●	●	●	●			
Fuchsia	●	●	●				
Galanthus	●						●
Geranium	●				●		●
Gladiolus	●						
Hebe	●	●	●				
Hedera		●	●				
Helleborus	●						●
Hemerocallis	●						●
Hosta	●						●
Hydrangea		●	●				●
Ilex	●	●					
Iris	●						●

	seed	softwood	semi-ripe	hardwood	root cutting	leaf cutting	division
Jasminum		●	●				
Kniphofia	●						●
Laburnum	●			●			
Lathyrus	●						●
Lavender	●		●				
Lonicera	●		●	●			
Lupins	●	●	●				
Magnolia	●	●	●				
Mahonia	●						●
Malus	●						
Mentha		●					●
Narcissus	●						
Nepeta	●	●					●
Nicotiana	●						
Paeonia	●						●
Papaver	●				●		●
Passiflora	●						
Philadelphus		●	●	●			
Primula	●						●
Pyracantha	●		●				
Pyrus	●						
Ribes				●			
Rosemary			●				
Roses	●			●			
Salvia	●		●				●
Sarcococca	●		●				●
Sedum	●	●				●	●
Skimmia	●		●				
Sorbus	●						
Strawberries	●						●
Syringa	●	●	●		●		
Thymus	●	●					●
Tomatoes	●						
Tropaeolum	●	●			●		●
Tulips	●						
Viburnum	●	●	●	●			
Vitis			●	●			
Wisteria		●					

as soft fruit. You can, if you really want to, grow most shrubs, trees, woody climbers and herbaceous perennials from self-saved seed, but again not the best named varieties.

Division

Some crops, such as potatoes, Jerusalem and Chinese artichokes, garlic and shallots, and some flowers, such as dahlias, naturally form tubers or storage organs, which we can dig up and separate very easily. Runnering and suckering plants such as violets and strawberries are obviously simple. Thicket-formers such as raspberries and bamboo, indeed any plant with a perennial root system that produces dispersed buds not all clustered together on a central core, can be divided up into many smaller plants. So most suckering shrubs can be divided easily. Almost all herbaceous perennials that form clumps can be divided as they have multiple buds and shoots that easily root; examples include hemerocallis, phlox, delphiniums, rhubarb and globe artichokes. Most benefit from this every few years, re-invigorating them by disposing of the dead centre and replanting the strongest shoots/chunks. However, there are always exceptions. Paeonies, hellebores and asparagus really resent such treatment and may sulk for a time afterwards, or they may spontaneously flower and die unless they are well looked after (and lucky). As a rule, the more fibrous the root system and the more shoots and buds on each part, the greater the chance of success by division. Big brittle roots with few buds may be more difficult or, as with yuccas, just take time. Annuals and trees are unlikely to succeed.

Cuttings

Some herbaceous plants, and a few woody ones, can be grown from quite small root cuttings. Others, such as some succulent houseplants, can be propagated by leaf cuttings. Indeed, with a bit of skill and resource, almost any living part of a plant can be grown on. However, I suggest you start with the most common methods. Hardwood or autumn cuttings can be taken from most shrubby plants with varying degrees of success. Don't forget that while a three-in-fifty success rate is abject failure for a nursery business, it may be quite sufficient for the home garden. Many shrubs and most herbaceous perennials can be successfully propagated by softwood cuttings, rooted during the growing season. This sort of cutting usually needs bottom heat and a cloche or propagator cover to succeed well; harder subjects might also need a mister. Most annuals and many biennials can only rarely be rooted by any method and oddly many trees are also reluctant to strike. You cannot fail with black, red or flowering currants, grapes and gooseberries – and, surprisingly, you should be able to multiply most roses by cuttings.

Layering

Layering is effective with everything that will take from a cutting, but is most used for those shrubs that won't take easily or quickly from cuttings, such as rhododendrons. Climbers are the easiest group to layer. This is a very convenient (if not lazy) way to gain an extra choice plant or two, but not a great method for producing large numbers.

Grafting

Not done by many at home, in practice grafting is relatively simple. Timing is important but otherwise it's not a difficult technique for anyone to try. Once mastered you can fit many sorts on the same tree, repair damage and missing branches and change varieties. And even if you fail the original usually springs back.

Grafting is usually done on deciduous trees and shrubs but can be used to produce tomato on potato, for example, or tomato on disease-resistant rootstock. Most bought-in fruit trees, other than stone fruits, as well as many ornamental trees and most choice shrubs and climbers have been grafted onto special rootstocks.

Budding

This is a little more demanding but also easily achievable by anyone with adept fingers. Most roses and stone fruits sold commercially have been budded onto suitable rootstocks.

This apple, *Malus* 'Yellow Ingestrie', would be a much bigger tree, fruiting later in life, if it was on its own roots. Grafting it onto semi-dwarfing stock makes it more suitable for a medium-sized garden.

the kit – propagating features & equipment

Seed bed and nursery bed

Bob: These are grandiose terms for a bit of prepared soil in a sheltered corner, protected from strong winds or heavy shade. Many gardeners prefer to nurture their young seedlings in a seed bed, rather than planting them in situ where they are to mature. Here, vegetables such as brassicas and leeks, and regularly replenished ornamentals, such as wallflowers and stocks, are sown, thinned and tended until they are big enough to transplant to their final positions. The soil for a seed bed needs to be sandy and light, moist but never waterlogged and not excessively fertile. Cuttings (often housed in a sand-lined slit trench), slow-growing ornamentals and temporary occupants 'heeled in' (roughly planted, usually lying over) occupy a nursery bed where they can grow large enough to move to their final site. The soil in the nursery bed needs to be weed free, moist but never waterlogged, heavier than a seed bed, i.e. loamier, less sandy and more fertile though not over-rich. In most cases well dug and weeded will do!

Cloches, cold frames and propagators

These make propagation success more likely, by keeping the desiccating effects of air and extreme cold away from seedlings, cuttings and young transplants. A cloche (traditionally a bell of glass) might today be made of plastic or sheets of glass. Some can be joined together in long runs for protecting rows of seedlings. Others, such as clear, plastic bottles with the bottoms and caps removed, are used for single plants. The main advantage of a cloche over a cold frame is that it can be transported from place to place as the season and crop demands. It therefore allows you to grow plants in situ and, because cloches are small, they require little attention or watering because the rainwater is able to seep in sideways (which it can't in a cold frame). On the whole, cloches are of most use to keen vegetable growers and for raising winter salads.

Cold frames are bigger, better insulated and more permanent than cloches. Some plants are placed directly in the soil, but more often they are grown in pots. Many gardeners transfer their plants to a cold frame in pots, after starting them off somewhere warmer, and keep them there until they are big enough to plant out. Cold frames are also useful for over-wintering plants. As they are more permanent and bigger than cloches, and the plants are usually in pots, all watering must be done by hand. The advantage of cold frames is that they are better insulated, so they keep the plants warmer, although the downside is that there is little ventilation and they can cook young plants on sunny days if the lids are not opened. Propagators vary, from large ones like cold frames (usually supplied with bottom heat by soil-warming cable) to seed tray-sized ones with plastic lids. The latter are a simple aid to growing from seed or cuttings, because the clear lids keep the air moist just like a cloche. Plants in propagators need to be watched and cared for like babies, as they are easily damaged while small. And be careful what you grow in them – some plants require shade or even darkness in order to germinate (see page 235).

Heat and moisture

The addition of some bottom heat is a huge aid to propagation, as a warm, moist compost will encourage seeds to germinate quicker and cuttings to root much faster. In the past, hot beds were created using fermenting manure, but these were difficult to manage and required reworking every other month or so. Even so, fermenting manure is still used today to create a short-term heated bed for starting melons, pumpkins, marrows and the like. Although many forms of heat can be used, most propagators and hot beds are warmed by electric pads, mats or, most often, special cables buried in sand. They are a superb aid to propagation, but because they are powered by electricity, you will need a competent electrician to install them safely. Once installed, the compost can be kept at a controlled temperature using a thermostat. Small seed-tray propagators are available with built-in electric heaters, or you can place ordinary trays on heated mats or staging. Large propagators, which take several trays, can be bought or made.

While bottom heat is useful for germinating seeds or rooting cuttings, further heating is also an advantage when raising tender plants. Electric or fan-assisted air heaters are ideal for propagating tender subjects, which can be started off in winter in their own protected environments (without having to heat the whole greenhouse). To propagate softwood or leaf cuttings, water misting is another great boon. This is traditionally done by hand, but automatic systems are available for large areas.

Almost every plant will benefit from a little bottom heat if it is available. It is the primary tool for starting off almost any plant early in the season. For germinating and growing on most tender seeds, it is essential (lettuces are one of the few exceptions, failing to germinate if they're too warm). For rooting softwood and leaf cuttings and tender crops, heat usually helps immensely. When in doubt, give warmth. A word of warning, though. Electricity is dangerous, especially in combination with damp conditions, and more so in combination with incompetence. So have a professional install everything that does not simply plug in! And do read the instructions.

Choosing and using propagating equipment

So how do you choose what propagating equipment you need? Well, it basically depends on what you want to grow. Most hardy annual flowers and the majority of vegetables are best sown in situ. However, a small seedbed becomes convenient when you grow many brassicas, leeks or salads for succession, or for raising biennial bedding plants and many hardy plants from seed. A nursery bed will be useful if you take a lot of hardwood cuttings or grow your own replacement plants, such as stocks or pinks. All of these plants will benefit from a cloche to keep off pests and protect them from harsh weather – although a cloche may make some plants rather soft in growth, so you should harden them off before transplanting them to their final positions.

A cold frame is worth having for propagating near-hardy plants in pots, such as fuchsias and pelargoniums, or for raising tender vegetables. A small propagator is essential for any

A cloche keeps the frost off these young courgette plants, but will cook the leaves unless it is propped open.

serious gardener, as many choice plants cannot be sown outdoors in the ground. A large, heated propagator will be useful to any keen gardener – almost as much use as a greenhouse. Few really need mist propagation equipment.

Crepis rubra is a member of the dandelion family and self-seeds merrily.

the next step

Once your seeds have germinated, you could just leave them to themselves. However, the results will not be ideal because, unless you were both skilful and lucky, it is unlikely that you will have just the right number of seedlings in just the right places. When sowing in situ or in a seedbed, you inevitably sow thickly to allow for poor germination and losses. The resultant stand will be either patchy or dense, with the seedlings growing like cress. Emergent seedlings must be thinned as soon as possible to prevent them either choking or checking each other. Early thinning is even more important if you are sowing in pots, cells or trays, where there is little root space.

Pricking out

Seedlings that were initially sown together to save space while germinating eventually get bigger and are ready to be given their own pot, cell or space in a tray. This is called pricking out and is usually done in place of, or at the same time as, thinning; it is most common with seedlings grown in pots or trays. Pricking out is not essential for emergent seedlings grown in a seedbed where space is not at a premium.

Don't underestimate the importance of pricking out – it has been shown that tomato seedlings pricked out within three days of emergence made plants nearly twice the size of those left together in their first pot for a week or more.
When choosing a container for transplanting, avoid using one that is too big. Tiny seedlings usually do best in small pots, cells or boxed trays until they are strong enough to colonise a larger ball of compost. And, just as importantly perhaps, where are you going to keep all those big pots? As they grow, the seedlings can be potted on into larger containers.

If your seedlings have been growing in a protected environment, such as a greenhouse or propagator, make sure you maintain the same conditions after pricking out or potting on – so, if they have been kept in a warm place, put them back there. Only when they have re-established in their new compost can you risk moving them.

pricking out a young seedling

1 Seedlings are big enough to prick out when you can handle them by their first leaves which have fully unfurled. It is riskier to touch either the stem or central tip.

2 These seedlings are already overcrowded – pricking out should have been done days ago.

3 Make sure the seedlings have been watered thoroughly well before attempting to remove them. This will encourage the compost to stick to the roots and help prevent them getting damaged. Rattle the pot, cell or tray to loosen the compost, then carefully tease out a rooted seedling, keeping the root intact. Use a pencil to help extricate the thread-sized roots. A pencil or dibber is helpful to tease the seedling from its container.

4 DON'T hold plants like this – you'll bruise the fragile stem.

5 Choose a small pot, cell or boxed tray. Fill with sieved sterile potting compost such as John Innes. Use a pencil or dibber to make a hole in the compost and transfer the seedling immediately. Firm gently but very firmly. Partly immerse the pot/tray in warm water until the surface appears damp, then immediately drain. Do not water from the top, or wet the compost, before pricking out. Once transplanted, place the seedlings back in the greenhouse, propagator or sheltered spot in the garden until they have started to grow strongly and need potting on.

Anne's tip for watering seedlings
Bob's probably right to play it safe, but I've watered all the seedlings I have ever pricked out from the top, and thousands and thousands of them have lived to tell the tale! Mind you, it is important to use a rose (sprinkler) on the end of the watering can. I also don't bother sieving bought-in potting compost, but that's a matter of personal preference.

Potting on

Pricking out is done to give each tiny seedling a bit more space to grow in. However, this is only the initial stage. As the plants get larger, they either need to be potted on (or 'up') into larger containers, or moved on to their permanent position in the garden. Every type of plant has different minimum needs for the amount of compost in which it can grow without checking or cramping the roots. In general, it is safer to pot on sooner rather than later, especially fast-growing annuals and vegetable crops in spring, because being potbound will check the plants and ruin their potential. Plants rarely need to be potted on in autumn or winter when growth is slow.

Buying in

Keen enthusiasts may grow everything from seed, but many buy in larger, slower-growing plants 'ready grown' to save time. However over recent years more and more people are also buying in seedlings and very small plants to grow on, thus avoiding the difficulties of germination and pricking out. Most frequently offered are summer bedding plants and specialist selections of such plants as fuchsias, pinks and chrysanthemums. These small plants are usually offered in the most popular varieties and are called plug, mini, cell-grown or just small plants. They are more expensive than seed but cheaper than fully grown plants.

potting on

1 It is impossible to tell by looking at the top of the plant if it is ready for potting on. One clue, though, might be if it keeps drying out between waterings. You need to examine the rootball, so knock the plant out of its pot and have a look.

If there are few roots visible, leave the plant to establish for a little longer.

2 If you can see lots of roots, now is the perfect time to pot on.

3 If there is a great mass of congested roots with no compost visible, tease them out under water...

4 ...and plant up immediately.

As with all gardening, it helps to read the catalogues and to choose early to get the best selection. The plug plants will arrive at the most suitable time by mail and should be inspected, approved and potted up as soon as possible. If they are dried out, soak the roots in warm water first. It is foolish to put even the hardy sorts straight outdoors, especially if you forget to harden them off as well! In every case it is better to pot up and hold such wee subjects in a greenhouse or cold frame until they are bigger and the soil is warmer. Half-hardy or tender plants will likewise need to be potted up but kept in the warmth until they are bigger, tougher and can be hardened off and planted out.

Choosing a pot and compost

As stated above, every plant is different in its requirements. Most want to have the biggest pot with the hugest quantity of the richest compost you can give them! Some can make do with much less and some actually give us more of what we want, such as flowers, if they are cramped! Generally, though, because of the need for economy of space, most plants are squeezed into smaller pots than they want. This being so, when potting on, choose a much bigger pot than the existing one if the plant is growing fast and a slightly bigger pot if it is not swelling by much. Likewise the strongest growing seedlings can have stronger composts. Initially all are best started in low fertility seed composts, such as the John Innes series, going into John Innes potting compost No. 1 if they are small and weak, or No. 2 if they are bigger and stronger. The biggest, toughest, most hungry plants will like John Innes No. 3 potting compost. Less professional results can be had by using any old multi-purpose compost!

Moving on

Plants in the open ground need to be moved on from the seed bed to the nursery bed in the same way as plants in containers need to be potted on. However, the term 'moving on' also refers to the move from propagator to bench to cold frame. Moves, if handled well and in good time, are nearly always beneficial, as they strengthen the plant and help it to grow bigger with a strong rootball equipped for coping with tough conditions. Moving on is especially important when building up a stock of wallflowers, stocks and brassicas. As the small plants are lifted from seedbed to nursery bed, the tap root is broken; on replanting in a nursery bed it forms a more fibrous root system, which is much better equipped for the final move to its permanent position than if it had grown as one big tap root. Likewise, cuttings in their second year and small perennial seedlings need lifting and moving on to a place with more space where they can become established before being transplanted to their final positions.

Hardening off

This is absolutely essential, otherwise all your hard work will be wasted. Little plants are easily killed by sudden changes in temperature and even as they get bigger and tougher, they are still susceptible. Hardening off involves exposing plants to changes in temperature little by little, rather than all at once. This applies as much to tough, old house plants, which need hardening off before they can be moved outside for summer, as it does to young plants. The secret with hardening off is to expose the plants to the outdoors on pleasant days in early summer and bring them back indoors at night. Then, after a week or so, they should be able to stay out more or less permanently until autumn (unless a frost is likely).

Little plants need extra care, ideally being moved through a series of protected environments that allow them to acclimatise in stages – propagator to heated greenhouse (or at least a frost-free, warm area), to cold greenhouse, to cold frame, to cloche before finally facing the elements unprotected. If you can't provide such specialist protection, then put the plants out by day and bring them in by night for at least three or four days (even for the toughest plants); the longer the better. Really tender plants will always need some extra protection. Be cautious with bought plants, especially tomatoes, peppers and tender bedding, because despite the purveyor's assurances, these will not have been hardened off, except, perhaps, by being well chilled while standing out for sale! Keep them in a protected environment initially and acclimatise them slowly or their progress will undoubtedly be checked.

Chapter 10

pests & diseases

Bob: No matter what we do, sooner or later some pest or disease is going to attack our plants – it's just what happens. But just as we can survive a cold, a pimple or a broken bone, plants can shrug off most pest and disease attacks with little damage, especially if they are well established. A fully grown plant might lose a great deal of leaf area, but that means light will fall more fully on the leaves that were once shaded. There is likely to be little detriment other than aesthetically – holes eaten all over the place might not look nice, but they are probably not doing that much harm. In the case of sweet cherries, pests can actively help by effectively doing our summer pruning for us, withering back the lush tips, checking the growth and forming more flower and fruit buds to make more cherries. It is interesting that you will probably lose more cherries to birds than to the aphids! Similarly, more crops, flowers and even whole plants and their foliage are lost to bad weather than to all the pests and diseases combined! There is little we can do about the seasons – we have to take each as it comes, and the weather has a greater effect than anything else on our plants.

Gardeners can become more sanguine and relaxed about many pests and diseases once they start to associate each noticeable attack with a naturally recurring cycle. Natural checks and balances do control the populations, but not very quickly. Some years you might have many ladybirds and wasps and no aphids, and other years it will be all aphids and caterpillars. Most pests that are especially troublesome in one year often disappear or become much less of a problem the next year or so, and over the years they will come and go, regularly or intermittently. Where an attack only leads to superficial damage or the crop is in such surplus anyway that some loss does not matter, then we have to ask ourselves whether the economic cost and labour of trying to control the attack is worthwhile. For example, if you already have a glut of apples does it matter if maggots have damaged some of them? Although in general many pest and disease attacks on established plants can be almost ignored or dealt with lightly, for small plants and seedlings action is crucial. The younger the plant the more easily it is overwhelmed, and so we need to take most care of them while they are smallest and keep them better protected until they are old and tough enough to fend for themselves, or until it no longer matters – there's no point worrying about blight attacking your outdoor tomatoes in early autumn, for example, as they'll be dead from cold in a week or two anyway. Without doubt, the healthier and stronger our plants, the better they are able to withstand pest and disease attacks, so our first and most important task is to grow them well. Only once this is accomplished is there any point in going on to use any other method of prevention.

There is a whole host of different ways to deal with any particular problem, ranging from relatively simple traps and barriers to more risky measures, such as highly noxious sprays. Even if you do not wish to be an organic gardener, it still makes sense to use the least invasive and ecologically disruptive methods first before resorting to chemicals. So here are some alternatives.

Companion planting: planting nasturtiums round the base of your fruit trees will not guarantee freedom from woolly aphid infestation, but usually slowly reduces their incidence and looks beautiful while providing edible leaves, flowers and seeds!

Growing crops such as carrots and lettuce in a cold frame will bring them on more quickly and protect them from the dangers of frost. A cold frame can also reduce attacks by birds, carrot root fly and even slugs and snails.

compost, like soil, must be kept moist but not waterlogged and fertility should likewise be balanced with sufficient nutrients to promote growth without forcing it and must be of a suitable acid/alkaline range, usually with plenty of humus, and grit, clay and sand to balance. All plants must have adequate airflow, but not draughts, especially under cover where carbon dioxide may be used up if insufficient ventilation is provided. Plants also require freedom from competition if they are to do well. It does not matter much whether the other plants are weeds or more of the same kind – each one needs sufficient soil or compost and light to flourish, so any overcrowding should be thinned to prevent the plants becoming weak or spindly.

growing healthy plants

As I have said, a strong-growing plant is more likely to withstand pest and disease attacks than a weak specimen. As gardeners, we must do everything we can to grow our plants well to prevent the problem arising in the first place – from choosing our plants wisely by only selecting healthy ones and rejecting any that are weak or disease-ridden, to planting or sowing on a suitable site with the correct micro-climate and the right kind of soil. We must avoid stresses, such as growing plants out of their natural season or exposing them to extreme winds. Under cover, we must ensure our plants never waterlog or dry out, that they never get chilled, cooked or just choked in stagnant humid air. Many moulds, mildews and rusts don't even start unless the plants are under water stress; thus it is crucial to keep their compost or soil moist, especially when the air is damp or stagnant. Most of these infections need to 'germinate' in a wet droplet and most become much less troublesome when the plants are in drier air – so open pruning can help make old congested plants healthier. So

introducing disease-resistant or alternative varieties

Resistant varieties offer immunity or near-immunity to many common pests and diseases. From the natural variation, breeders have selected strains that do not suffer as much from this or that problem. Generally speaking, there are more varieties available with resistance to various fungal and bacterial diseases (mildews, rusts, moulds and rots) than to pests – I guess because hungry pests are harder to deter. Because they have been selected and bred for their resistance, they don't always provide the best quality in terms of cropping, flavour, sweetness or perfume. Nonetheless, most resistant varieties are well worth growing, especially in the vegetable garden where freedom from (or at least resistance to) any given problem is important. The range of resistant plants and seeds is huge and includes everything from scab-free apple varieties to parsnips that are less prone to canker, leeks that get less rust, blackcurrants and gooseberries that don't succumb to mildew, carrots that suffer less from root fly and lettuces that attract fewer aphids on their roots. A word of advice, though – don't buy a variety just because it is resistant to some pest or disease unless that problem does affect your plants anyway. Seed companies like to boast that such and such a variety is resistant or even immune to some particular disease, but you may find that this disease only affects that plant once in every dozen years, or is only ever a problem in commercial greenhouses. Another consideration is that although a resistant variety may be immune to a particular pest or disease now, it may not be so next year when the pest or disease has mutated.

If disease-resistant varieties aren't for you, you might like to try growing an alternative, trouble-free plant in place of one that is susceptible to disease – celeriac, for example, is much easier to grow than celery, especially if you only want it for cooking, rather than in salads, kohlrabi is much less troublesome than cabbage or turnip, while the Asian pear suffers fewer problems than European sorts. Almost all plants may suffer attacks from common pests such as birds, rabbits, dogs, cats, kids, slugs and snails; however, rare or unusual plants seldom suffer from as many problems as those common plants that everyone grows – there are plenty of pests and diseases to trouble roses and apple trees, for example, but few bother with zaluzianskya or mesembryanthemum.

Resistance is often just a matter of coming up with a neat solution – for example, roses with glossy, shiny leaves generally suffer less from leaf problems than those with matt leaves. In the vegetable garden, tomatoes that are grafted onto multiple-resistant KNVF rootstocks can be introduced into soils that would otherwise have been too infested with disease to make cultivation possible.

encouraging natural killers

The natural population of parasites and predators in our gardens would gladly exterminate every pest around (as well as every friendly bug and almost everything else, including each other!). They want to kill and my advice is to help them – they will certainly control pests better than we can. In general, the friendly predators are the quick movers, big and small – birds, beetles, wasps, hoverflies, ladybirds and hosts of others. They chase after their prey while it is busy eating our plants. If we can increase their numbers sufficiently, then our pest problems will disappear. So help our friends by providing water for them to drink or to wash or live in (frogs, newts and dragonflies). Give small predators long grass, rough bark mulches and deep layers of leafy, lush ground-cover plants to move about under. Provide winter homes or hibernation and nesting sites for all – from bird boxes and hedgehog nests, to toad and bat boxes and ladybird hotels. Supply them with food sources all year round – nectar and pollen-bearing flowers, for example – and extra treats such as seeds for birds and cat food for hedgehogs. And last, but not least, fill your gardens with as many attractant companion plants as you can – such as *Convolvulus tricolor*, *Phacelia tanacetifolia*, *Limnanthes douglasii*, buckwheat, clover and vetches. Whatever you do, try to avoid using poisonous sprays unless you really have to, or you will probably end up killing more friends than enemies. The enemies will breed faster and recolonise.

You can't have too many nest boxes. Choose different sizes to suit the various birds in your area, and do remember to clean them out after use or other birds may not be tempted to move in.

thinking ahead

Pests and diseases come in cycles and many attacks are triggered by changes in weather, soil or growing conditions. By using observation and cunning, we should be able to keep ahead of problems and prevent them from occurring by simply altering the plant's growing conditions. Keeping the soil moist is a very effective way of preventing flea beetle damage during the week or so after the brassica seed emerges, when it is at its most vulnerable. Likewise, maintaining a humid atmosphere in the greenhouse with frequent misting or spraying discourages red spider mite. Keeping some plants, such as grapes, roses and gooseberries, wet at the roots and dry about their heads usually prevents mildew. Careful timing is important too. For example, the carrot fly is active when cow parsley flowers, so then is not a good time to thin carrots. Early potatoes nearly always miss the blight, while broad beans sown in autumn and over-wintered are usually too large and well grown to be vulnerable by the time the aphids arrive in summer.

Using a rotation system in the vegetable bed has the benefit that the crops are moved away from where they were the previous year to another spot where there are less likely to be any pests or diseases waiting for them. Another method is to change how we cultivate – many gardeners grow onions from sets instead of seed, for example, because sets do not suffer as much from onion fly. Tomatoes grown under cover do not suffer blight as often or as early as the same varieties outdoors. Even simple measures, such as removing the soft tips from broad beans as soon as enough flowers have set, can prevent aphids finding anywhere to colonise. Prompt action can stop a problem in its tracks – gooseberry sawfly caterpillars, for example, are easy to pick off straight after they have hatched when they are all on one leaf, but are not so easy to deal with after they have spread to the entire bush.

Fleeces, fine mesh netting, even old net curtains can all be used to exclude pests from crops such as the carrots hidden here.

fitting mechanical barriers

These are very effective against many of the larger pests and some diseases. Nets and fruit cages to keep out birds need little explanation. Fleeces and finer mesh barriers work in the same way against cabbage white butterflies, carrot flies and even aphids. Clear sheet covers are useful to prevent blight in potatoes and tomatoes, to keep leaf curl off peaches, and to keep the rain, and thus blossom wilt, off cherries.

Cloches can be used in the same way on smaller plants and also offer some protection from rabbits, deer and squirrels. A good deterrent for slugs and snails is to place a ring of copper or rigid plastic embedded in the soil around susceptible plants, or to surround plants with nasty substances such as soot or wood ash. Wire baskets, wire netting, humming lines and criss-crossing string or wires on sticks all act as barriers and stop birds and cats from disrupting seed beds and dismembering succulent transplants. Even humble sheets of cardboard can be useful if laid around cabbages as they prevent the cabbage root fly from laying its eggs in the soil near the plant's stem. Simply cut a square with a slit from one edge to the middle and slide it around the stem of each plant, flat to the ground. On a larger scale, old carpets, membranes and ground-cover materials can all be used to trap pests and disease spores underground – these are especially useful against pear midge and gooseberry sawfly. To protect container plants from slugs, snails and vine weevils, stand the container on 'feet' in a saucer of water and the moat will form a natural barrier.

installing traps

Traps are useful to reduce the number of pests reaching our plants in the first place, while usually doing no harm to other creatures. Sticky papers have been used to trap flies for years; sticky yellow bands and boards are useful in the greenhouse as they trap all sorts of flying pests such as pollen beetles and whiteflies, but must be taken out if predatory or parasitic controls are to be introduced. Flea beetles are trapped by sticky cards waved over their heads and thrips by sticky paper laid under the plants. Specially baited sticky traps are set in orchards to lure pests with the smell of a mate. Cloth and cardboard bands wrapped around tree trunks entice many pests, who think it's a nice bit of thick loose bark to hide in, rather than a trap. Earwigs are caught in bamboo tubes or in upturned pots of straw on top of canes. Millipedes and wireworms can be attracted to hollowed out potatoes or to potato and carrot 'chips' hidden in the soil or under leaves. Slugs can be trapped underneath wet carpet, wet cardboard and especially buttered cabbage leaves, or drowned in 'slug pub' saucers of fermenting beer and fruit juice – but don't forget to put in a few sticks to allow any trapped ground beetles to climb out. Wasps are attracted to jars half full of water, smeared inside with jam and fitted with aluminium foil lids pierced by pencil-thin holes. If put out in time, they are a good way to trap wasp scouts early in the season and stop them from bringing the rest of their swarm to eat your fruit. Mouse traps are advisable among stored packs of seed or fruit and vegetables – unless you have a cat, of course.

playing hide and seek

Spreading out susceptible specimens and hiding them among other plants is a good way of tricking pests and diseases. It also prevents them being hit all at the same time. Smelly combinations work best by confusing the pests – so planting onions alongside carrots or planting strong-smelling herbs around the edge of beds is a good way of keeping pests away from their original target. Some strong smellers, such as marigolds (*Tagetes* spp.), will deter whitefly from greenhouses.

Of course, you don't just have to use plants to provide camouflage smells – seaweed, garlic, weeds such as nettle and indeed any other spray with a strong smell will all help mask the scent the pest is searching for. There is a nastier option to the hide-and-seek game, where we leave a sacrifice to fob off the pest and save our plant. After planting out a row of bedding plants, lettuces or cabbages try scattering a few shredded bits of surplus transplants or wilted or damaged leaves in between the rows – hopefully these will lure the slugs for a day or two, giving the transplants time to toughen up.

introducing companion planting schemes

Companion plants are those that benefit the plants growing near or around them. For example, many crops and garden plants are legumes, naturally rich in nitrogen, which is produced by bacteria living in nodules on their roots. So an ideal companion scheme might be beans and sweetcorn, with the beans benefiting from growing up the sweetcorn and the

Companion planting on a raised bed. Mixing plants together, rather than having a concentration of a single plant (which may be vulnerable to specific infestations), makes it harder for any pest or disease to spread.

sweetcorn profiting from the nitrogen-rich soil. Conversely, it is definitely not a good idea to grow beans near onions as they seem to sicken each other. Although there is still a great deal to be learnt about this method, it is worth noting that alliums, especially garlic and chives, have long been reputed to guard fruit trees and roses against fungal diseases, while *Tagetes minuta* has been used effectively for years to decrease parasitic nematode eelworm populations. And have you noticed how a grass sward with clover in it stays green and grows faster than one without clover?

introducing biological controls

Many of the predators, parasites and pathogens long used commercially by large institutions to control pests or disease under glass are now available to the home gardener by mail-order from adverts in gardening magazines. Some can be used to control pests outdoors, such as *Bacillus thuringiensis*, available as a spray to control many sorts of caterpillar, but the most widely available are for controlling pests under cover – whitefly, red spider mite, aphids and mealybugs, for example. Each will have its own instructions, but in general all you do is simply let out the nearly invisible bugs to eat your existing bugs. Whitefly is controlled by *Encarsia formosa* (a minute wasp) and red spider mite by *Phytoseiulus persimilis* (a minute predatory mite). Aphids can be controlled by *Aphidoletes aphidomyza* (predatory midges) or *Aphidius* spp. (parasitic wasps). Mealybugs are controlled by *Cryptolaemus montrouzieri* (predatory ladybirds) or *Hypoaspis miles* (predatory mites). Thrips are eaten by *Amblyseius* spp. (predatory mites) and scale insects by *Steinernema* spp. (predatory nematodes) or *Metaphycus helvolus* (parasitic wasps). Vine weevil grubs are killed by watering their compost with the parasitic nematode *Heterohabditis megidis* or *Steinernema carpocasae*, and best of all slugs and snails can be killed if you water on *Phasmarhabditis hermaphrodita* (also parasitic nematodes). If in doubt, ask a supplier because more biological controls are being introduced all the time.

direct action

This involves removing and destroying the pest to prevent further damage, either by hand picking – which works well for small numbers of slugs, snails and caterpillars – or, as a last resort, by spraying. Hand picking, especially by torch at night, solves a lot of mysteries and damage in one fell swoop! Whatever you do, resist throwing slugs, snails and the like over the garden fence. They will probably return. Slugs, in particular, will come back to a kill, so if your transplants were half eaten last night, you had better go out and hand pick again tonight before they're gone entirely. Spraying poisons should be the last resort but if you have to spray, always follow the instructions and make sure the spray is suitable for the plant. In the first instance, try spraying the pests with a jet of water as knocking them flying across the lawn may reduce an attack enough to save any other effort. If a safe spray is what you want, then soft soaps, special modern sorts, which kill pests by choking them in a drying soap film, are fairly risk free. The organic gardener would next choose something like quassia, pyrethrum and derris, and for fungal attacks copper and sulphur compounds such as Bordeaux. Most mildews, rusts and moulds are best prevented by growing healthy plants and practising good plant hygiene, but if problems are anticipated then the early and regular application of these compounds can prevent them starting and escalating. However they are ineffective once a severe attack has got away. The non-organic gardener will use whatever chemical alternatives are currently still available. Whatever you choose, please save the bees and spray last thing in the evening when they have gone to bed.

Tagetes marigolds are very good at deterring whiteflies from finding your tomatoes – but will not drive them out if they are already established.

identifying pests & diseases

Matt: As EU legislation disarms gardeners, making alternative 'organics' mainstream, we are delighting in untainted crops but need to constantly review our tactics against a wily, combative enemy. Gardeners now have to accept that control, rather than eradication, will become the norm and tasty – not blemish free – is the future for healthy gardens and gardeners. Chemical controls change regularly in line with legislation – see your local retailer for current options.

It is not possible to cover every pest or disease here, so I will just deal with some of the most familiar foes.

Glasshouse red spider mite

Red spider or 'two-spotted mite' attacks many indoor plants and can also be a problem in the garden, particularly at the end of hot dry summers.

Initially, upper leaf surfaces become pale and mottled and, as an infestation worsens, leaves and stems are wrapped in fine silk webbing. Leaves lose their colouring, become papery and dry and eventually fall off. Look closely and the tiny mites are just visible with the naked eye or a hand lens.

Red spider mites thrive in warm, dry conditions. They dislike humidity so, where possible, misting your plants has some effect. Predatory mites, *Phytoseiulus persimilis*, can be introduced as a biological control. These need good light and daytime temperatures above 21°C (70°F) to thrive and are effective between mid-spring and mid-autumn. Several weeks before they are introduced, use sprays based on vegetable oil or fatty acid to keep numbers down.

Insecticides containing bifenthrin are effective, provided the red spider mites in your greenhouse are not a resistant strain.

Scale insects

There are more than 25 different species of scale insect in Britain. Sap-sucking adults, found on the leaves and stems of a range of indoor and outdoor plants, hide under protective shells that vary in shape and colour.

Wisteria scale, one of the largest, is up to 1cm (½in) long! Plants are weakened; 'honeydew' secretions on leaves become sticky and affected by a black sooty mould, particularly in damp conditions. Adults stay under the protection of their 'shell' and don't move, but newly hatched nymphs crawl over the plant in their search for a place to settle – and this is the time they are at their most vulnerable. Indoor scale insects breed throughout the year, when all stages are present; outdoors, a single generation hatches in mid-summer.

To control scale insects on fruit trees and roses, treat with an environ-mentally friendly winter wash on a mild dry day in early winter. Treat ornamental plants with imidacloprid; organic fatty acids or vegetable oils are effective, although several applications are needed – the advantage being that they can be used on fruit trees and bushes in leaf. Wiping tough, leathery, smooth leaves gently with a soft soapy cloth dislodges scales.

Biological pest controls include the parasitic wasp, *Metaphycus helvolus*, which attacks soft and hemispherical scale under glass in summer.

Whitefly

These are familiar on ornamental plants and vegetables, indoors and out, as small white-winged insects usually hiding underneath the leaves, where they suck sap and excrete 'honeydew'. Foliage becomes sticky and coated with a black sooty mould, particularly in moist conditions.

To control whitefly, hang yellow sticky traps above or among plants. Composts containing imidacloprid can be used for containerised ornamental plants. Use thiacloprid as a spray or drench. Introduce *Encarsia formosa*, a predatory wasp, or *Delphastus*, a type of ladybird, under glass (check population levels beforehand using sticky traps). Use organic sprays based on vegetable oils or fatty acids. One novel method of removal is to knock the leaves and suck up the whitefly with a vacuum cleaner as they fly up into the air – but beware of causing mechanical damage to plants!

Potato blight

Spores are spread by wind and rain in warm humid conditions from mid-summer onwards, when temperatures exceed 10°C (50°F). Brown or black patches appear first on tips and margins of leaflets, which curl up and wither.

The disease then spreads rapidly to leaves and stems and finally the plant collapses. Spores are then washed down to the tubers, skins become discoloured and a reddish-brown rot appears. This, together with any secondary infection, reduces the tuber to a foetid, liquefied mass. Potato blight rapidly devastates crops, whether they are stored or still in the ground.

Tuber infection can be reduced by 'earthing up' or mulching with a thick layer of organic material like hay or straw. Remove infected foliage immediately to slow its spread and prevent spores spreading to the tubers; don't harvest the crop for at least three weeks after removing infected foliage to allow time for skins to thicken up and spores on the surface to die. Do not leave blighted tubers in the soil; lift even the tiniest ones and dispose of them away from the garden. Always plant seed tubers from a reliable source. Early maincrop varieties are more prone to blight, so plant early

to give them time to mature before it appears. Planting alternate rows of different resistant varieties can improve cropping. Check tubers in store regularly and remove any that are rotting.

Apply Bordeaux mixture, copper oxychloride or mancozeb before plants become infected. Listen out for mention of 'blight infection' or 'Mills period' on farming programmes or the weather forecasts on *Gardeners' Question Time* – these are the ideal climatic conditions for infection. If the weather changes and it becomes dry and sunny, this can just stop blight spreading. Some varieties show degrees of resistance, including 'Colleen', 'Premiere', 'Cosmos', 'Lady Balfour', 'Pomeroy', 'Orla', 'Remarka', 'Cara', 'Milva', 'Valor', 'Verity' and 'Arran Victory'. 'Sarpo Mira', the first to score 100 per cent in commercial evaluations against blight is ushering in a new era of blight and virus resistance. More varieties, including 'Sarpo Axona', are due to follow – roll on the blight-resistant revolution!

Tomato blight

Potato blight also appears on tomatoes and their relatives. Brown, watery, rapidly spreading patches appear on leaves and stems; patches of brown rot appear on fruit. Infected tissues die rapidly.

Potatoes are usually infected first, so follow all the recommended controls for potato blight to reduce the chance of it spreading to your tomatoes. Tomatoes grown under glass are usually less prone to infection. Spray outdoor tomatoes with mancozeb or Bordeaux mixture to protect against attack. Keep greenhouses well ventilated. Do not save seed from infected fruit. Remove and destroy infected plants immediately. The cultivar 'Ferline' shows some resistance, but not always. Smaller-fruited varieties are less likely to be infected.

Powdery mildew

Dry whitish powder coats the upper surfaces of leaves, but can spread to the undersides, shoot tips and flowers. Plant growth is stunted and distorted, particularly on young foliage; fruits split and crack. On rhododendron leaves, yellow patches appear on upper surfaces with brown felty blotches below.

Powdery mildew often affects woody and herbaceous plants, such as roses, apple trees, sweet peas and plants in hanging baskets, but beetroot, parsnips and spinach leaves can be affected too. Mildews can spread to cultivated plants from closely related weeds, so weed control is important.

Dryness at the roots increases susceptibility, so keep plants well watered (without splashing the foliage) and mulch to keep the soil moist. Improve air circulation around plants by pruning. Open vents or install fans in greenhouses. Don't plant too densely, plant vegetables at the correct spacing and avoid high-nitrogen fertilisers, which encourage vulnerable soft sappy growth. Grow plants in their preferred position so they are not under stress and at risk of infection. Grow resistant varieties. Prune out infected parts immediately and ensure that white patches on stems (the resting stage) are pruned

out of roses during winter pruning. Collect and burn or dispose of all infected debris. Many local authorities now collect for composting and the temperatures created on their giant heaps is sufficient to kill spores.

Spray with myclobutanil, penconazole, flutriafol, sulphur or fatty acids. Check the label before buying because pesticides can only legally be used on the range of plants specified. There are no fungicides for use on most vegetables, so try an alternative method of control. Wipe mildew from gooseberry fruits, for example, and they will still be edible.

Bicarbonate of soda at 5g per litre controls mildew. Researchers in Brazil discovered that milk solution was effective on courgettes and boosted the plant's immune system too. A weekly spray of one part milk to nine parts water reduced the severity of infection by 90 per cent. In New Zealand, researchers found skimmed milk to be equally effective and the reduced fat content decreased the chance of odours. The whole plant needed to be sprayed. However, as neither product is legally approved for powdery mildew control, I am not allowed to recommend them!

Carrot fly

Carrot fly affects carrots, parsnips, parsley and celery. Females, attracted by the smell released when plants are damaged or thinned can smell one molecule of 'eau de carotte' a mile away! Creamy yellow maggots up to 9mm (½in) long tunnel through roots, rusty brown scars appear where tunnels on the roots collapse and reddening of leaves may occur. In severe infestations the roots are inedible, susceptible to secondary rots and not suitable for storage. Two or three generations of carrot fly can occur between summer and autumn.

Sow in early summer to avoid the first generation. Harvest before early autumn to avoid the second generation. Surround the crop with 60cm (24in) barriers of clear polythene to exclude low-flying females or cover crops with horticultural fleece. Sow sparsely to avoid thinning – if you have to thin, firm and water the rows immediately afterwards. Rotate crops. Cultivars 'Fly Away', 'Maestro', 'Resistafly' and 'Sytan' and fast-growing varieties such as 'Nandor' are less susceptible.

'Autumn King' types appear to be more susceptible. Grow carrots on a windy site. You can intercrop with four rows of onions to one row of

carrots and the protection will last until the onion leaves stop growing, when the bulbs start to form.

Apply a 5cm (2in) mulch of grass clippings before carrots are 10–15cm (4–6in) high, then top up with 1cm (½in) every week for four weeks to make it more difficult for females to lay their eggs in cracks in the soil. Be warned, slugs and snails also love these conditions. Alternatively, create ridges of soil at least 5cm (2in) high around roots (which has the added benefit of stopping the tops from becoming green).

Vine weevil

Adults are about 10mm (½in) long, matt black with pale orange spots, with antennae bent at an angle. Vine weevils hide in the dark during the day, can be seen moving slowly on leaves at night, 'play dead' if disturbed and nibble notches in leaf margins. Rhododendron, primula and evergreen euonymus are among their favourite foods. Only females have ever been found, each laying one thousand eggs per season, without the help of a male! The larvae are plump, white and C-shaped, with pale brown heads and mainly – but not exclusively – feed on the roots of containerised plants, which simply wilt and die. When lifted from the compost, there are no roots attached.

Go on torch-lit hunts on spring or summer evenings, check plants and walls, pick off adult weevils and crush them. Shake shrubs over an upturned umbrella to catch adults, check under pots or on the underside of staging in the greenhouse where the beetles hide during the day – they lurk anywhere dark, under sheets of hessian, old tiles or coloured plastic too. Take a loose roll of corrugated paper, tied with string or a rubber band, and put it in the greenhouse. Adults will hide inside during the day and can be collected and crushed. Other preventative methods include mulching pots with a layer of gravel or putting gauze over the drainage holes of pots so the females cannot lay their eggs. Alternatively, smear sticky barriers, such as petroleum jelly or insect barrier glue, around the rims of pots or glasshouse staging. Encourage predators, such as birds (robins love the larvae and bantams the adults), frogs, toads, shrews, hedgehogs and predatory ground beetles.

Apply biological control nematodes as a drench according to the supplier's instructions. These are more effective in pots of open potting compost, such as peat or coir, than in the open ground. Results are poor in heavy or dry soil.

Compost mixed with imidacloprid controls larvae for up to 12 months. Wash old compost off the roots before repotting. Applying thiacloprid as a drench in mid- to late summer controls larvae, preventing damage later in the season. Unless you have a soil steriliser, do not re-use old compost, even when grubs are removed, since eggs may still be present.

Honey fungus

Honey fungus (*Armillaria*) spreads between plants by means of black 'bootlaces', which are found about 20cm (8in) below the soil surface, both in the soil and on the roots, growing about 1m (3ft) every year. Plants under stress, due to poor growing conditions, tend to be most vulnerable, although some species are more susceptible than others.

When infected, trees, shrubs, other woody plants and herbaceous perennials will die back and their leaves can discolour and wilt. Death will usually follow, sometimes rapidly, but often after several years. Flowering or fruiting plants can perform magnificently out of season before they die. Pull off the bark, particularly around the base – if infected, it will come away easily and the trunk underneath will be covered with sheets of white mushroom-smelling mycelium. Gum oozes from the trunk, particularly of conifers. Clumps of honey-coloured, pale-stemmed toadstools may appear at the base or near the roots of infected plants in autumn, but are not a usual source of infection – at night they may phosphoresce. The 'mushrooms' can be eaten when young for sweet revenge (but only if you know what you're doing and are certain of their identity)!

To control honey fungus, dig out the stumps and roots of all infected woody plants thoroughly and burn them immediately; do not use the chippings as a mulch. If removal is impossible, treat with ammonium sulphamate to kill the stump and hasten decay.

Feed and mulch regularly to keep plants healthy. Once honey fungus appears in your garden, only plant resistant species. Alternatively, create raised beds with a barrier of landscape fabric in the base. To prevent honey fungus spreading, bury a vertical barrier made from thick plastic or butyl pond liner 30–40cm (12–16in) deep in the soil.

Susceptible plants include birch (*Betula* spp.), cedar (*Cupressus* spp.), cotoneaster, forsythia, hydrangea, privet (*Ligustrum* spp.), apple and crab apple (*Malus* spp.), apricot, cherry, peach and plum (*Prunus* spp.), rhododendron, currant (*Ribes* spp.), rose (*Rosa* spp.) and wisteria.

Semi-resistant plants include abutilon, bamboo, Indian bean tree (*Catalpa bignonioides*), plumbago (*Ceratostigma* spp.), Judas tree (*Cercis* spp.), quince (*Chaenomeles* spp.), choisya, clematis, smoke bush (*Cotinus* spp.), elaeagnus, beech (*Fagus* spp.), kerria, and passion fruit (*Passiflora* spp.).

Clockwise from top left: a classic example of aphid damage; the giant lupin aphid; ladybirds, lacewings and hoverflies all help to keep your aphid population down.

Aphids

No gardener really needs a description of these horticultural horrors that suck sap, excrete 'honeydew', encourage a black sooty mould and introduce viruses to plants! They protect themselves by making leaves pucker and curl, by producing a woolly coating or by hiding on plant roots, and they can travel hundreds of miles on air currents to land in our gardens.

Aphids come in a range of colours from traditional green to pink and whitish grey, and sizes from 2mm (⅛in) to the giant lupin aphid, about 4.5mm (¼in) or more long. Most aphids can be found clustered in rapidly expanding colonies on young shoots and under leaves, which become distorted.

Rub off small infestations between finger and thumb. To remove colonies on strong growth, try blasting them off with a jet of water, but beware of damaging your plants; or make it more fun and more of a challenge with a high-powered water pistol – do this early in the day to discourage fungal growth. Use organic contact insecticides containing pyrethrum, rotenone, fatty acids or vegetable oils. You can also use imidacloprid as a spray or drench.

The biological control *Aphidius*, a small parasitic wasp, lays eggs on immature aphids and occurs naturally in the British Isles. *Aphidoletes* is a small midge whose larvae eat aphids; both can be bought from specialist suppliers.

Ladybirds, particularly their larvae, are voracious feeders on aphids. To encourage them into the garden, don't tidy up too much in autumn but leave dry plant debris, loose bark and hollow stems as hibernation sites.

Lacewings and their larvae are aphid eaters too. Encourage them to over-winter in your garden by buying or making nesting chambers for them. To make your own, cut the bottom off a large plastic drinks bottle, roll up a piece of corrugated cardboard long enough to reach to the end of the bottle and push it inside. Make a small hole on either side at the base of the bottle and push a thin piece of wire through to hold the cardboard in place. Leave the cap on the bottle to stop water from getting in and hang it out in the garden from mid-summer onwards. Place chambers at least 3m (9ft) from trees or buildings and bring them into a cool shed from early winter, returning them to the garden in spring. Make sure you replace the straw and attractant in purpose-built chambers annually.

Hoverflies like to munch on aphids too and can be attracted by planting food sources. They prefer small, simple flowers, such as fennel and dill, and members of the daisy family, as well as the poached-egg plant (*Limnanthes douglasii*), *Convolvulus tricolor* and buckwheat.

Blue tits eat more aphids than any other garden bird – one family eats as many as 100,000 aphids a year. Encourage them in your garden by hanging pieces of fat in fruit trees and above fruit bushes. Avoid using high-nitrogen fertilisers that encourage soft aphid-friendly growth.

Put down old tiles as a hiding place for ground or rove beetles and centipedes, which eat the larvae of lettuce root aphid. Sow lettuce varieties that are resistant to root aphid, such as 'Avoncrisp' and 'Avondefiance'. Grow crops under horticultural fleece.

To prevent ants 'farming' aphids in woody plants, smear a band of grease around the stem or trunk to stops the ants climbing up.

Plant 'sacrificial' crops, such as nasturtiums, to attract black bean aphids. Once they are heavily infested, lift and destroy the plants.

Left: A solitary citrus in its role as a slug trap.

Mealybugs

Most mealybug species are found on indoor plants but some attack garden plants, such as ceanothus and New Zealand flax (*Phormium* spp.). White waxy covered clusters, like tiny woodlice, hide in the most inaccessible places including leaf axils or between twining stems, sucking sap, reducing vigour and excreting 'honeydew' that encourages a black sooty mould. Heavy infestations may cause early leaf fall.

Buy healthy plants and put them into quarantine for several weeks before introducing them to the greenhouse. Remove dead leaves and prunings, as these may have mealybugs or eggs on them.

Use imidacloprid as a spray or drench for root aphid. Use organic winter wash on peaches; scrape loose bark off vines to expose hidden mealybugs before treatment. Spread newspaper under vines to collect the scrapings, then burn or dispose of them away from the garden. Spray with fatty acids or vegetable oils, giving each plant several applications. The biological control *Cryptolaemus montrouzieri* (predatory ladybirds) can be used under glass; both adults and larvae feed on mealybugs. *Leptomastix*, a tiny wasp, parasitises citrus and grapevine mealybug.

Slugs

Several slug species forage on the soft tissue of a wide range of plants. They favour moist conditions and are particularly active in spring, when damp weather and soft foliage abound.

Use biological control nematodes; these are most effective on moist, well-drained soils and less so on clay. Sow seed in pots and cover transplants with plastic bottles with the bases removed as cloches (check that no slugs have become trapped inside the bottles a few days after transplanting). Wait until plants are well established before mulching. Make traps using lettuce leaves or the scooped out remains of citrus or melon skins, laid cut-side down, placing them near vulnerable plants. Put out 'slug pubs', jam jars or saucers part-filled with stout – making sure the lips of the jars are at least 2cm (1in) above soil level to stop any slug-eating ground beetles from falling in. Empty traps daily. Go slug hunting on mild, damp evenings. Pay special attention to organic mulches, where slugs like to hide. Leave out large sheets of hessian, cardboard or plastic sheeting on the ground for the slugs to hide under (ground beetles and centipedes that feed on slugs and their eggs will be attracted to the damp conditions too). Dispose of slugs in a nearby field, hedgerow or on waste ground a long distance from your garden. Alternatively, destroy them in hot water or a strong salt solution – or adopt your own gruesome methods of destruction!

Encourage other natural predators, such as birds, frogs, toads, hedgehogs and slow-worms into the garden. Lure ground and rove beetles by digging a trench about 7.5cm (3in) deep. Cover the base with a layer of pebbles to provide somewhere for the beetles to hide under and leave them to eat any slugs that fall into the trench. Provide upturned flower pots for frogs and toads, log piles for hedgehogs and upturned tiles for ground and rove beetles. Rake over the soil during winter to expose slug eggs to birds. Keep ducks and chickens.

Most plants, once established, tolerate slug damage. Chemical controls include scattering metaldehyde slug pellets around vulnerable plants at the manufacturer's recommended rate (avoid spreading them too thickly as this is unnecessary and wasteful). A liquid formulation can be applied to ornamental plants and the soil. Controls based on aluminium sulphate and ferrous phosphate pellets are also available. Other controls include copper-impregnated mulch mats, barriers and tape, bran, sharp grit, vermiculite, ground porous rock, traps and repellents.

Slugs dislike travelling over open ground so surround raised beds with grass or slabs. Slugs attack potatoes from late summer so lift tubers by early autumn to reduce damage. Grow slug-resistant varieties, including 'Kestrel', 'Pentland Dell', 'Spey', 'Romano' and 'Golden Wonder'. Sow 'sacrificial' crops, such as lettuce, that are irresistible to slugs. Practise good hygiene, removing leaf debris and decaying plant material.

Snails

Snails are simply slugs with their houses on their backs! Like slugs, they adore chomping on soft tissue but they can also climb and damage trees – they often attack young growth on laburnums. Protected by their shells, they are less dependent on high levels of moisture and because they need calcium to form their shells, they are less common on acid soils. The common garden snail causes the greatest damage to plants; other species are less of a problem.

In general, snails are controlled in the same way as slugs (see page 275). However, the nematode used against slugs is unlikely to control snails. Snails often hibernate over winter in upturned flower pots or crevices in walls and can be removed by hand. Provide an 'anvil' stone for thrushes so that they can smash the snail shells and eat the contents. I have heard about someone who collected snails, fed them on bran for three weeks as a purgative, then ate them!

Magnesium deficiency

Magnesium, part of the green pigment in leaves, is essential for plant growth. Deficiency is most common on light, acid or sandy soils where it is easily washed from the soil and is worse in wet seasons. Excessive use of potassium fertilisers causes deficiency, because when potassium is available in high concentrations, it, rather than the magnesium, is absorbed.

Deficiency is most common late in the season, with yellowing between leaf veins and around the margins. It appears on older leaves first. Red-leaved plants, such as beetroot, turn red or orange tints; in severe cases, the same discoloration appears on green-leaved plants and if left untreated, the leaves will die. Magnesium deficiency is quite common in fruit and vegetables, particularly tomatoes, lettuces and apples, and in rhododendrons.

Treat soils in autumn or winter with magnesium sulphate or calcium-magnesium carbonate (Dolomitic limestone), but not if you have neutral or acid soils as it makes them more alkaline. Magnesium sulphate (Epsom salts) is an effective foliar feed in summer. Mix 200g to 10 litres of water (8oz per 2½ gal) and apply after flowering. Reduce the use of potash fertilisers where necessary.

Nitrogen deficiency

Nitrogen is essential for growth of leaves and shoots. Where deficiency occurs, older leaves are affected first. Leaves may be small and pale, growth is slow and lacklustre and flowering and fruiting may be reduced. Brassicas develop yellow, orange, red or purple tints; potato crops are poor.

Nitrogen deficiency can occur where unrotted woody material is applied as a mulch. Since nitrogen is needed to break it down, it is temporarily unavailable to the plants. Mulches should be fully or partially rotted before applying; general or high-nitrogen fertiliser should be sprinkled on the soil before mulching.

Nitrogen deficiency is more common on light soils with a low nitrogen content. Leafy crops, such as brassicas, have high demands, so practise regular crop rotation to prevent soil becoming depleted. Top and soft fruit need moderate supplies of nitrogen; carrots need very little. Legumes such as peas and beans produce nitrogen in nodules on their roots and they can benefit future crops – especially brassicas or similar leafy vegetables – if roots are left in the soil after harvesting.

To prevent nitrogen deficiency, apply general or high-nitrogen fertiliser, such as sulphate of ammonia, nitrochalk or dried blood, hoof and horn. Improve the soil with well-rotted organic matter and plant 'green manures' (see page 133) to prevent nitrogen being washed away in winter. Improve drainage on wet soils or mulch with grass clippings.

Iron deficiency

The symptoms of iron-induced chlorosis are often seen in acid-loving plants, such as rhododendrons and camellias, grown on alkaline soils where they are unable to absorb iron from the soil. Yellowing occurs between the leaf veins and, in extreme cases, leaves go almost white with brown patches along the margins.

Transplant acid-loving plants into raised beds or containers of acid compost. Water with sequestered trace elements; in hard water areas use rainwater, cooled boiled water or distilled water from a dehumidifier. Test the soil: if it is slightly alkaline, raise the pH with sulphur.

High phosphate levels in acid soils can also cause iron deficiency.

Phosphorus deficiency

Phosphorus is needed for growth and ripening of fruits and seeds. It is also important for seed germination. Spinach, carrots, lettuces, currants, apples and gooseberries are the most susceptible to deficiency.

Symptoms are similar to nitrogen deficiency: growth is weak, leaves are small and become dull green and purple, flowering and fruiting is poor, fruits are small and taste acidic. Phosphorus deficiency is more likely to occur in areas of high rainfall or on acid soils because phosphorus washes easily through heavy clay or shallow chalk soils.

Apply bonemeal, natural rock phosphate, superphosphate, the delightfully named 'basic slag' or a general NPK.

Potassium deficiency

Flowering, fruiting and general growth are affected by potassium deficiency. Brown patches appear on leaf blades, margins or tips, and spots on undersides; leaves become blue-green and margins may roll up and become soft. Older leaves are affected first. Deficiencies occur more often in light soils or those with a high acid or alkaline pH.

Improve your soil by adding organic matter. Apply sulphate of potash or high-potash fertiliser annually to soft and top fruit. Prevention and cure can be achieved in the short term by feeding with liquid comfrey or seaweed meal. Add wood ash via the compost heap and apply as a mulch.

Chapter 11

gardening under glass

Bob: Any covered area enhances the value of a garden, allowing you to grow a wider range of plants over a longer season. Walk-in, and even sit-in, areas are pleasant both for you and for your plants. An important consideration is that no matter how big your greenhouse or conservatory may be at the outset, it will very soon seem too small. Don't just get the biggest you can afford, get an even bigger one. No matter how big and empty it looks initially, it will be more than full by the end of the first year. Economies of scale help a bit, as larger houses cost less per area covered and lose less heat proportionately than smaller ones. (However, they still cost more in total!) If you are considering building a greenhouse or something similar, listen to the advice of everyone else who has ever had one – I have never met anyone who said they wished they had built their greenhouse or conservatory smaller!

Is the most expensive necessarily the best? If you can afford an expensive greenhouse, it is probably worth the extra outlay – but only if it's the one you really want. A small greenhouse is a valuable gardening asset and it costs less than an average holiday, but it is a complete waste if what you really want is a sit-in conservatory. If you are after economical crops and have plenty of land, a huge polythene covered tunnel is for you – it will cost about the same as a small glass greenhouse and ten times as much to heat, but it will provide you with masses of space for your money. A proper conservatory might cost you a fortune, but it should also add good value to your property (whereas any greenhouse probably will not – and I hate to speculate on what a wind-shredded polytunnel does!).

Another thing to bear in mind is the very different repair, repainting and replacement costs of each type in terms of time and labour.

choosing a structure

Glass and wooden greenhouses

A traditional greenhouse is probably more pleasing to the eye than any other type. There are two styles: the half-section form, which can be attached to a wall or house as a lean-to, and the full freestanding variety. Wood, being an excellent insulator, is snug and relatively cheap to heat. The downside is that because the wooden base and lower half often extends to waist level to save glass and conserve heat, the growing area is restricted to benches or raised staging.

Another drawback of wood, even hardwood, is that it does need regular treatment and, of course, the glass needs to be cleaned at least once a year. You might also find that styles usually come with insufficient venting. Even so, a traditional wooden greenhouse is a good choice for the gardener with specimen plants in pots and for those with children, as the wooden lower half is much safer. It may be easy or difficult to fix extra insulation in winter depending on the construction. In summer extra shading can be arranged by washes or screens.

Tender plants such as this *Allemanda* can be kept under glass in the winter and moved outside once any fear of frost has passed.

A Victorian greenhouse on the grand scale costs less to build than it does to run, but allows a vast range of plants and gardening 365 days a year.

Glass and metal greenhouses

Glass and metal greenhouses are usually a tad cheaper than wooden ones, easier to self-assemble (a relative point), slightly brighter because the metal supports are slimmer, slightly colder because metal cools down rapidly, sometimes more draughty and often less attractive. However, they need less maintenance than wood. Extra insulation is usually relatively easy to install, as long as the appropriate fixings are secured for the type of metal bar used, and summer shading is possible with washes or screens. Glass to ground level enables borders to be grown in.

Plastic or polythene-covered walk-in tunnels or greenhouses

Despite what many people think, these are remarkably sturdy structures if well built. The cost per unit area covered is remarkably low. The downside is that although they can be made draught proof if the ends are well constructed, they are very expensive to heat as the plastic is so thin, and likewise ventilation can be difficult in hot weather. The diffused light they provide suits many plants, and shading is almost never required, but the light is not especially good for growing tomatoes, aubergines and a few others who like it brighter. Maintenance levels are high – the plastic needs to be washed annually and should be replaced every five years or so once it becomes opaque and brittle.

Matt's tips for choosing a greenhouse

● Timber has a natural empathy with the garden. Cedar is rot resistant and long lasting but needs treating to retain its colour; check that other timbers like rosewood have been properly treated to increase longevity.

● Aluminium comes in a range of colours, so that you can choose whether to have white (which stands out) or green or pastel shades to blend in with the background.

● It is worth paying extra for toughened safety glass, especially if you have children. Some greenhouses have plastic frames with polycarbonate glazing that is lightweight and safe, diffusing light in summer and, being double skinned, insulating well in winter.

● Ensure that the doors are wide enough for your wheelbarrow. Check that the greenhouse is high enough for you to enter with ease – not bang your head on the ventilation – and have sufficient space to work comfortably under the eaves. The height can be raised by building up the brick foundations but you'll need to make a step or ramp either side of the doorway to compensate. Make sure there is enough room by the door to turn the wheelbarrow in the greenhouse and put a hard surface by the entrance to avoid wear and tear.

● Smaller greenhouses limit the number of plants that can be grown and are difficult to heat and ventilate in summer; the minimum size for easy gardening is 2.4 x 1.8m (8 x 6 ft). If you intend to grow crops like tomatoes in a border, the minimum practical width is 90cm (36in).

Conservatories

These can vary from ramshackle Victoriana to modern, double-glazed luxury. In general, you have to decide whether your conservatory is a room to live in or a home for your plants. We, and our clothes and furnishings, prefer a drier atmosphere to most plants and don't care if it's freezing in the conservatory at night when we are tucked up in bed. If your conservatory doubles as a living room, stick to plants that like arid conditions, such as cacti, succulents and certain house plants. If it is a room for your plants, then do not plan on including electrical items, books or soft furnishings as they are unlikely to endure the humidity. The greatest advantage of a conservatory is its proximity to the rest of the house, making services and central heating easy to connect. The glass may need shading in summer and automatic ventilation should be installed to prevent high temperatures harming plants. Of course, being part of the house it is also a potential security risk and should be secure!

Sunrooms or orangeries

Whereas a conservatory generally has a glass roof, a sunroom – or orangery as it once would have been called – only has a glass front, usually (sensibly) facing the sun. In winter, when the sun is low it shines in to warm the room. In summer, when the sun rises higher during the heat of the day it is obscured by the roof, and optional awning, to give a cool, light but shaded room. Apart from placing house plants on the windowsills, sunrooms are not really suited to growing many things. However, they are excellent for over-wintering citrus plants, provided you keep them misted and watered.

Doors, paths, floors, borders and bases

Sliding doors are most convenient, provided they are not too flimsy. Otherwise go for outward-opening ones, which take up less internal floor space. If possible, try to include double doors in larger constructions. An additional set of netting doors will keep out many pests in summer, while still allowing for ventilation. Paths should be paved or concrete with rough surfaces to prevent slipping when wet. Obviously proper conservatories deserve tiled floors, whereas polythene tunnels can make do with bark mulches or – my favourite – a piece of old carpet. In every case, make sure the floor is level and solid as you will be moving heavy things around. If you

An extension of the house or an extension of the garden? The most successful conservatories are a bit of both.

are planning on having plants growing in the soil in borders, then you may want to improve this before building. If you are installing a fixed solid floor, don't forget to include drainage for drips and washing down. Always check with your local authority about the need for planning permission and what building regulations might apply. Heavy, well-fixed foundations and a secure base are essential and should not be economised on.

easy to fix to the sides of a greenhouse, however freestanding styles are more suitable under polythene or in a conservatory. Staging is often slatted to provide air flow and it may also be banked to expose more plants to the light and to raise them closer to the glass, to warmer air higher up. A potting bench needs to be substantial or it will rock. It may conveniently have storage underneath. However, be careful not to take up valuable growing area with junk. A chair – comfortable – is permissible!

equipping the greenhouse

Staging, potting benches and storage

Staging, potting benches and storage are usually overlooked initially, but they are quite essential. Most types of staging are

Winter protection

Don't forget that winter will eventually come. Water in pipes and containers may freeze, as may solutions of garden chemicals. Plastic may become brittle and automatic vent openers can stop working. Without adequate heat, non-hardy

Staging, especially banked staging, allows better access, more plants to be displayed and each to get more light.

plants will soon die. To cut down on heat loss, fix extra insulation (often bubble plastic) inside. Take care to provide adequate ventilation, because the reduced light and increased humidity will make your plants more prone to moulds. More heat plus ventilation is usually the (costly) answer.

Heating

It goes without saying that if you haven't got enough heat to keep your plants warm on the coldest nights, all your initial outlay and efforts will be utterly wasted. Electric thermostatic fan heaters are expensive to run (even though they are mainly needed at night when rates are cheaper) and need professional installation, but they are extremely reliable and hassle free, making them the most common choice. Paraffin stoves and solid-fuel boilers are awkward, while gas- or oil-fired boilers only really make sense for the larger greenhouse. For advice on heating for propagation, see pages 256–57.

Greenhouse health and hygiene

Health and hygiene are more of a problem under cover because the natural checks and balances found naturally outdoors are absent. Predatory insects rarely find their way inside, unless they are lured by the attractive smell of their prey, and once inside pests can breed unchecked. Infection and its spread is rife because we keep our greenhouses so snug and warm and cram our plants close together. Under glass, we (wrongly) tend to ignore rotation and grow the same plants year after year in the same border soil. We grow them soft and lush and so they're more prone to attack and infection. And we often heat the lot all winter, allowing our pests to avoid frost and thrive all year round.

Pest and disease controls

Begin by following the suggestions on pages 264–68. Many of the points made there apply to gardening under glass, although you might have difficulties trying to incorporate a pond or hedgehog den in a small greenhouse! Prevention under glass is key, so we must put greater reliance on ensuring that our plants are healthy. As the area is contained, it is worth buying in beneficial insects, with the likelihood that they will stay around.

The single biggest difference between growing plants outdoors and growing them under cover is that we can do little about the weather outside, but we can alter the growing conditions inside. The most important factor for pest and disease resistance is healthy plants grown without any check.

Only if our plants are healthy can they shrug off attacks, and that means controlling their conditions carefully to ensure they are never stressed or checked. (Checking causes tissues to harden and the plant finds it difficult to resume growing, resulting in stunted growth and split fruits and roots.) Plants grown too softly and lushly with excess water and fertiliser will have soft tissues prone to attacks by pests or disease, so we must not spoil our plants with too much coddling.

Watering

Watering is crucial. Any shortage of water and plants stop growing, their sap becomes thicker and more appealing to pests and, in the worst cases, they wilt – a serious sign that damage has been done! Water stress makes them prone to mildew and rust. Under cover, watering must be adjusted to the season and the day – even in cold weather, the sun can still be bright and your plants may need more water than you imagine. Most plants are best watered in the morning, so they have the water to call on during the heat of the day, whereas watering in the evening can leave them damp and cold at night. However, if you find they need watering at other times, do it then! Warm water is less stressful than cold. If the compost is very dry, add a drop of soap to the water to help it wet better. Over-watering is as dangerous as under-watering – it washes out nutrients from the soil and rots roots – so do not let plants stand in water and make sure they can drain. Automatic watering systems may be worth investing in.

Misting and spraying

Controlling the air humidity helps keep plants healthy. Some plants prefer it drier, some moister and some, such as tomatoes, want it moist when flowering, but dry at other times. In general, greenhouse air tends to be too dry for many plants in summer and too damp in winter. We can help plants that love humidity by misting and spraying clean rain water

Bob spraying his beloved seaweed solution.

(tap water may contain too many residues). This should be done earlier, rather than later, in the day so that plants are dry by nightfall, and never in very hot, bright, dry conditions, as the plants can scorch. Automatic systems are available.

Ventilation

Much of the skill of keeping plants happy under cover is to supply adequate ventilation. All plants need a change of air, as stagnant air soon causes diseases and pests. In summer, you cannot give too much air, so fan assistance may help. In winter, ventilation will waste heat but it is a necessary evil. The problem in winter is that damp air encourages moulds – it makes the air warmer, making the moulds mould faster. In general, if it's not too cold and windy it's best to open up all ventilation as early in each day as possible and close up in late afternoon to retain warmth. If you miss opening up, and it gets steamy inside, do not open suddenly but bleed cooler air in gradually – any sudden chill will shock your plants. And if you miss closing, do it as soon as you remember – even after midnight – as the coldest time is usually at four or five o'clock in the morning. In spring when the air is cold but the sun is bright, plants may use up all of the carbon dioxide, especially if the greenhouse is kept shut to save heat. In this case, place fermenting bottles of yeast, sugar and water in the greenhouse to provide this important gaseous nutrient (commercially, it is provided from pressurised bottles). Automatic vents and fans are very good investments. Remember, ventilation means air, not draughts!

Temperature control

We all think about heating to keep the temperature up to minimum temperatures in winter, but we often fail to consider the effects of over-heating on hot days when the greenhouse is shut up. There is always a problem under glass with the temperature rising, especially with plants raised above the ground, which is not where they find themselves in nature! Automatic vents will let excess heat out and keep the air near the glass cooler, but you may also need extra fans in a crowded or large greenhouse to move air around and help to balance hot and cool places. In general, we tend to keep temperatures too regular with automatic thermostats, when, in fact, many plants prefer cooler nights and hotter days.

Shading and lighting

Under glass, though not so much under plastic, it can get too bright and this can scorch the foliage of some plants, especially cucumbers and gardenias. Very hot, bright conditions also favour pests, such as red spider mites. Shade is beneficial, whether it's a piece of paper placed over germinating seeds, a net curtain laid over seedlings or a cooling wash on the glass. In conservatories, automatic roller blinds and so on are available. Conversely, for the very keen among us, we can add additional light to promote growth or extra flowering during the winter. Although expensive, boosting a plant's growth aids its resistance to pests or disease.

Quarantine

One of the disadvantages of having a nearly sealed eco-system is that natural controls don't find their way in – but neither do most problems unless we help them. Many pests, such as vine weevils, mealybugs and scale insects, and many diseases are only likely to appear if we bring them in. If you germinate only from bought-in seed in sterile compost in a new construction you may go for decades before problems ever show. On the other hand, you can get the lot on one imported plant! Each and every plant should be inspected thoroughly, roots and all, and then ideally held somewhere else for several weeks to ensure it is not carrying some woe. Do not overlook such simple steps – I never had mealybugs until I accepted one infected plant.

Introducing predators and parasites

The enclosed space under cover restricts the ecology you can build up to control pests – as previously mentioned, a pond is usually out of the question! However, as a greenhouse is virtually sealed it is possible to use commercially available biological controls in the knowledge that they can't get away. There are predators, parasites and even diseases available to control almost every greenhouse pest, and they are very effective if introduced correctly and in time. Some natural allies can be encouraged, of course. For example, all spiders are carnivorous and they can be coaxed in with string frames for their webs (it keeps them out of pathways), hollow stalks for day time nests, and drinking water in plastic bottle caps.

Growing companion plants

Companion plants can be grown under cover and, because the space is nearly sealed, some are extremely effective. As

anecdotal as the evidence is, there is no doubt that the pongy smell of French marigolds emanating from a greenhouse prevents whitefly ever venturing in, however it does not drive them away if they are there already. Having flowering plants may attract in pollinators, but make sure they can find their way out again. 'Sacrificial' plants are also useful. Basil seems to lure aphids off tomatoes; broad beans act as a magnet to red spider mites and sweet tobacco attracts whitefly. Once these 'sacrificial' companions are infested, they can be pulled up and composted, taking the pests with them.

Hygiene

Prompt action whenever any pest or disease is spotted is certainly important to prevent them contaminating other plants. Often a finger and thumb can squeeze the problem away, or a few leaves promptly picked can take away the primary infection. Daily inspection and grooming is vitally important when growing plants under cover. Bacterial and viral diseases spread quickly in warm, damp conditions, so be especially vigilant about rot and decay and eliminate them as soon as you find them. Always sterilise secateurs, knives and other tools before and after use. Beware of water butts in the warm. These can become full of diseases that may be lethal to seedlings, although they rarely bother mature plants.

Fumigation and smoking

Fumigation and smoking used to be common, but are rarely practised today. Although there are a few specialist fumigants and smokes that can be used on certain plants with safety, in general the majority die! Sulphur candles are still available and lethal to us as well as to plants, but for the traditionalist who wants a sterile environment they are fairly effective. The essential point is to use enough candles to penetrate every crack and to keep the greenhouse closed up long enough to allow the fumes to work. Read and follow the instructions! Nicotine has been withdrawn and most other smokes and fumigants are no longer available to amateurs, who are better off using a steam device to clean.

Basil and French marigolds are good companions to tomatoes.

Steam cleaning, pressure washing and disinfecting

Steam cleaning and pressure washing are safer ways of getting a greenhouse scrupulously clean, but be careful not to blow the panes out! They can be hired rather than bought, which is sensible because you only need to use them every year or so. Make sure they are supplied with full instructions. Either will clean the glass really well, even if you choose not to sterilise the insides. Alternatively, a good scrubbing with detergent in water will clean algae off glass (which can absorb more than half the light the plants need). If you are sterilising the insides, do not forget to wash the pots and trays as well.

greenhouse techniques

Cold, cool or warm?

A cold greenhouse is just that – without any heat it is subject to the weather and will heat up in the sun and cool down dramatically at night. However, depending on the construction and the site, an unheated greenhouse should just keep the minimum temperature in a mild winter sufficiently high to over-winter citrus or mimosa in a mild area. The greatest use of an unheated greenhouse is to extend the growing season, enabling us to plant out our tomatoes up to a month earlier in reasonable safety, and extending the crops for

Tomatoes may succeed outdoors but are earlier and guaranteed under glass.

about a month or even two before the autumn frosts come and kill them off. An unheated greenhouse is also a great place for growing flowers, as they don't get battered by wind or rain and their scent is trapped in with you. Once you add sufficient heat to keep it frost free, it becomes a cool greenhouse. This is what you usually need for over-wintering citrus, daturas (*Brugmansia* spp.), choice fuchsias and so on. The heat makes it possible to grow earlier crops, later crops and, indeed, year-round salads and flowers. A warm greenhouse is one with a minimum temperature similar to that of your bedroom and it is needed for orchids, tough bananas, birds of paradise (*Strelitzia* spp.), and other exotica. The cost of heating is more than repaid by the range of interesting plants you can grow all year round. Indeed, you may wish that planning regulations would allow you to knock down your house and make it into a big warm greenhouse! There is no need to go for excessive heat and humidity, except for a few rare plants, but then if you need to keep the temperature up in the sauna range it becomes a stove house!

Choosing plants

Most gardeners manage to grow almost anything they want with the aid of a cold greenhouse, a heated propagator inside it and a sheltered garden outside. Nevertheless, they will still need to make a choice as it's not possible to grow everything under cover where space is often very limited! When choosing what to grow, be imaginative – you could go for foliage plants to give you year-round interest and colour, depending on your degree of heat. The weather being kept off allows for some spectacular shows and these will endure much longer than most flowers. In a conservatory, it is probably more important to choose well-formed or well-shaped plants with good foliage. Indoor topiary, trained climbers and tender wall shrubs all offer great potential and aesthetic interest without cropping or even blooming. Many flowering plants have great perfumes, which are more intense when grown under cover – and many, such as the daturas (*Brugmansia* spp.), gardenias, citrus and hoya are all good conservatory subjects and would also do well in a warm greenhouse. Cool and cold greenhouses can have excellent shows of 'normally' outdoor flowers, and over a much longer season. They are especially good for growing cut flowers to bring into the house. Food crops are usually absent in a true conservatory, but don't forget that Mediterranean herbs and citrus will do well there in winter. At the other end of the scale are polytunnels. People always imagine polytunnels are useful only for utilitarian crop producers, but they can be extravagantly planted with gorgeous flowers for your own, very private show! I use mine for pineapples, bananas and guavas, and new potatoes in time for Easter. However, it's your space so grow what you want.

Extending the season

There are several stages of growing under cover depending on the type of structure you have. On a basic level, you can use it merely as a potting shed and giant propagator to nurture plants for the outdoor garden, with few plants or crops actually reaching maturity, except say for tomatoes in summer. Add a heated propagator and you prolong the growing season, giving you an earlier start and a slightly longer season. Introduce warmth under cover and you can go for even longer seasons – though without extra light the

Oranges and other citrus flourish in a warm greenhouse. Who could fail to enjoy a display such as this?

Early flowerers such as apricots need hand pollinating most years.

range of crops and flowers would still be limited in mid-winter. With heat you can bring on fruits and vegetables months ahead of outdoor plants – and safe from the birds. The range of plants you can grow will also depend on whether you have basic equipment or a sophisticated greenhouse with hot beds or soil-warming cables.

Forcing plants

One of the problems in winter is that there is insufficient light for plants to actually do much real growing. Plants that store up energy underground can be coaxed into growth by providing warmth, often from underneath. Plants of asparagus, seakale, rhubarb and chicory all benefit from being brought into the warm (and usually dark) indoors, where they are forced to throw succulent new shoots for our culinary delight.

Orchard house forcing

This is a marvellous technique, the idea being that fruit trees, grapes and soft fruits, such as strawberries and raspberries, are grown in containers so they can be moved in and out of cover to 'force' fruiting. It makes optimum use of a cool or cold greenhouse or polytunnel, but can also be used to great effect with warm greenhouses – provided ventilation is good. By moving fruiting plants under cover from late winter, we give them a sudden improvement in conditions and they think it is spring and start producing early. By bringing more specimens of the same plant in at fortnightly intervals, it is possible to

have a favourite fruit cropping continuously for more than half the year. Obviously good management is necessary, especially hand-pollination, thinning and good ventilation. Once the crop is harvested, the plants are hardened off and spend the rest of the year outdoors. They are pruned when put out and the sojourn outdoors usually removes pests and diseases, ensuring cleaner crops when they are brought back in again. Without doubt, this orchard house method is the most sensible way to get a wide range of some fruits over a longer season and is especially suited to grapes, enabling almost any choice variety to be grown successfully and cropped every year! And you can grow half a dozen or more sorts in the space taken by just one specimen growing permanently in the ground and trained under cover. Peaches, apricots and cherries are all very good choices for this method. Strawberries are also good – bring the plants in in early spring and keep them up high and as near the glass as possible without touching, and you will be rewarded with (light) crops months before the outdoor ones.

Hand-pollination

This is crucial for some crops under cover and very simple to do. Take a small, fluffy soft paintbrush, cotton wool ball or the traditional (but certainly not politically correct!) rabbit's tail and simply touch the male flowers to gather the pollen,

A soft fluffy brush is ideal for pollinating by hand.

take it to the female flowers and brush it on their parts. How do you tell the difference? Basically, male flowers (and some 'bisexual' flowers) have pollen – a commonly yellow, slightly sticky fine dust. Female flowers, on the other hand, give off no pollen but have small sticky receptors and quite often small fruits forming behind the flowers, especially the squash and cucumber family. If a flower is 'bisexual', it may not be self-fertile, so treat it first as a male and again later as a female. As to what needs pollinating – well don't do it unless you want seeds and fruits, so leave ornamental flowers untouched and they will bloom for longer. Citrus, peaches, apricots and most other forced fruits, especially strawberries, need careful regular hand-pollination. Melons and watermelons must be pollinated by hand; aubergines, okra and peppers may need it; tomatoes usually do better if it's done. I've never hand-pollinated grapes, but early sweetcorn must be done carefully. Indoor cucumbers are different – every male flower (remember no fruit behind it) must be removed before it opens or you will end up with pollinated indoor cucumbers, which taste bitter.

Rotation

Although rotation is very important outdoors, it is often overlooked under cover where a few common crops are repeated year after year (see pages 134–35). Ignoring rotation under cover is a recipe for disaster, especially if all you grow is tomatoes. If this is the case, avoid growing tomatoes in bags or containers as this causes too many problems with limited root runs and insufficient water holding capacity. Instead, enrich the bed or border soil each year with compost and organic fertilisers. As soon as the tomatoes are finished, scrupulously remove all traces of them and sow green manure (see page 133) or salad crops of corn salad and claytonia. Dig these in a month or two before planting out the next crop of tomatoes. If after several years your tomatoes do consistently very badly, then dig out a trench the length of the border and swap the soil with some good loam-rotted down turves. Even if this has to be done every five or ten years, it is still less work than carrying bags in and out every year together with all the extra watering they require! With more space and a variety of crops you can work out a rotation of sorts and in the case of a large

polytunnel, there is enough space to have a sophisticated arrangement. If you're growing plants in pots or containers, don't think you're exempt from problems – pests and diseases can build up in the fabric. Whatever you do, don't be so foolish as to re-use potting compost twice – and never ever for the same sort of plant!

Chillis – these are *Capsicum* 'Hot Banana' – are easier to grow than tomatoes.

Chapter 12
planting with containers

Matt: You can grow almost anything in containers, as long as they are large enough to support the plants you choose to grow. The opportunities are endlessly exciting – from annuals, trees and herbaceous perennials, to flowers, fruit and vegetables.

Containers can certainly be used for growing acid-loving plants, if your garden soil is alkaline, or tender specimen plants that can go outdoors in summer but need protection in a greenhouse in winter. Yet there is so much more to container gardening than that – think laterally and don't be afraid to experiment.

Containers without drainage holes are perfect for bog plants. A pot in my garden is home to a display of *Equisetum hyemale*, an ornamental horsetail, which glows an ethereal green when the late evening sun shines through the stems, red-flowered *Lobelia cardinalis* with beetroot-coloured stems and *Houttuynia cordata* 'Chameleon', sporting attractive variegated foliage. I divide the display in spring, when the contents become congested, and top it up regularly with water – it can never be over watered! The container is just the right thing to keep the rampant houttuynia in check and protects the lobelia from the predations of slugs and snails.

Containers are ideal for carnivorous plants too. My hardy *Sarracenia purpurea* subsp. *purpurea* and *Sarracenia flava* share a blue glazed bowl by the patio, their peat compost retained by a piece of naturalistic timber that would normally be at home in an indoor aquarium. The other half of the container, with black glass chippings in the base for a contemporary effect, is the 'pond' and provides water for the birds, whose mineral deposits supply added liquid feed!

Left: Containers add character to an elegant terrace.
Right: Arum lilies in a glazed pot are an eye-catching focal point.

Co-ordinating designs work really well in containers. Planted in a colour scheme to celebrate gold, silver and ruby anniversaries, they make ideal presents – if, that is, you can bear to give them away! Create your designs at a local nursery or garden centre, buying the container and plants at the same time so you can be sure your ideas will work.

Wildflowers work well in pots, too. Either plant them in 'plugs' into loam-based compost or, for a more natural effect, plant the 'plugs' into a strip of turf in a shallow tray or pot. Containers are great for filling gaps in the garden. Use them to brighten up areas where displays have faded, putting them in position when they're about to flower and removing them once they've finished their job. Pots of lilies or annual climbers are ideal for this.

choosing containers

Containers give you another opportunity to use your imagination! Clean up colourful old paint tins, removing oil-based paint with white spirit and warm soapy water, and punch several drainage holes in the base with a nail and you have a simple, attractive, low-cost container. Galvanised buckets can take the place of more expensive contemporary containers. It is easy to create your own designs. Buy a cheap pot, grout the rim and cover it with mosaic tiles from a specialist shop or DIY store (make sure the tiles don't overlap the rim because their edges are very sharp, as I have found to my cost!). If you feel adventurous, you could tile the whole pot or simply cover it with grout, adding pieces of broken pottery or china as ornamentation. Alternatively, buy paint tester pots from a DIY store and paint with a couple of layers to complement or contrast with the contents; lining terracotta pots with plastic or using a plastic pot as an inner sleeve ensures the 'paint job' lasts longer. Or you could spray plastic containers with paints used for metal, like Hammerite or car body paint, following the manufacturers' safety guidelines. There's a fantastic range of colours available, and you can change the colours each season according to the display.

A green concrete container proves that pots shouldn't be boring.

Herbaceous perennials are perfect in containers, especially if you are a little late to plant traditional hanging baskets and pots. Herbaceous perennials are at their best from late summer onwards, when other plants in containers are flagging. Although perennials are quite expensive to buy, they can be incorporated into your flower borders after the display is over, so you should get your money's worth!

Ceramic sinks or troughs make wonderful water features.

Most garden centres stock a wide selection of containers to suit your needs – from terracotta pots and fibreglass window boxes to heavy stone troughs and wooden barrels. When choosing, try to find styles that complement the garden design and suit your practical needs. The size of the pot should relate to the plant or plants it contains. Small pots need regular watering and those with narrow bases are more likely to be blown over if planted with relatively tall specimens. It is easiest to fill large containers with compost and plant them in situ, rather than planting them and then moving them. If you have to move a heavy container, use a purpose-built pot trolley or a sack barrow. Avoid moving large containers in wheelbarrows, in case they tip up.

Terracotta

Terracotta containers come in all shapes and sizes. Before buying, check the labels to make sure they are frost-tolerant, if that's what you need. Vulnerable pots must be brought indoors before the first frosts, or, if this isn't possible, should be wrapped in bubble wrap (this also helps prevent the rootball freezing) and raised off the ground using bricks,

blocks of wood or pot 'feet' to improve drainage. Another option is to place vulnerable pots in a sheltered corner of the garden, against a sheltered wall or even in the bottom of a hedge, covered with leaves for insulation. Terracotta looks natural and weathers attractively, is cool in summer and warm in winter. It is also easy to tell when a terracotta pot needs watering, as it becomes paler in colour. Also, if you tap the side you can tell by the sound it makes whether it needs water or not – a resounding 'ring' tells you the compost is dry; a 'flat' sound shows the pot is well-watered. Being porous, terracotta containers need watering more often than some other materials such as plastics, particularly during the heat of summer. One way to reduce the need to water is to line the pot with polythene or an old plastic bag to prevent moisture loss through the sides. Alternatively, pot up your plant in a plain plastic container and use the terracotta pot as the outer sleeve. If you have new terracotta pots, it's a good idea to soak them in a bucket of water before planting, otherwise they absorb moisture from the compost, causing it to shrink away from the sides of the pot.

Plastic

The quality and range of designs of ornamental plastic containers has improved immeasurably over recent years. Gone are the days when they were flimsy, faded rapidly and looked 'cheap and nasty'. In most cases, it is difficult to tell the difference between plastic and the genuine article, whether lead, terracotta or reconstituted or natural stone. Plastic containers today are less likely to fade in the sun than their predecessors and are excellent in locations where weight is a consideration, such as balconies and roof gardens. They are also cheaper than their lead, terracotta or stone counterparts and don't lose nearly as much moisture through their sides. On the downside, plastic doesn't have the insulating properties of terracotta and so the roots can overheat in summer and become cold in winter; neither does it weather attractively. Fibreglass containers are similar, though longer lasting, and are more expensive.

Stone and metal

Reconstituted or natural stone containers look very attractive and weather well, but they are very heavy, difficult to move and don't always have drainage holes in the base. If this is the case, you will need to put your plants in a plastic pot and use the stone container as the outer sleeve. Alternatively, you can line the base with a deep layer of drainage material and take care with watering. Architectural salvage yards are a good source of cast-iron and natural stone containers. Cast-iron containers should be cleaned to remove loose rust, then treated with rust-inhibiting paint to increase their longevity.

Galvanised containers might look attractive in contemporary settings, but they are often thin and some have sharp edges. They also become hot if they are placed in the full heat of the summer sun, damaging the roots; lining them with sheets of polystyrene helps. Many lose their lustre with time as the zinc oxidises, but you can combat this by painting them with a layer of yacht or letterbox varnish. I've used the latter successfully on the hinges of my garden shed to retain their silver colouring.

Wood

Wooden containers are very popular. However, the traditional half barrel is becoming more difficult to find and increasingly expensive. Wood is a good insulator and great for protecting plants' roots. To increase the life of wooden containers, paint the inside with bitumen. Alternatively, line them with polythene before planting or put plastic pots inside. Half barrels are heavy to move, even when empty, so always use a sack barrow or trolley. 'Versailles' tubs are made of wood and look very attractive when painted in any colour, although white tends to discolour and needs regular repainting.

A display of succulents – perfect for a stone trough.

creating a water garden in a half barrel or pot

Half barrels make a great feature in a small garden and brighten up any corner or balcony. You will need either a half barrel or a glazed pot, a minimum of 30cm (12in) in diameter. To make a glazed pot waterproof, fill the hole in the base with epoxy resin. Half barrels that began life as sherry or whisky casks should be waterproof – even if they leak a little when first filled, the wood should expand to plug the leak. Check the stamp on the bottom of the barrel to confirm its authenticity – if there isn't one, the barrel may not be waterproof and should be lined. Use a sack barrow or trolley to move the container to its final location – preferably a level, sunny site – before filling with water. If using a glazed pot (which may not be frost-proof), it is a good idea to dismantle the display in winter, keeping plants wet in a frost-free place.

1 Put containers in place before filling with water. Check the container is level using a spirit level and correct using wood or slate wedges. If necessary, line barrels with butyl pond liner. Lay the liner over the barrel and gradually fill with water as you tuck in the sides. Trim the liner to size, just below the edge of the barrel, using a sharp knife and tack it to the side with roofing tacks or double-sided tape.

2 Line the base of the barrel with a 5cm (2in) layer of washed gravel.

3 Plant your aquatics in open-sided baskets...

4 ...standing them on bricks inside the container to raise them to the correct height. As the stems grow longer, gradually reduce the height of the bricks until the plants sit on the bottom of the pond but still emerge from the barrel. The wonderful spiral plant shown here is *Juncus effusus* f. *spiralis*, the grass-like one is a species of *Acorus*. The waterlilies *Nymphaea* 'Pygmaea Rubra' or *N.* 'Pygmaea Helvola', both with a spread of 30cm (12in), are perfect in small barrels, but you will need an oxygenator such as Canadian pondweed to keep the water clear.

5 When topping up, add water slowly, directing the flow around the sides of the tub to avoid disturbing the plants.

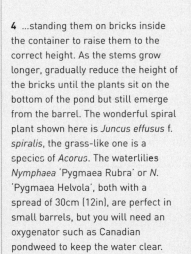

Drainage

Unless you are creating a pond in a pot or growing bog plants, containers must have drainage holes. Ideally, these should be at least 12mm (½in) in diameter, although slightly smaller holes will do if there are more of them. The drainage holes in large containers should be about 7.5cm (3in) apart. Drill holes with a metal bit, or a masonry drill for terracotta. To stop the bit from moving around on slippery metal or ceramic surfaces, stick a piece of masking tape in place and drill through that.

Before filling your container with compost, include a good layer of drainage material in the base, up to 5–7.5cm (2–3in) deep, depending on the size of the pot. Fragments of broken terracotta pots make ideal drainage material. These can be smashed into smaller pieces with a hammer. For safety, put them in a sack beforehand to prevent the pieces flying around – this will also make it easy to collect up the pieces. Bottle corks, broken polystyrene packaging material, washed stones from the garden, gravel or stone chippings all work well too. If using smaller materials such as gravel, cover the drainage hole first with a large stone from the garden or a piece of terracotta to stop the gravel from falling out.

Compost

Compost should suit the needs of the plant. John Innes No. 3 with up to 50 per cent added multi-purpose compost is ideal for specimen plants, such as shrubs or trees, and provides weight for improved stability as well as good moisture and nutrient-retaining properties. Soil-based John Innes compost has, on average, enough nutrients to last about six weeks. Multi-purpose compost can be used for temporary displays, with added John Innes to improve moisture retention. Specialist composts are available for citrus plants, acid lovers and alpines – or you can mix your own (see page 136–137).

When filling the container, firm the compost in gently with your fingers and don't compact it too much. Never fill it to the brim because the compost will overflow when you water the pot, but leave a 2.5–5cm (1–2in) gap, depending on the size of the pot. Mulching with gravel, slate, or glass or stone chippings reduces both weeding and moisture loss.

making an alpine trough

Alpines are traditionally planted in old stone troughs, but it's worth having a go at making your own, as old ones are becoming scarce and expensive.

1 Mix two parts sieved coco fibre with one part cement and one part sharp sand on a board.

2 Make a hollow in the centre, add water and mix into a paste.

3 Upturn a large cardboard box and cut a piece of small-gauge wire mesh 12mm (½in) smaller all round than the base of the box.

4 Turn the box the right way up and trowel a 2.5cm (1in) layer of the cement/sand mixture into the base, making sure you fill the corners.

5 Take a second box, 2.5cm (1in) smaller all round than the first (so when you put one box inside the other, there should be a 2.5 cm (1in) gap all round). Turn the smaller box upside down, place the wire mesh over the base and push several pieces of dowelling rod through both cardboard and mesh to form drainage holes.

6 Take the dowels out, turn the mesh right side up again (so that the holes will match when you add the smaller box) and place inside the larger box, on top of the cement/sand mixture. Now add another 2.5cm (1in) layer of cement/sand.

7 Place the smaller box inside the large box and feed the dowels through the holes.

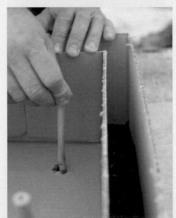

8 Measure the sides of the inner box and cut four more pieces of mesh slightly larger than the sides. Push the mesh into the gaps between the two boxes, making sure it doesn't protrude above the rim.

9 Put bricks in the inner box to prevent the sides from collapsing and support the outer box with more bricks.

10 Push more of the cement/sand mixture into the gap between the two boxes and use a dowelling rod to force the mixture into the corners.

11 When the mixture reaches the top of the sides of the largest box, cover the 'trough' with a sheet of plastic.

12 Leave to set for 2 or 3 days, then peel away the cardboard around the sides of the 'trough' and remove the inner box. After a week, push out the dowels.

planting an alpine trough or pan

Containers must have a drainage hole, covered with a piece of broken terracotta to prevent the compost from falling out.

1 Make a mix of equal parts John Innes No. 1 and grit. Fill the trough to within 5cm (2in) of the rim, to allow for watering.

2 Water the alpines thoroughly before removing them from their pots.

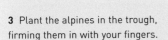

3 Plant the alpines in the trough, firming them in with your fingers.

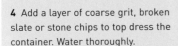

4 Add a layer of coarse grit, broken slate or stone chips to top dress the container. Water thoroughly.

Left: Sinks on brick plinths are perfect for eye-level viewing.

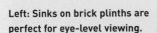

tip

● There are plenty of other ways to display alpines to bring them towards eye level and enhance your viewing pleasure. If you have an old wooden table, you can turn it into a fabulous display. First paint the table top with wood preservative to prevent it from rotting, then drill drainage holes in it and screw a 'frame' of 10 x 5cm (4 x 2in) around the edge. Fill with compost and alpines for an eye-catching table-top display.

Feeding and watering

Plants in containers need regular feeding and watering because they are unable to send out their roots in search for moisture and nutrients as they would do in nature. Check the individual requirements of each plant and water accordingly. Tender plants prefer tepid water and hate cold showers! During the growing season, most plants need watering regularly each time the surface of the compost starts to dry out, but in winter watering can be kept to a minimum as long as the compost remains slightly moist. You'll notice I say most plants – this is not always the case, so check the individual plant's requirements first. Water plants in containers thoroughly, giving them a good soaking until the water runs out through the drainage holes.

Mix slow-release fertiliser into the compost at planting time and moisture-retaining gel into temporary displays. Don't add too much gel, as it can push the plants and compost out of the container as it expands!

Re-pot specimen plants every two or three years, before the container becomes congested with roots. If necessary, trim off one third of the roots before replanting in fresh compost. In the intervening years, top dress annually in spring by raking out the top 5cm (2in) of compost and replacing it with a mix of fresh compost and slow-release fertiliser. An old culinary fork does the job impressively well. If plants are too old or too large to re-pot, give them regular liquid feeds and then, once they start to show signs of stress, either plant them out in the garden or re-propagate and start again. Always check a plant's individual needs before re-potting – clivia and cymbidium, for example, prefer being pot bound.

planting a container with a specimen plant

1 Put a layer of drainage material in the base of the pot, making it 5–7cm (2–3in) deep, depending on the size of the pot.

2 Gradually build up layers of John Innes compost, firming it with your fingers.

3 The compost should be high enough to leave enough space for watering when the plant is potted up. Water the plant thoroughly, allow it to drain, then ease it from its pot over the container....

4 ...and tease out the roots.

5 Place the plant in the centre of the pot and fill around the sides with compost, firming with your fingers or a piece of cane or dowel. The final soil level should be roughly 2.5–5cm (1–2in) below the rim of the container to allow for watering. Water the plant thoroughly.

6 Cover the surface with a layer of ornamental mulch to conserve moisture, about 2.5–5cm (1–2in) thick, depending on the size of the pot.

planting several layers of bulbs

This is a great way to prolong spring displays.

1 Depending on the size of container, choose at least two types of bulb that flower consecutively, like daffodils and tulips. Place a 2.5cm (1in) layer of drainage material in the base.

2 Cover with a layer of multi-purpose compost, with 20 per cent added perlite or grit for drainage, about 5–7.5cm (2–3in) deep.

3 Bulbs should be planted three times deeper than the size of the bulb, so larger bulbs form the bottom layer. Arrange the first layer on the surface of the compost mix, spacing them about 1cm (½in) apart.

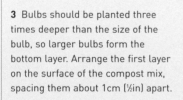

4 Fill the gaps between the bulbs with compost, leaving the tips exposed.

5 Place the next layer of bulbs in the gaps.

6 Top up with compost to within 2.5cm (1in) of the rim, water thoroughly and label the container to remind yourself what to expect!

growing fruit in containers

Apricots, figs, apples, nectarines and many other tree and bush fruits are perfect for container cultivation. They can be protected against the weather and given exactly the conditions they need. Some appreciate greenhouse protection throughout the year for earlier crops of improved quality, others stay indoors over winter and after two to three weeks of acclimatisation spend the rest of the summer on the patio as a specimen plant. When choosing tree fruits for containers, always buy them on dwarfing rootstocks.

Growing early flowering fruits, such as apricots and peaches, in containers under glass will protect blossom from cold weather and leaves from peach leaf curl, but you will need to pollinate by hand (see pages 288–89). Those flowering later in the season, when the greenhouse windows and doors are open, will be visited by insects but it is probably best to hand pollinate as well to be sure of a crop. In a container in my garden I grow an apple called 'Calville Blanc d'hiver' that makes wonderful Tarte aux Pommes. Traditionally, it would have been grown by Victorian head gardeners against a sheltered wall or in a pot under glass. Apples and pears need pollen from other compatible varieties that flower at the same time.

Blueberries, cranberries and their acid-loving relatives, which thrive on peat and need a pH of 4–5.5 in free-draining compost, are ideal in containers, although two or three plants are generally needed for a good crop. They should be mulched with wood shavings and watered with rainwater. John Innes No. 2 is good for soft fruits and No. 3 for trees, while an annual top dressing with nitrochalk is beneficial for alkaline-loving stone fruits. Gooseberries and red or white currants can be grown as ornamental half standards in containers, making a talking point by a doorway. Arguably they make better ornamentals than culinary fruits as there are so few recipes exploiting their virtues.

Figs, which have a reputation for taking over the garden, can be constrained in pots. I asked Terry Read, whose nursery holds the National Collection of figs, which ones he recommended before buying mine. I now have *Ficus carica* 'Rouge de Bordeaux', which he described as one of the best, *F. c.* 'White Marseilles', renowned for its sweet taste, and *F. c.* 'Osborn's Prolific', with its unbelievably sweet and syrupy tasty golden flesh. Figs in pots need to be given high-potash fertiliser once a week from late spring until harvesting. Prune out the growing tips after four or five leaves and re-pot in spring.

Apricots can be grown in containers on 'Pixie', a dwarfing rootstock. Two new varieties, *Prunus armeniaca* 'Tomcot' and *P. a.* 'Flavourcot' flower profusely and are worthy to stand alongside old favourites such as *P. a.* 'Moorpark'.

Vines also grow happily in containers. Victorian head gardeners grew them so that the pots could be brought into the centre of the grand table and the grapes picked straight from the plant. They are started as one-year cuttings, transferred into 30–45cm (12–18in) pots and the growth trained round the type of flat frame that is used to support weeping roses. Once the vine has grown around the frame, tie it in. Allow the vine to produce two bunches of grapes in the first season and, in later years, only one bunch per spur at 30cm (12in) apart.

Treat bush and tree fruit as specimen plants, repotting every two or three years and top dressing annually in spring in the intervening years.

Most strawberry planters are too small for growing strawberries, which are better grown in beds and borders.

Citrus add a little Mediterranean magic to the garden.

growing vegetables and herbs in containers

Any vegetables can be grown in containers, though deep-rooted ones such as parsnips, those with a long growing season, like Brussels sprouts, or those needing plenty of space, such as pumpkins, are more challenging. The best for pots are fast-growing summer crops such as French beans, peppers, courgettes, tomatoes, spring onions, beetroots, carrots, turnips, lettuces and 'cut and come again' or seedling crops. Most of these are raised in pots, trays and modules and transplanted later.

Vegetables that are sown in containers under glass will crop much earlier than those sown outdoors. French beans can be sown in heat in late winter for an early crop in late spring and early summer, lettuces in late autumn for winter cropping. Ornamental vegetables look fantastic in containers. Why not be adventurous and plant them up for summer? You'll be surprised how attractive they are. A great combination is lettuce foliage, carrot leaves and upright spring onions, with crimson 'Tumbler' tomatoes and beetroot, and Swiss chard 'Bright Lights'. Try combining vegetables with flowers and herbs for even greater impact. 'Pickwick', a red-flowered, bushy runner bean that doesn't need supporting, is worth growing in a pot as a specimen plant, so are the small peas 'Half-pint', as well as radishes and lettuces. Vegetables like aubergines and French beans have obvious ornamental value, particularly the mottled lavender aubergine 'Listade de Gandia' and the dark purple pods of the bush French bean 'Purple Teepee'. Vegetables in containers need watering regularly and feeding twice a week with a diluted general fertiliser until established, changing to high-potash fertiliser once a week for those producing pods or fruits. Ensure they are in a sunny position and turn the pot regularly for balanced growth. Harvest regularly to prolong the production of flowers, fruits or leaves and to retain their ornamental interest. When selecting containers for growing vegetables, make sure there is sufficient space for root growth. Many of the vegetables mentioned here will grow equally well in a window box, but avoid planting them too densely as rooting space is restricted. If growing vegetables from seed, harden off as necessary before planting out once the danger of frost has passed.

Small crops of potatoes can be grown in 30–45cm (12–18in) pots filled with multi-purpose compost, which helps protect them from slugs. Early potatoes, such as 'Rocket', are ideal for growing in this way. Some seed companies offer potatoes in late summer for growing in containers so you can enjoy new potatoes with your Christmas dinner, provided they are positioned in a frost-free place or greenhouse.

Herbs such as thyme and marjoram that thrive in sunny Mediterranean climates can be grown individually in small pots and need little watering. Most herbs dislike windy locations and enjoy some sunshine, so they should be kept away from frost pockets and wind tunnels. Fast-growing plants like parsley are happiest in deep containers and will struggle in cramped conditions. Rosemary and dwarf marjoram both grow well in hanging baskets. Mint can be controlled by growing it in containers, but most other large perennial herbs such as lovage or angelica are easier to manage in the open ground.

Protect permanent plantings of herbs such as bay over winter by wrapping them with horticultural fleece and putting them in a sheltered corner of the garden or under cover. Mulching the surface with a layer of gravel or stone chippings reduces evaporation.

A simple yet stylish container featuring chives and Black Tuscan cabbage.

planting a strawberry planter with herbs

Strawberries don't grow very well in strawberry pots, but herbs flourish! To ensure even watering throughout the pot, follow point 2 below; alternatively, fill the tube from the centre of a kitchen roll with horticultural grit, plant the container, then gently ease the cardboard tube from the compost.

1 Line the base of the planter with a 2.5cm (1in) layer of drainage material.

2 Take a 2.5cm (1in) plastic pipe, cut so it's long enough to reach from the base of the planter to just above the final level of compost, and drill holes in the sides so it's like a colander. Insert the pipe in the centre of the planter.

3 Fill the bottom half of the planter with John Innes compost with added grit, firming it around the pipe, until it reaches just below the level of the lowest planting hole.

4 Depending on the size of the rootball, push one of the herbs through the planting hole from the outside....

5 ....or (preferably) wrap the foliage in plastic from an old fertiliser sack and thread the herb through the planting hole from the inside out.

6 Build up another layer of compost and repeat the process. Top up the compost until it is just below the top of the plastic pipe.

7 Fill the pipe with gravel.

8 Place the pot in a sunny position and rotate it regularly for even growth.

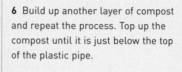

hanging baskets

Local garden centres and DIY stores now stock a huge range of hanging baskets in contemporary or traditional styles. Traditional designs have improved considerably over recent years and many are now made of plastic to reduce weight, some incorporate a water reservoir attached to the base, reducing the need for watering, while others have hinged sections that open up for ease of planting. If you're going for a traditional style, make sure there are enough large spaces in the sides for planting. Many baskets look more like ornamental hanging containers than baskets, with less space for the plants – this may offend the purists, but some are beautifully ornamental in rustic designs. Conical hanging baskets made from willow, sea grass or even braided leaves are deeper than traditional styles and are ideal for large plants, particularly those with architectural foliage that offsets the bold shape of the basket. Others in the traditional semi-circular design are made from moss, banana leaf rope and cocoa palm.

When fixing the basket to a wall, make sure the bracket is robust enough to take the weight of the basket and its (watered) contents. There are several different sizes available to suit the various sizes of basket, so make sure you choose the correct one. I would also recommend changing the thickness of the chains so they don't break and fixing a swivel attachment to allow the basket to be turned for watering, maintenance and even growth. You can buy retractable systems so the basket can be pulled down for maintenance then returned to its usual height.

Planting hanging baskets

If possible, buy your plants as soon as they appear in the garden centre (when there is the greatest choice available). Try to buy on the same day they were delivered, before they have been on the shelves too long. Always choose healthy plants, avoid any with yellowing leaves that look weak or impoverished, ones with roots pushing through the base of the trays or pots, or those in dry compost. Hanging baskets are planted with multi-purpose compost or multi-purpose with

Nasturtiums have edible leaves, flowers and seeds.

added John Innes – straight John Innes is unsuitable because it is the wrong consistency and too heavy. If you have a greenhouse, start your hanging baskets early in the season and keep them in the warmth until they are fully established. Pinching out the stems (removing the growth tips) and removing flowers, so that all the plant's energy is concentrated into forming new growth, will get your plants off to a good start. Acclimatise them to the outdoors gradually, initially putting them out in a sheltered spot during the day for two weeks to harden off before hanging them out permanently once the danger of frosts has passed. If you don't have a greenhouse, wait until the weather has warmed up before planting and keep your hanging baskets in a sheltered spot until the plants are established. Listen to the weather forecast and beware of late frosts.

Be adventurous when choosing plants for hanging baskets and try planting foliage instead of flowers, or houseplants, herbs or vegetables, making sure they are suitable for the location. Lobelias, busy Lizzies, fuchsias and ferns flourish in shade; helichrysums, pelargoniums and petunias love sunshine. That said, most plants will tolerate a range of conditions. Hanging baskets look best if they are colour themed. Don't let your basket be noticed for the wrong reasons. Look out for incidentals, like the cerise pink petunia that has sneaked into a basket of pastel colours, and remove them immediately. It's surprising how often they are simply left in place and complained about, spoiling the entire display for a season.

Watering and feeding hanging baskets

The best time to water hanging baskets is early in the morning, so that the plants are prepared for the coming day. In the heat of summer, plants need plenty of water and should be checked at midday, if possible, and in the evening too. Multi-purpose compost is difficult to re-wet once it dries, so water regularly and mix swell gel into the compost to prevent it drying out completely. It's a good idea to put a container display underneath your hanging basket to catch the drips, rather than allowing excess water to drain away. The best, and safest, way to water a hanging basket is using a lance as this delivers water right into the heart of the basket and helps to avoid wetting the foliage and flowers, which can damage them and encourage disease. You can make your own lance by attaching a hose to a bamboo cane, leaving the end of the hose overhanging by 15cm (6in) to create a bendy 'spout'. This is much safer than standing on a ladder and watering with a can, but if you have to do this make sure the ladder is secure and the watering can is lightweight and filled only with as much water as you can carry safely. It's easier to have a tall stepladder and hold the can at arm's length than trying to water at head height. Ideally, install an irrigation system – it saves considerable time and effort and makes watering more efficient.

Plants in hanging baskets need regular feeding as there are lots of roots packed into a small space. Until the plants are established, feed at the same time as watering using soluble plant food dispensed through a container at the end of the hose. Alternatively, you can use a lightweight watering can or add slow-release fertiliser to the compost mix. Start with general fertiliser, then change to a high-potash fertiliser, such as tomato feed, once the baskets are established; apply once a week to boost flowering. Deadhead regularly to prolong the display and check regularly for signs of pests or disease.

ten unusual ideas for hanging baskets

- If you have a sheltered spot, or one where your plants will be protected in bad weather, try a winter or early spring display of bulbs, heathers and pansies with evergreens, such as ivies, euonymus or santolina.

- In spring, plunge small pots of flowering bulbs in hanging baskets. These can be taken out and replaced with new plants once they've finished flowering to keep the display looking fresh.

- In autumn, use cuttings of shrubs for leaf colour, stems and berries. These can later be planted out in the garden to mature.

- Plant salads in summer – purple-fringed lettuce and ruby chard work well with 'tumbler' tomatoes or herbs. Harvest crops when they are small for a continuous supply of flowers, fruit and leaves.

- Wire two baskets together to make a sphere and fill with succulents, or sow with grass seed to create a globe of grass.

- Use wildflowers, such as primroses and cowslips in spring.

- Grow bedding plants, such as *Bidens ferrulifolia* or purple petunias, using a single variety in each basket.

- Grow strawberries with tomatoes. Place the basket by the back door on a special pulley device for ease of maintenance and harvesting.

- Use hanging baskets indoors, with trailing houseplants over the bath.

- Use houseplants like *Syngonium* or *Begonia rex* to create 'tropical' summer displays.

Go on, pick one!

Baskets respond well to TLC – plenty of water, regular deadheading and not too much sun.

Rejuvenating hanging baskets and containers

By the end of the summer, hanging baskets and containers often suffer from 'burn out'. Flowers fade and the plants are exhausted from the effort of flowering, despite your tender care! But it's possible to boost your baskets for a final flourish. Lightly trim them with a pair of shears to remove flowers and any seeds that have escaped your attentions (seed production weakens plants and prevents them from flowering). Take a close look at the basket, then slowly and methodically pick through the flowers and vegetation, removing dead or diseased material and checking for pests and diseases.

If the compost is dry, dunk the whole basket in a large bucket of water or a water butt and soak thoroughly. If you are unhappy with your basket, work out why and make notes for next year – maybe you should have used a larger basket, or added controlled-release fertiliser or water-retention granules. List plants that have been successful and remember to use them next year.

Finally, put the basket or container somewhere away from scorching sunshine and feed with a high-nitrogen fertiliser to give the plants a boost. Once re-growth appears and the plants are revitalised, revert to feeding with a high-potash fertiliser to encourage flowers, then sit back and enjoy!

planting a hanging basket with a loose fibre lining

There's a whole range of flexible, fabric and other natural recycled and recyclable materials that can be used to line baskets. Avoid sphagnum moss for conservation reasons. Solid-sided hanging baskets made from ceramic or woven materials lined with plastic can be planted only from the top. However, many have the advantage of a built-in water reservoir that prevents the compost drying out too rapidly.

1 Unclip the chains and stand the basket securely on a bucket or flowerpot at a good working height.

2 If using sisal, moss or similar, line only the bottom half of the basket; otherwise put the whole liner in place to prevent the plants falling out. If using black polythene, carefully cut holes in the sides for planting.

3 Firm in 'moss', ensuring it is evenly spread.

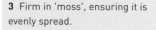

4 Cut a circle about 15cm (6in) in diameter from a plastic compost or bin bag. Put it in the bottom of the basket to stop water flowing straight through.

5 Mix water-retaining gel and controlled-release fertiliser into the compost and fill the bottom half of the basket. Or use multi-purpose compost with 20 per cent John Innes (soil-based) compost added. Soil-based compost combined with the water-retaining gel ensures that the baskets don't dry out as quickly. Don't add extra moisture-retaining gel – it expands impressively and an overdose will push the compost and plants over the top of the hanging basket when water is added. Follow the manufacturer's instructions.

6 There is a range of basket designs. With baskets with large holes, you can simply push the rootballs through the gaps into the compost. For baskets with small holes, wrap the foliage in a strip of plastic from a fertiliser sack and feed the plant gently through from the inside to avoid damaging the rootball. If using moss, finish lining the basket, gently firming it around existing plants. If using wire or plastic baskets, make sure the base is well covered by plants. It's all about burgeoning baskets – there's no sight more dispiriting than a hanging basket with a bare bottom!

7 Fill the basket with compost, leaving at least 4cm (1½in) between the compost and the top of the basket to allow for watering. Put the main plant in the centre and firm gently with your fingertips...

8 ...then fill the rest of the basket with plants.

9 Hang the basket in place and water thoroughly. Watering is critical. Check hanging baskets daily. In the height of summer, they may need watering twice a day, morning and evening. Feed regularly – there are a lot of roots packed into a very small space. Pinch out flowers until the plants are established.

index